JESUS OF NAZARETH

JESUS OF NAZARETH

GÜNTHER BORNKAMM

Professor of New Testament,
University of Heidelberg

Translated by Irene and Fraser McLuskey
with James M. Robinson

1817

HARPER & ROW, PUBLISHERS
New York, Hagerstown, San Francisco, London

TRANSLATOR'S PREFACE

Jesus von Nazareth first appeared in November, 1956; a second edition was published in June, 1957, and a third in March, 1959. The translation incorporates the improvements in a few matters of detail introduced by the author into the subsequent German editions or transmitted by him for the English edition.

The body of this translation was prepared by Irene and Fraser McLuskey, who wish to acknowledge the very substantial help received from Miss Isabel S. Muir, M.A., and Dr. L. S. Salzberger Wittenberg. Mrs. M. R. Gordon rendered invaluable help in the preparation of the original manuscript. Responsibility for the final form of the translation is assumed by the undersigned.

It should be noted that Scripture quotations are given from the Revised Standard Version,* except in a few instances where the author's interpretation necessitated a diverging translation.

JAMES M. ROBINSON

CONTENTS

FOREWORD

IN recent years scholarly treatments of Jesus of Nazareth, his message and history, have become, at least in Germany, increasingly rare. In their place there have appeared the numerous efforts of theologians turned poets and poets turned theologians. They are not to be criticised here. However, no small danger is hidden in this change in so significant a field of research. It would indeed be fatal if here, where there lies a task so promising and unavoidable, demanding though it is, scholarly research were to leave the field or even withdraw into an area to which the experts alone have access.

Many are of the opinion that the way of historical critical research has proved a false path for this subject matter and should be given up for good. I do not hold this view and cannot see at all that it is necessarily a way of unbelief, and that faith should forswear it and is bound so to do. How could faith of all things be content with mere tradition, even though it be that contained in the Gospels? It must break through it and seek behind it to see the thing itself, and perhaps in this way to understand the tradition afresh and to regain it. In this attempt faith is on common ground with all who are genuinely concerned with historical knowledge. Certainly faith cannot and should not be dependent on the change and uncertainty of historical research. To expect this of it would be presumptuous and foolish. But no one should despise the help of historical research to illumine the truth with which each of us should be concerned.

Admittedly the difficulties in the way of arriving at a reasonably assured historical knowledge in the field of the tradition about Jesus have increased. That is inherent in the nature of the sources, with which right away the first chapter of this book will be more particularly concerned. Their investigation has, in point of fact, greatly enriched our understanding, but at the same time has made our knowledge of the historical Jesus ever more uncertain. It has also driven the ship of enquiry so far in another direction that the map of the actual history of Jesus, once so clearly marked, must in the opinion of many today be in all honesty left blank. I cannot myself share this extreme scepticism, although I am not blind to these difficulties and to the limitations of our knowledge, and although a considerable area must be left open for different judgments and opinions.

This book is intended to inform not only professional theologians on such questions, uncertainties and findings of historical research, but also the laymen who wish, so far as possible, to arrive at an historical understanding of the tradition about Jesus and are not content with edifying or romantic portrayals. Whoever does not bring energy and patience to it should not read this book. Especially in the present state of research, unaccustomed reflections and thoughts will be asked of the reader. Perhaps some will find it hard to make their way through the first chapter and will lose heart. They should not hesitate to skip it and perhaps read it later. Nevertheless, it stands at the beginning for a set purpose, because it will clear the ground for the argument of the following chapters.

The subject of this book is in many respects a special one. This is especially the case because we are all so familiar with it through Christian tradition, and yet at the same time this very tradition has become strange and unintelligible to many. If the journey into this often misty country is to succeed, then the first requirement is the readiness for free and frank questioning, and the renunciation of an attitude which simply seeks the confirmation of its own judgments arising from a background of belief or of unbelief. This book could not have been written without the real hope that on its part it might help the reader who is estranged from the heritage of the Church to a new and fresh meeting with the person and message of Jesus. The experience that the greatness of the subject and the limitations of our ability are out of all proportion to one another will, I hope, constitute a bond between reader and author. This will not need repeated expression in what follows. Also I may assume that only the foolish will miss "edification" and personal testimony, and confuse the objectivity proper to a scholarly exposition with an indifference incompatible with the experience of the Emmaus disciples: "Did not our hearts burn within us while he talked to us on the road . . . ?"

The texts are purposely not quoted from the Luther version familiar to us. The reader will best follow them in a modern translation. Sayings which occur more than once in the Gospels are usually only given according to one Gospel, and without reference to the parallels, which in a Greek or English harmony are quickly seen, and are also usually noted each time in our own Bibles. As I cannot imagine the reading of this book without the Gospels open beside one, I have often done without fully printed quotations, and in their place so expressed their inner meaning that most readers will immediately recall well-known stories and words. In addition I have here and there indicated in the paraphrase what seems to me essential for the understanding of a saying.

The choice of the texts is determined for the most part by critical considerations as to the reliability of the sources. Nevertheless, let it be expressly stated that I do not consider the texts quoted as alone genuine. On the other hand, there are certain quotations among them in regard to which I concede the possibility that they are later creations, or even consider this likely. However, it is not apparent why a word or a story which was first formulated by the Church should not in content possess historical genuineness.

The arrangement of the notes at the end of the book enables the reader to obtain from the outset a clear picture of the whole, and then thereafter to examine the arguments for particular assertions and to pursue specific questions further. Much that is mentioned in the notes and appendices is really only for the theological fraternity, and the non-theological should not burden themselves with it. Happily the boundaries between the two are not too sharply defined, and to some of the laity it will not seem unimportant at least to have a glimpse of the theological task.

The references had to be limited for considerations of space. The extent of the subject compelled a choice in the questions dealt with, apart from the limiting factor of the bounds of one's own knowledge.

GÜNTHER BORNKAMM

Heidelberg
June 1956.

Chapter I

FAITH AND HISTORY IN THE GOSPELS

No one is any longer in the position to write a life of Jesus. This is the scarcely questioned and surprising result today of an enquiry which for almost two hundred years has devoted prodigious and by no means fruitless effort to regain and expound the life of the historical Jesus, freed from all embellishment by dogma and doctrine. At the end of this research on the life of Jesus stands the recognition of its own failure. Albert Schweitzer, in his classic work, *The Quest of the Historical Jesus,* has erected its memorial, but at the same time has delivered its funeral oration.

Why have these attempts failed? Perhaps only because it became alarmingly and terrifyingly evident how inevitably each author brought the spirit of his own age into his presentation of the figure of Jesus. In point of fact the changing pictures of the innumerable "Lives" of Jesus are not very encouraging, confronting us as they do with now the "enlightened" teacher of God, virtue, and immortality, now the religious genius of the Romantics, now the teacher of ethics in Kant's sense, now the protagonist of social theory. But that could be just an argument for a genuine, historical enquiry, enabled by a sharper criticism even of the presuppositions and ideals provided by its own age, to start afresh on the old task and to better purpose. Has all the life gone out of research? Does it lack today a sympathetic exponent? If that is so we would have reason to speak of a scholarly fade-out, in which research has perhaps found itself the victim of its own hypercriticism. In truth this state of affairs has deeper causes, and compels us to affirm the futility of any renewal of attempts at Lives of Jesus now or in the future.

This judgment is based on the special nature and character of the sources to which we owe almost exclusively[1] our historical knowledge of Jesus. These are the Gospels of the New Testament, mainly the first three (Mark, Matthew, Luke). We call them commonly the synoptic Gospels because they are interconnected and interdependent, a fact which becomes evident as their respective records are looked at "synoptically". (See Appendix I.) The Gospel according to John has so different a character in comparison with the other three, and is to such a degree the product of a developed theological reflection, that we can only treat it as a secondary source. Admittedly the synoptic Gospels themselves are not simply historical sources which the historian, enquiring after Jesus of Nazareth as a figure of the past, could use without examination and criticism. Although their relation to history is a different one from that of John, they none the less unite to a remarkable degree both record of Jesus Christ and witness to him, testimony of the Church's faith in him and narration of his history.

Both should be continually distinguished in the understanding of the Gospels and in each individual part of their tradition; on the other hand, both are so closely interwoven that it is often exceedingly hard to say where one ends and the other begins. Mathematical certainty in the exposition of a bare history of Jesus, unembellished by faith, is unobtainable, in spite of the fact that the critical discernment of older and more recent layers of tradition belongs to the work of research. We possess no single word of Jesus and no single story of Jesus, no matter how incontestably genuine they may be, which do not contain at the same time the confession of the believing congregation or at least are embedded therein. This makes the search after the bare facts of history difficult and to a large extent futile.

It follows that anyone who takes upon himself the aim of this book, to give an historical presentation of Jesus and his message, sees himself, in relation to his readers, in an embarrassing position. Quite understandably the reader wishes to know what actually happened, what took place then and there, what was said then and there. In no case can these questions be set aside. Nevertheless, we must learn to restrain them, and must not grant them the urgency normally accorded them. Under their pressure we already find ourselves far too much in a completely hopeless position. It is to be noted that the insistent question "what actually happened" in no wise brings us to the point. Such questions can actually lead us astray. So much at least is clear: were we to accept uncritically everything handed down to us as historical (in the usual sense), we would be subjecting the Gospels to an investigation alien to them, and forcing upon them an understanding of the history of Jesus quite unsuited to them. But on the other hand, this is also true: should we reduce the tradition critically to that which cannot be doubted on historical grounds, we should be left ultimately with a mere torso which bears no resemblance to the story set forth in the Gospels. In the course of research both paths have been sufficiently trodden. Each movement has resulted in a counter movement. In contrast to a blind and uncritical approach, historical criticism appeared with perfect right on the field, and destroyed the foundation, thought to be so secure, on which the other relied. And then in turn came the constantly renewed efforts of the conservative historians and theologians, who sought with more or less good fortune to restore some of its limbs to that torso; only themselves to be succeeded by an even sharper criticism which removed the limbs still remaining. And so there resulted in the history of research an agonising alternation between critical and conservative tendencies, sad for any who in the spirit of scientific enquiry seek enlightenment, and even more painful for those who as believers seek after the history of Jesus.

No one should think that he can escape the aforementioned difficulties with a violent solution, as with one blow upon the Gordian knot. Without the process of criticism and counter-criticism there is no knowledge of historical truth in this field or in any other. Such a process teaches us to examine more strictly, to find better grounds for our arguments, not to rest on mere tradition, nor to succumb to a criticism entirely uncontrolled. Since research has learned to engage in untrammelled historical investigation and no longer to be content with Church dogma and doctrine, such questioning is entrusted to research. Genuine faith is certainly not dependent upon the course of this research. But when anyone, out of a concern for the understanding of history, has embarked upon these questions, he will hardly keep a good conscience if thereafter he is driven in desperation to take refuge from the problem of investigation and its frequently controversial results in what is considered the safe fold of Church tradition.

All the same, it must be our concern to extricate ourselves from this dilemma. We shall be well advised, prior to the historical questions concerning the reconstruction of just exactly how the sequence of events ran, to solve the question as to the understanding of the history and person of Jesus found in the Gospels. It is basically different from that familiar to modern thought. To the original Christian tradition, Jesus is not in the first instance a figure of the past, but rather the risen Lord, present with his will, his power, his word. Jesus Christ—no other than the rabbi from Nazareth, whose earthly history began in Galilee and ended on the cross in Jerusalem: and yet at the same time the Risen One, the author of salvation, and the fulfilment of the divine decree. The interest of the Church and her tradition does not cling to the past, but to today; and this Today is not to be understood as a mere date in the calendar, but as a present appointed by God, and together with it a future made accessible by God. In light of this Now and To Come accomplished and decreed by God and opened up through the crucifixion and resurrection of Jesus, the Church understands the past in the history of Jesus before Good Friday and Easter. This she includes in her message, but always as a history which pertains to the present and opens up the future (cf. for example Acts x. 37-43). This understanding of the history of Jesus is therefore an understanding from the end backward and to the end forward. This understanding is built into all the traditions collected together in the Gospels.

That is already apparent in the oldest brief sermonic and confessional formulae, in which we have before us the original form of the Gospel long before there were Gospels committed to writing. (Acts iii. 13 ff.; iv. 10 ff.; v. 30 ff.; compare especially 1 Cor. xv. 3 ff., etc.)[2] They all speak with extreme concentration simply of the death and resurrection of Jesus Christ and proclaim thereby the end of this old age and the breaking in of the new world of God in salvation and judgment. The primitive Christian proclamation confines itself so exclusively to this history—a history which shatters the horizon of all events confined to this world and shifts the ages, that it can pass over the pre-Easter life and work of

Jesus to an extent which seems astounding to us (2 Cor. v. 16). Doubtless Paul and the authors of other New Testament writings knew extremely little of the detail which is known to us from the Gospels.

Neither do the Gospels, which for the first time make the pre-Easter history of Jesus their theme, differ essentially in their understanding of this history from the older formulations of the message of Salvation (the Gospel or Kerygma). They also grow out of the proclamation and are in its service. As an example of this, the description of the few days of the passion occupies so disproportionate a space that one could describe these books, not without reason, as "Passion narratives with extended introduction" (M. Kahler).[3] Whatever of reliable historical recollections may have been preserved in this part of their records (see pages 153 ff.), it is certain that the Gospels in their treatment did not follow out a chronological interest, but wished to proclaim what the Risen Lord said to the disciples at Emmaus: "Was it not necessary that the Christ should suffer these things and enter into his glory?" (Lk. xxiv. 26). In the relating of past history they proclaim who he is, not who he was. What the passion narratives show applies also to the Gospels as a whole: what belongs to the past in the history of Jesus should always be investigated and understood in relation to its significance for the present time today and the coming time of God's future.

Because the earthly Jesus is for the Church at the same time the Risen Lord, his word takes on, in the tradition, the features of the present. From this standpoint are to be explained two apparently conflicting characteristics of the tradition which nearly every page of the Synoptics presents: an incontestable loyalty and adherence to the word of Jesus, and at the same time an astonishing degree of freedom as to the original wording. The word of Jesus is preserved, and yet not with the piety of an archivist, nor is it passed on like the utterances of famous rabbis with expositions attached.[4] In fact, one can go on to say this: the tradition is not really the repetition and transmission of the word he spoke once upon a time, but rather *is* his word today.[5] From this standpoint alone can we grasp the different renderings of his word in the tradition. It is not a sufficient explanation to say that popular, oral tradition always tends to alter, adorn, and omit, as well as to preserve: although, of course, the laws of popular tradition and the forms which it habitually takes are without question to be seen in the Gospels.

For the clarification of this contemporary nature of the word of Jesus, let us here refer to a single obvious example, to which we can find many parallels. When one compares the different versions of Jesus' parable of the Great Supper (Mt. xxii. 1 ff.; Lk. xiv. 16 ff.), one sees that Luke tells it differently from Matthew, and moreover provides the older text. A rich man invites his friends to the feast, but the guests refuse the invitation with plausible though fatuous excuses. The account in Luke remains in the quite natural setting of a parable. In Matthew the telling is strengthened by lurid features. The man of means has become a king. The meal has become the marriage feast for his son. The servants (no longer only one) are maltreated and killed. We read further in Matthew that the infuriated king sends out his armies against the thankless and murderous guests and burns down their city. One sees at once that this is no longer a simple parable. Each special feature demands interpretion and understanding. The king is a standard picture of God. The king's son is the Messiah. The marriage is a picture of the joy of the Messianic age. In the fate of the servants we recognise the martyrdom of God's messengers. In the military campaign we recognise the Jewish war, and in the destruction of the city, the catastrophe of A.D. 70. The old people of God, having become rebellious, will be rejected and a new people will be called. But this new people is still a mixture of good and bad on the way to judgment and the final separation of the unworthy. (Only in Matthew does the parable end with the rejection of the man who came to the wedding without a wedding garment.) In Matthew's version we find clearly worked into the parable of Jesus his own story, a picture of Israel and the picture of the early Church. The word of Jesus long ago has become today's word.

Luke, at least at first, has better preserved the original character of the simple parable, but he also reveals the tendency of the word of Jesus to become contemporary. He makes the servant of the nobleman go out not only twice but three times; after the first refusal he is sent to the poor, lame and crippled *in* the town, and after that once again to those in "the highways and hedges" *outside* the town. There can be no doubt that the evangelist intended to represent thereby the advance of the mission from Israel to the heathen world.

One learns from the example of such a text how strongly the tradition collected in the Gospels has been influenced by the believing interpretation of the history and person of Jesus. The understanding of the "once" of the history of Jesus in its significance for the "today" of his lordship over the Church and for the divine consummation that lies ahead was able to lead to what in our terms would be considered a relativisation, often even to an elimination of the historical boundaries between the period before and after Easter. The history of the tradition shows that frequently not only the words of Jesus spoken while he was here on earth (as in the parable mentioned above) soon took on a post-Easter form. For words spoken by the Risen Christ also became words of the earthly Jesus. In principle this is the same process. We have to reckon with it wherever circumstances and questions of the later Church are presupposed in a saying coming from the tradition. In the course of this book we shall meet frequently with such examples. Such sayings will originally have been declared to the Church by her inspired prophets and preachers, as the Revelation of John shows in its Letters to the Churches (Rev. ii and iii). The extent to which the Church's faith and theology have formed and added to the tradition of the history of Jesus appears most clearly in the legends and in a story's legendary embellishments, as these increase from one evangelist to another. This is especially evident in the infancy narratives of Matthew and Luke, and in the Easter stories of all four evangelists. This tendency is frequently found to have been raised into the realm of phantasy in the later non-canonical Gospels, of which fragments remain in considerable number.

The tradition's lack of historical concern appears in its style of storytelling. The modern historian to whom where and when, cause and effect, inner development and personality are all important questions, receives small satisfaction. As a rule, historical and factual notes serve only to frame and to connect the individual scenes. They confine themselves to indicating time in general terms (thereafter, on that evening, a few days after, etc.). Equally stereotyped are descriptions of place (house, road, field, lake, etc.); descriptions which are used in quite different ways by the different Gospels. Every reader has only to compare the romantic expansion of precisely these exterior features of the history of Jesus in many sermons and children's lessons, and in the literature relating to the life of Jesus, with what is contained in the actual text. With the text, too, let him compare the frequently irreverent and senti-mental discussions of what took place in the soul of Jesus. We should learn from this that we would be well advised not to try to help out the "defectiveness" of the text in the interest of a more realistic story, but to stick to the subject which the text has in view.[6]

Only in more recent times have the character and form of the tradition become the subject of more detailed investigation, a task which has been the especial province of so-called form criticism.[7] It has revealed laws of tradition which stem from pre-literary, oral tradition and which are still preserved unchanged in the first three Gospels. Observing these laws is an excellent aid in distin-guishing the essential from the non-essential in any passage. But the results reach further. They prove the unique character of the Gospels compared to all other kinds and classes of ancient his-toriography and literature. Above all these laws of tradition teach us to look for the connection between the entire Jesus tradition and the faith and life of the Church, out of which that tradition arose and for which it was meant. The extent to which the Church was responsible for its formation need not be stated here in detail. It is more important to recognise the existence of its responsibility. The critical exegete and the historian is therefore obliged, in questions concerning the history of tradition, to speak often of "authentic" or "inauthentic" words of Jesus and thus to distinguish words of the historical Jesus from "creations by the Church". Even today he usually incurs the horrified reproach of theologians and laity that he is merely destructive. This critical task should, however, be understood in principle as pointing out a very positive factor, namely the interpretation of the history of Jesus in terms of his resurrection and the experience of his presence. We should not, therefore, dismiss as mere fancy or invention what criticism might term "inauthentic" and "creations by the Church". Such an erroneous conception appears frequently both among supporters and opponents of criticism. While the one declares that under no circumstances is the Church to be credited with such a degree of creative phantasy, the other holds that precisely this assertion is required of us. Meanwhile we should ask ourselves whether the categories employed here really suit the case. Though one should not deny the part played by subjective experience and poetic imagination, the tradition which first grew out of the faith of the Church is not to be dismissed, by reason of its foundation and origin, as the mere product of imagination. It is an answer to Jesus' whole person and mission. It points beyond itself to him whom the Church has encountered in his earthly form and who proves his presence to her as the resurrected and risen Lord. In every layer, therefore, and in each individual part, the tradition is witness of the reality of his history and the reality of his resurrection. Our task, then, is to seek the history *in* the Kerygma of the Gospels, and in this history to seek the Kergyma. If we are asked to differentiate between the two, that is only for the purpose of revealing more clearly their inter-connection and inter-penetration.

A long tradition, whose spell we cannot so easily escape, has alienated us from this understanding of the history of Jesus, and has made it the sole—or at least the first—essential for us to enquire into the historical happenings. This applies to those who cling to the tradition and secretly or openly consider historical-critical research an attack on the foundations of Christian faith. It applies equally to those who draw their weapons for attack on the Christian message from historiography and criticism. It is for this reason that we needed to speak here in such detail, although by no means exhaustively, of the understanding of history implicit in the Gospel tradition, and of its disagreement with our way of thinking. In view of the position we are in today, all these considerations as to method were unavoidable, although they may well have put the patience of the reader to a severe test. Unfortunately we show this patience and freedom too infrequently; some of us because the work of historical-critical theology is regarded as purely destructive, and others of us who defend it, because we have never faced the theological problems posed in such research. In consequence historical criticism and Christian faith have parted company to an almost hopeless degree, and one of our noblest tasks, both exacting and rewarding, has been left unfinished. But in this fashion the recognition of the truth is clouded for us and rendered impossible. This truth does not lie before us as self-evidently and openly as we might think. Perhaps other times have been more fortunate. For us the way lies through precisely that narrow pass of such considerations concerning principle and method as have engaged us.

What has been said so far must in no way discourage us from raising the question of the historical Jesus at all. True, it may appear as if scholarship and faith, from opposite points of view, would wish to dismiss it as an impossible question. Representatives of critical biblical scholarship dismiss it because they consider the entanglement of confession and report, of history and faith in the Gospels so indissolubly close, that they consider every quest of the historical Jesus entirely vain. The supporters of believing tradition dismiss it because from the very start they dispute the suitability of critical historical scholarship for this subject, and consider the unqualified recognition of the tradition in its given form the first requirement of faith. Both offer solutions senseless and forced. There is no need of long discussions in defence of our position that critical research cannot allow itself to be ordered off the field. Such discussions would, in any case, be fruitless in face of dogmatic prejudices. If what we have said about the character of the Gospels is true, it is clear that research is faced with a great number of questions and tasks. The torrent cannot be halted, no matter how much of its water has strayed from its course. We shall have to set about building real dams until these waters subside and the dry land becomes visible again. But it cannot be seriously maintained that the Gospels and their tradition do not allow enquiry after the historical Jesus. Not only do they allow, they demand this effort. For whatever the opinions of historians on matters of detail, none can dispute that the tradition of the Gospels is itself very considerably concerned with the pre-Easter history of Jesus, different though this interest is from that of modern historical science. The Easter aspect in which the primitive Church views the history of Jesus must certainly not be forgotten for one moment; but not less the fact that it is precisely the history of Jesus before Good Friday and Easter which is seen in this aspect. Were it otherwise, the Church would have been lost in a timeless myth, even if for some irrelevant reason or other she had given the bearer of this myth the name of Jesus. The Gospels are the rejection of myth. To whatever extent mythological conceptions from time to time find access to the thought and faith of the early Church, they are given once and for all the function of interpreting the history of Jesus as the history of God with the world. As the language of the New Testament puts it: the "once" of Jesus' history as God's "once and for all", certain to faith.

Nothing could be more mistaken than to trace the origin of the Gospels and the traditions collected therein to a historical interest apart from faith—irrespective of whether that historical interest were to be considered questionable or wholesome. Rather these Gospels voice the confession: Jesus the Christ, the unity of the earthly Jesus and the Christ of faith. By this the Gospels proclaim that faith does not begin with itself but lives from past history. Of this past history we must speak, as do all the Gospels, only in the past tense: and this precisely because of the present in which faith has its being.

In another respect also, faith's interest in pre-Easter history must be made clear. The following question could be posed concerning the post-Easter Church which lived in the assurance of the presence of the risen Christ and in the hope of his speedy return: Did not the Church fall into a strange anachronism? She made herself contemporary with her earthly pre-Easter Lord. She made herself contemporary with the Pharisees and high priests of long ago. She made herself contemporary with the first hearers of Jesus who heard his message of the coming of God's kingdom; with the disciples who followed after him; with the sick whom he healed; with the tax collectors and sinners with whom he sat down at table. But what may appear here as anachronism corresponds exactly with the Church's understanding of herself and her situation. She made herself one with those who did not already live by faith, but who at the beginning were called to obedience and faith by the word of Jesus. In this she confessed at the same time that her faith can be nothing else but following her earthly Master who is yet to face the cross and resurrection. The Gospels are therefore at the same time the rejection of an eschatological fanaticism which denies the temporal order and proclaims the glory of God's world as already present.

What then of the other question raised by scholarship? With regard to our sources, is an exposition of the history and message of Jesus a sensible undertaking capable of being carried through? Shall we retrogress and once again attempt a detailed description of the course of his life biographically and psychologically? Certainly not. All such attempts, as often as they are undertaken, are doomed to failure. They can only be carried through with a lack of criticism which alleges everything to be historical, or with the display of an imagination no less uncritical, which arbitrarily stops gaps and manufactures connections precisely where the Gospels omit them. They only obscure the fragmentary and incomplete nature of our detailed knowledge and efface the boundary between what is historically certain and uncertain. It is not our most urgent task to establish the possibility or probability of this or that miracle story which criticism calls a legend, or to save this or that word for the historical Jesus which on very good grounds can be shown to have sprung from the faith of the later Church. Such manœuvres, even if called for here and there, can change nothing in the total situation.

Nevertheless, the Gospels justify neither resignation nor scepticism. Rather they bring before our eyes, in very different fashion from what is customary in chronicles and presentations of history, the historical person of Jesus with the utmost vividness. Quite clearly what the Gospels report concerning the message, the deeds and the history of Jesus is still distinguished by an authenticity, a freshness, and a distinctiveness not in any way effaced by the Church's Easter faith. These features point us directly to the earthly figure of Jesus.

It is precisely historical criticism which, rightly understood, has opened up our way anew to this history, by disposing of attempts along biographical, psychological lines. We can now see more clearly. Although the Gospels do not speak of the history of Jesus in the way of reproducing the course of his career in all its happenings and stages, in its inner and outer development, nevertheless they do speak of history as occurrence and event. The Gospels give abundant evidence of such history. This opinion may be boldly stated, despite the fact that on historical grounds so many of the stories and sayings could be contested in detail, despite tendencies evidently active in the tradition, despite the impossibility of finally extracting from more or less authentic particulars a more or less assured whole which we could call a life of Jesus.

As everyone knows, the Gospels tell the story of Jesus in "pericopae", i.e. in brief anecdotes. These story scenes give his history not only when pieced together, but each one in itself contains the person and history of Jesus in their entirety. None requires explanation in terms of previous happenings. None is directed at later events for the unfolding of what has gone before. We are always being held in the beam of this scene and this scene only. The circle of light is always sharply defined. The description of those who appear in it are limited to the essential. The meeting of Jesus with certain people, which through his word and deed becomes an event of supreme challenge and significance, is clearly and sharply illuminated. This way of telling his story has its exact counterpart in the transmission of his words. Here again each word stands by itself, exhaustive in itself, not dependent on context for its meaning or requiring a commentary on it from some other word. In the same way the so-called discourses of the Gospels—the Sermon on the Mount, the Commissioning of the Disciples, the Parables—are in reality not discourses, but collections of such sayings.

What then is shown us in this style of transmission? Surely these are all characteristics of a popular and unhistorical transmission, evidence that the Gospel tradition, in origin and purpose, is directed to the practical use of the believing Church, to whom mere history as such means very little. Surely the historian is forced thereby to criticise this tradition, which often enough is silent where he seeks an answer, naïvely generalises where he enquires after the individual element in each case, and frequently blurs the distinction between history and interpretation. These are legitimate questions. And yet we must never lose sight of the fact that, precisely in this way of transmitting and recounting, the person and work of Jesus, in their unmistakable uniqueness and distinctiveness, are shown forth with an originality which again and again far exceeds and disarms even all believing understandings and interpretations. Understood in this way, the primitive tradition of Jesus is brim full of history.

Chapter II

PERIOD AND ENVIRONMENT

THE history of Jesus is to be found neither in the documents and annals of the Roman state nor in Jewish historical writings. World history in general took scarcely any notice of him. The few non-Christian sources in which he is mentioned at all are quickly enumerated.[1] Modern man is apt to attribute to them a special significance, as they appear to him impartial. The most important one is a note in the Annals of the Roman historian Tacitus (beginning of second century), which refers to the first persecution of Christians under Nero (A.D. 64). An extensive fire had laid the greater part of Rome in ashes. The hated emperor himself was accused of having started the fire. Hence he threw suspicion on the Christians, who were reputed to be the "enemies of mankind", and put many of them to death in cruel spectacles. In this connection Tacitus gives the following explanation of the name "Christian": "This name originates from 'Christus' who was sentenced to death by the procurator, Pontius Pilate, during the reign of Tiberius. This detestable superstition, which had been suppressed for a while, spread anew not only in Judea where the evil had started, but also in Rome, where everything that is horrid and wicked in the world gathers and finds numerous followers" (Ann. 15, 4). This is really the only useful note in Roman literature. For the next one, which is to be found in the Life of the Emperor Claudius (ch. 25, 4) from the pen of the imperial biographer, Suetonius (second century), if it refers at all to Christ and Christendom, must be classified as entirely incorrect. "Claudius expelled," it says, "the Jews from Rome who, instigated by Chrestus [sic], never ceased to cause unrest." This passage may perhaps contain vague memories of unrest called forth in the Jewish community in Rome by the penetration of Christianity, in which case the Roman historian described Jesus as a Jewish agitator. For the history of the Christians at the beginning of the second century there is, finally, an important description of them in a famous letter of Pliny the younger, governor of Asia Minor, to the Emperor Trajan (A.D. 110). He, too, calls them representatives of a gross superstition and reports of them, among other things, that they gather together on a certain day and "sing a hymn in honour of Christus as in honour of a God" (Ep. 10, 96). It is at once noticeable that this is not an independent source; its content goes back to an interrogation of the Christians themselves.

One expects better information from the Jewish historian Josephus, whose extensive account, *Jewish Antiquities*, appeared about the year A.D. 90. Josephus, born about 40 as the son of a priestly family in Palestine, temporarily even a disciple of the Pharisees, was himself involved for a short time in the Jewish war for freedom, until he sided with the Romans, and there attained questionable honours as historian at the court of Domitian. We find in him important information about the Jews as well as about the Essenes, and John the Baptist. Jesus, however, is only mentioned in an incidental note, when the trial and the stoning of "James, the brother of Jesus, who is called Christ" is mentioned (XX, 9, 1).[2]

Even less productive is what the Talmud reports later about Jesus' appearance and end. It betrays no independent knowledge whatsoever and is nothing but a polemical and tendentious misrepresentation of the Christian tradition. It makes Jesus into a magician, seducer and political agitator, and tries to justify his condemnation.[3]

These pagan and Jewish sources are of importance only in so far as they confirm the fact which was also otherwise well known, that in the early days it never occurred even to the fiercest adversary of Christianity to doubt the historical existence of Jesus at all. This was reserved for an unrestrained, tendentious criticism of modern times into which it is not worth while to enter here. To our knowledge of the history of Jesus, however, the non-Christian allusions to him contribute practically nothing. We learn from them that contemporary historiography, so far as it knew of Jesus' appearance at all, considered it anything but an epoch-making event.[4]

In no way do the first Christian sources themselves wish to correct this impression, and prove in the aforesaid sense Christ's greatness and importance in world history. Neither do they interpret him as the preacher of a political programme, nor as leader of a popular movement in the struggle against Roman foreign rule, nor even as the opponent of the emperor in Rome.[5] It is, therefore, no coincidence that we learn from the Gospels exceedingly little of the history of the Jewish people, of the Roman empire and the great problems of world politics. Such allusions occur, if at all, only on the margin, and prove only this, that Jesus' person and history belong to a certain period, and that his word, as well as that of his followers, is directed to a particular historical environment. This, indeed, is important enough. Hence we look first of all for a picture of this environment.

1. THE JEWISH PEOPLE

Small, insignificant, doomed to being a weak nation in a remote, infertile land, the Jewish nation in Jesus' time[6] was anything but a historical world power. Since the return from the Babylonian exile (586-538 B.C.) it had become a temple congregation and had lost its own political independence, apart from a few weak traces, to a long succession of foreign powers; from the Persians to Alexander the Great, from him to the Egyptian Ptolemies; again, a hundred years later, to the Syrian Seleucids; finally, after a short interlude of Parthian rule, to the Romans. In this history, full of changes, small Israel was, however, in no way a mere plaything without a will of its own. It still possessed something which was completely its own among the oriental nations. Its God was different from the gods of the world around it, and the faith in this God was the vital nerve centre and the sustaining power of this nation. Through the power of this faith, not only ancient Israel but no less post-exilic Judaism did its best to hold aloof from the changing foreign powers, although the land lay in the magnetic field of their aspirations. Again and again it repelled the influences of their cultures and religions, and never produced anything like Babylonian or Egyptian science, not to mention anything of the type of Greek philosophy and science. Historically, therefore, it gives the impression of a strangely backward structure. And yet the Romans, as once the Persians and the Diadochi rulers, had to take into account its individuality if they were to establish their rule in this country, which, although small, was important owing to its boundary position. The measure of freedom and concessions, of donations and privileges, which was granted to Israel for the securing of its position as a religious unit is astonishing, and as much a sign of its uniqueness as of the political shrewdness of its foreign rulers which, however, was not always apparent.

It was in this very connection that the passion of the revolt against the Syrian king Antiochus Epiphanes was kindled, when in the year 168 B.C. he dared to occupy Jerusalem, desecrate the sanctuary, plunder the temple treasures and, by the introduction of Hellenistic cults, tried to put an end to the Jewish religious community. These events were the cause for the Jews' memorable struggle for freedom under the leadership of the Hasmonaean Judas Maccabaeus and his brothers. He gave back to Israel for the last time its political independence for a century, and appeared, after making the high priest king and extending his dominion to the extent of the old realm of David and Solomon, to be renewing once again the old glorious days of Israel. Jewish history and poetry have amply glorified the heroism, the courage to confess, the readiness to die of the Maccabaean soldiers of the faith, just as, by contrast, the erection of an altar to "Zeus" in the sacred area of the temple by Antiochus long remained, even into Christian literature, an obvious symbol and apocalyptic sign of dreadful pagan blasphemy.[7] Nevertheless, the history of the Maccabees was not really the time of a rebirth of Israel. Their government developed rapidly into a history of unscrupulous power politics and a struggle of various interests among the different dynasties. In consequence the people who were faithful to the law and who had once energetically supported and fought in the battle for their faith soon found themselves in sharp opposition to the family of princely priests and to the secularisation instigated and encouraged by them.

The fate of the Maccabaean epoch was sealed when the Roman general Pompey appeared in Syria in 63 B.C. and was called in as an arbitrator by the last Hasmonaean sons, Hyrcanus II and Aristobulos, quarrelling over the throne. For at the same time a deputation from the city of Jerusalem implored him to eliminate the unworthy rule. Pompey, in reply to these requests, gave the answer with his army. Jerusalem was conquered. The temple area, fortified by the inhabitants, was besieged and occupied. The general himself and his Romans entered the Holy of Holies, to the horror of those faithful to the law. They took Aristobulos with them as a prisoner to Rome, and Hyrcanus was once again reinstated as "High Priest and Ethnarch" (i.e. deprived of the royal title). Thereafter the true rulers of the country were the Romans. The intrigues and the struggles for power had, however, not yet come to an end. In their course Hyrcanus and his energetic minister, the Idumaean Antipater, succeeded cleverly in taking advantage of the new situation in Rome caused by Caesar's victory over Pompey. They won Caesar's favour and gained for the land of Judaea the privileges of exemption from payment of taxes and military service. Above all, however, the Jewish community in Jerusalem was granted the right of jurisdiction in its own affairs. The true beneficiaries in this political game were, however, no longer the Hasmonaeans, but rather Antipater and his sons, who soon overcame the weak Hyrcanus. Although the father was forcibly removed, the foundation was laid for the rule of the Herodian dynasty which now followed.

Herod, Antipater's son, sought as did his father the favour of Rome and, at the instigation of Antony and Octavian (later the Emperor Augustus), was nominated king of Judaea by a resolution of the senate in 40 B.C. At first a favourite of Antony, he also won over Octavian ten years later when he had become sole ruler of Rome, and received with the confirmation of his royal crown the rank of prince and ally of Rome, and a dominion embracing almost all provinces of Palestine. As ruler by the grace of Rome and in honour of Rome he displayed tremendous splendour. Colossal secular buildings in the Hellenistic-Roman style, fortifications, the founding of new cities and temples for the cult of Augustus proved to the entire land his active, lavish rule; but at the same time, and by the names he gave his creations, he showed the power of Rome to whom he owed his dominion.[8]

Through Herod, called the Great, Jerusalem received also the splendid appearance which it showed in the time of Jesus and until its destruction: in the north-west corner of the city the strongly fortified royal castle which became later the official residence in Jerusalem of the Roman procurator, and, above all, the new temple building, begun in the year 20 B.C., pompously erected according to the old plans of Solomon with its powerful outer walls and gates, halls, courts and sacred buildings. Immediately beside it—symbolic of his rule—lay the previously erected citadel which Herod named Antonia, in honour of his patron at that time.

All this, however, cannot delude us. The "great" Herod was a Hellenistic-Oriental despot, even although he formally belonged to the religious community of Jerusalem and, by his marriage to the Hasmonaean Mariamne, tried to give his royal dignity an air of legality. Since as an Idumaean he could not invest himself with the hereditary priesthood, he gave it away all the more unscrupulously to compliant members of the old families of priests, only to remove them again without further ado when political considerations demanded it. To the people he remained a foreigner, a vassal of Rome, and was hated for his lavishness and for the murderous rage and tyranny which he displayed in his own home.

When the king died in the year 4 B.C., the representatives of the Jewish community requested of Augustus the removal of the Herodian rule. But the emperor carried out the will of the deceased and divided the country among his sons: the area in the north-east fell to Philip; Galilee and part of the land east of the Jordan to Herod Antipas, later the sovereign of John the Baptist and Jesus; Samaria and Judaea with Jerusalem to Archelaus. All three dominions remained, however, insignificant puppet states of short duration, almost all of whose rulers finished up later as Roman exiles in Gaul. The first to go was Judaea which, after the brutal and incompetent Archelaus had been deposed (A.D. 6) was immediately joined to the Roman province of Syria, only retaining its own administration under a Roman procurator. He resided in the seaport of Caesarea, was military commander-in-chief of the area and responsible for the levying of taxes and for the customs duties which were collected in each area by Jewish tax collectors. He was also supreme administrator of justice. To the Sanhedrin in Jerusalem had been left, however, the power of jurisdiction in religious offences and crimes, with far-reaching competence even including the death penalty. Yet the police power relating to public order and the "right of the sword" in the punishment of political crimes belonged solely to Roman jurisdiction.[9]

In the practising of their religion the Jewish people even under the Roman rule were at first quite unrestricted. The consideration for their religious sensibilities even went so far as for the Roman troops to refrain from marching into Jerusalem displaying pictures of the emperor, which were particularly offensive to the Jews, although individual procurators like Pontius Pilate (A.D. 26-36) took pleasure in reversing this practice to provoke the Jews. Taken on the whole, the administrative and legal organisation of the country clearly reveals the political wisdom of the Romans. In spite of this they signified to the people only the foreign rulers whom they had to endure reluctantly, and only the least provocation was necessary to fan the passive or active resistance of the people. Brutality and mismanagement by incompetent procurators aroused this hatred in full measure, although open revolt occurred at first only in isolated instances.

Only later, after the death of the last Herodian, Agrippa I (A.D. 44), who by the emperor's favour had received once again for a short period the royal title and the old dominion of the first Herod, did the country become directly Roman territory. From now on the rebellions never ceased. Their leadership lay in the hands of a party of Zealots, small at first, and by no means supported by the people as a whole and their religious groups. It was formed four decades earlier on the first occasion of a taxation of the country[10] by the emperor, and had set before it a programme for the forcible liberation of the people of God from the foreign rule, which did not shrink from violence and murder. Josephus describes these Zealots as being almost wholly bandits and a crowd of partisans. There is no doubt, however, that this rebellious movement was filled with a theocratic ideal and fervent Messianic hopes. The open conflict started up in Caesarea and above all in Jerusalem (A.D. 66). The Roman occupation forces, but also the high priest who tried to smother the rebellion, were no longer equal to the situation and were slaughtered. Even the legate of Syria, Cestius, when approaching with a strong military force from Damascus towards Jerusalem, had to turn back before the courageously defended city, and suffered during his retreat heavy losses from the rebels. With this the struggle for liberation from Rome was begun. It ended in the year A.D. 70 with the siege of Jerusalem by Vespasian who in the same year was made emperor, and with the conquest of city and temple by Titus, the carrying off of the sacred vessels of the temple, the elimination of the Jewish community and the deportation of innumerable of its members. The triumphal arch of Titus at the south-east side of the forum in Rome, through which even today no believing Jew will pass, has remained up to the present the documentation of this victory.

In surveying this troubled history one will notice with some surprise that it contributes only in an indirect way to the understanding of this people. What normally applies to every nation, that through its history it both receives and expresses its nature and character, applies to the Jewish nation only in a very limited measure. It proved its vital forces not so much in its changing history as this passes over the people and draws them painfully enough into its whirlpool, but rather in spite of this history.

This means that its vital forces resided in that which with tenacious steadfastness in each particular period set itself against or withdrew from each succeeding rule. Here lies the reason for the fact that this people survived the never-ending succession of political catastrophies after the exile even until the complete loss of its national existence.

This applied to Judaism in a quite unique sense. True, even in other nations one notices here and there indestructible vital forces which slumber underneath the surface and give a people the possibility to rise anew even after the heaviest defeat. Any assessment, however, which takes into account only the factors normally decisive for a people—geographical position, natural ability, environment, history, culture and so forth—misses Israel's uniqueness. We must therefore speak now of the religion of this people. This is the law of its life.

2. THE JEWISH RELIGION

The God of the Jewish faith, in contrast to the gods of the Oriental and Greek religions, has no myth, no image, and no cult practices whereby men may share in the natural-supernatural powers of the deity. Certainly, there are mythical elements in Israel's religion, too: the ancient Oriental myth of the creation struggle between the deity and the monster of the primeval world has left behind numerous traces, especially in the psalms.[11] Mythical elements have permeated Israel's expectation of the Messiah and still colour the pictures of its ultimate apocalyptic hope.[12] Cult and piety also are interspersed with ideas and motifs which to a large extent the history of religion finds again in soothsaying and magic, in sacrificial and cleansing rites. It is noticeable, however, that such elements are strongly modified. They are relegated to the margin and made subservient to a completely different understanding of the deity. The history of the Israelite-Jewish religion is marked by a continuous struggle against myth.

For Yahweh is Creator and Lord, and as such radically superior to world and nature. This never means for Israel's faith the banishment of God into an ideal metaphysical other-worldliness. This is in no way so. No other religion is as unsuitable as Israel's for any dualistic and Platonising interpretation.[13] Yahweh is rather the God who from the beyond creates, commands, judges and saves. History is the field of his revelation and of his deeds. This does not mean that from the experiences of history one infers that there is a God, or that historical occurrences are crystallised into myths. In this sense the God of Israel is precisely not a God of the people or of history, for he is there before the people and history, "from everlasting" (Hab. i. 12), and it is he who makes and determines history in his sovereign power, the God of Israel and at the same time Lord of all nations. "The Lord, God of Hosts, he who touches the earth and it melts, and all who dwell in it mourn, and all of it rises like the Nile, and sinks again, like the Nile of Egypt; who builds his upper chambers in the heavens, and founds his vault upon the earth; who calls for the waters of the sea, and pours them out upon the surface of the earth—the Lord is his name" (Amos ix. 5 f.).

Israel is the people of this God. At its beginning stand its *election* and its *liberation*, which have separated it from all other nations and set its life and history on a foundation upon which no other can live. The desert is the place where it has met its God, where through terrible signs it learned his will, and for all time received the law of its life. "Election" and "covenant", "law" and "promise" determine from now on its life and its history, ideas all of which express that this people no longer has its being in itself, but that it is dependent on this great and powerful otherworldly God, who marvellously guides and sustains, who by his law both directs and judges. "But the Lord has taken you, and brought you forth out of the iron furnace, out of Egypt, to be a people of his own possession, as at this day" (Deut. iv. 20: cf. also iv. 32 ff.). This, then, is Yahweh's power. The natural frontiers of a nation are no frontiers to him. He is no national God (Amos ix. 7). "Behold, to the Lord your God belong heaven and the heaven of heavens, the earth with all that is in it; yet the Lord set his heart in love upon your fathers and chose their descendants after them, you above all peoples, as at this day" (Deut. x. 14 f.).

True, Yahweh, in making a *covenant* with his people, has tied himself to this people. But not unconditionally. For he judges the nation by their obedience and disobedience, and visits it just because it is his people (Amos iii. 2). "Covenant" and "election" are Israel's pride and confidence, and are themselves the foundation of the history of the nation. On them is founded its unequalled self-confidence. But never do they become natural, historical qualities on which the nation can count as a matter of course. Whenever this happened, there rang with sharp incisiveness the immediate "NO" of the prophets, recalling Israel to its origin and shattering its security by the announcement of the divine judgment.

This makes the *law* (Torah) by which Israel lives something fundamentally different from an expression of its own essential nature, its ethical views, from the expression of its own inherent feelings and ideas, from a national culture raised to a philosophy, from its philosophical "understanding of the universe" or whatever we may call it according to Greek or modern ways of thought. Rather is it for Israel the expression of God's sovereign will, given to the nation against their own wish or will, under thunder and lightning. The story of the giving of the commandments on Mount Sinai is inextricably tied with the story of the wrath of Moses and the judgment on the people who, wearied of their invisible God, make an idol of their own will and dance round the golden calf (Ex. xxxii). So little is the law the natural custom of the people, so little is the individual naturally at home in the land and in the nation, that the faithful has to pray: "Open my eyes that I may behold wondrous things out of thy law. I am a sojourner

on earth: hide not thy commandments from me!" (Ps. cxix. 18 f.)
Thus is the law the joy and pride of the people, and yet remains
always in Yahweh's hand. Hence the prayer of the faithful: "And
take not the word of truth utterly out of my mouth; for my hope
is in thy ordinances" (Ps. cxix. 43). From the earliest times to the
latest it has never been the case that the law was deemed valid
because it seemed common sense or because its principles were
understandable and convincing. Rather is it valid solely because
it is a divine demand. The sole task of interpretation is to relate
the Torah to the manifold situations of life in each particular
period. Even the weirdest oddities of Jewish casuistry betray this
understanding of the law.

Without a doubt the religion of ancient Israel underwent in
Judaism after the Exile a tremendous narrowing down and hardening. "The Lord of all peoples had become the party leader of the
legalists, obedience to the ruler of history had become a finespun
technique of piety" (Dibelius).[14] Similarly, worship and sacrifice
in Judaism are seen as a ritual obligation. But even in its perversion,
the original understanding of God's power and law, to which
both the ancient and the changed Israel owes its being, is recognisable. Here lie the reasons for the fact that in comparison with
the empires surrounding her, she creates the impression of being
so backward in her historical developments, a strangely archaic
structure which never departs from its own most primitive historical origins.

Here is another way of putting it: Israel lives by the conviction
that for her all things come from God. And this is meant in a
strict, definitive sense. It determines the individuality of this people
and of its religion long before there is a properly developed
expectation of the final consummation. The time during which
this expectation of the final consummation took clearer shape is
the time of the Exile and the subsequent centuries up to Israel's
historical end. Originally Israel's expectation for the future was a
purely temporal hope. It was directed towards the coming of the
Messiah, the recovery of the lost land, the purging of the nation
of all pagan and alien influences, and towards the redeeming of the
promise given to David and his heirs. This hope persisted right
through to the time of Jesus and to the time after the political

catastrophe of the nation. The 17th Psalm of Solomon, which is to be found in a collection of psalms of the Pharisees, and the prayer of Eighteen Petitions, which to this day is said by the faithful Jew, express it most clearly indeed.

These temporal-political expectations, however, no longer satisfied a good many people in the era of late Judaism. They were extended and elevated by a hope which represents the coming and the manifestation of the Kingdom of God and the salvation of Israel, no longer in the limitations of this world, but in universal, cosmic dimensions. The myths of the Babylonians and Persians supplied colours and ideas for this, and brought a sinister, dualistic trait into the Jewish expectations. Thus, since the Book of Daniel, the Jewish expectation of the end is changed into apocalypticism, and creates for itself new forms of expression and images. One in particular is the conception of the two aeons; this present, passing aeon which, under sin and curse, has become old and tired and is drifting towards a dreadful catastrophe, and the new coming aeon of God in glory and joy, which the righteous shall see. There is also the conception of a heavenly "Man" (Dan. vii. 13) who comes on the clouds of heaven to judge the world and who will gather the chosen into a sacred people. There is further the conception of Satan and his army of angels who spread temptation and horror, but also of the angels of God who carry out his decrees. Then, too, the doctrine of the resurrection of the dead found its way into Jewish theology at this time.

All these new elements, however, became part of genuine Jewish thought and hope. Nowhere is the dualism carried so far as to endanger the uniqueness of God and faith in his creation. In any case we should really not speak with regard to apocalypticism of a metaphysical or mythical, but only of a historical, dualism. Time and history present great puzzles which the roaming imagination of the apocalypticist tries to fathom and to solve with calculations, with dividing into periods and with visions. But Israel's fate and future in the midst of world happenings are the real subject even of apocalyptic dreams. Its history remains the centre, its ancient prophecy is interpreted anew, only now enlarged into cosmic dimensions. Righteousness and evil are determined by Israel's law alone, and salvation and rejection by the eternal judgment. So also the mysterious "son of man" bears the features of the Messiah. In general the visionaries of the various apocalypses consciously hide behind the mask of the great men of God of Israel's origin and history. Even the Book of Daniel, originating as early as the days of the Maccabees (second century B.C.), presents itself as a tale told by a pious interpreter of dreams of the Babylonian epoch long ago. Especially, however, do the names of the later apocalypses (Apocalypses of Enoch, Abraham and Elijah; Ascension of Moses, Ascension of Isaiah; the Apocalypses of Baruch and Ezra, etc.), show how the choice of ancient and revered names, of whose authority the editors and collectors made use, became an established part of the style of writing for this literature.[15]

It is difficult to imagine adequately the extraordinary circulation and effect of these books and their expectations in the age in which Jesus lived. Even if they pass themselves off frequently as secret writings, we have nevertheless no reason to believe that they were only known to special circles. Their ideas inspired in Jesus' day even the teaching of the Pharisees and other groups. Only in later days was apocalypticism excluded by a scribal, legalistic Judaism. Without this background, as we shall see, the message of Jesus and early Christian theology also can never be understood.

3. GROUPS AND MOVEMENTS

The picture of Judaism and its religion in Jesus' day is, however, not so uniform as might be assumed after the sketch given above. It comprises many different and separate groups and tendencies. As the Gospels themselves indicate, the most influential is that of the Pharisees.[16] They appear for the first time in the period of the Maccabees under the aforementioned name of "the Pious" (Chassidim), who, after an initial alliance, soon formed a sharp opposition to the secularised priestly aristocracy. Their programme is the rigorous and uncompromising keeping of the Torah in all spheres and situations of daily life. Even their name (the Separated Ones) probably points to the fact that they kept themselves apart from the Hellenising leaders of the people as well as from those whom they called disdainfully "Am-haaretz"—i.e. the people from the country, who were not expert in the law. The Pharisees are a lay movement, joined closely together in a community of their own. The Pharisees quite definitely are innovators; not, as is often erroneously thought, a conservative reactionary group. For their zeal is aimed at this: the law is not to be left merely in its sacrosanct letter, but is to be interpreted as obligatory for the present day, and to be applied to all problems of private and public life. Certainly on this foundation there grows a theology; but no longer a priestly one, directed towards the worship in the temple. It is the theology of the teacher in the synagogue. The appearance of the synagogue in Judaism after the exile[17] with its worship limited to the reading and exposition of the scriptures, confession and prayer, for which there is no parallel in the ancient history of religion, is one of the most important historical presuppositions of the Pharisee movement and of the Jewish scribal teaching. Hence Pharisees and scribes are frequently found in close connection. The exposition of the scriptures, developed and practised in this movement, led to the addition to the authoritative letter of the Torah a no less obligatory exposition, which on occasion indulged in the oddest subtleties of casuistry. The entire life of the individual from morning till night was ritualised to the minutest detail, with prayer and cleansing regulations, with rules for eating and for relations with other people. Above all, the observance of the Sabbath rest became an inexhaustible topic, as we know from Jesus' numerous conflicts and disputes, and also from the literature of the rabbis. Is it permissible on the Sabbath to rescue an animal which has fallen into the well? To eat an egg laid on the Sabbath day? To keep food hot on the fire? May one get engaged? These and other questions could be easily enumerated, little as one wishes to question the considerable measure of moral wisdom and religious sincerity which is also to be found in this tradition. Nevertheless, there developed, on the ground of Pharisaism and the scribal teaching connected with it, that formalistic legalising of the law, and a corresponding detailed technique of piety, to which Jesus' message of the divine will stands in sharp contrast. The nature and spirit of the later Judaism of the Talmud have their origin here.

The authority and position of the Sadducees among the people is a much weaker one.[18] Unlike the Pharisees the class element plays a definite part in their case and forms them into a caste. They belong mainly to the circles of the privileged priestly families in Jerusalem. Even their connection with the temple and temple traditions makes it clear that, in contrast to the Pharisees who were scattered all over the country and represented the religion of the synagogue, they only exercised a small influence on the people. As far as their teaching is concerned, they differ from the Pharisees in that they reject the "tradition" of the scribes and with it newer ideas, like the teaching of the resurrection of the dead, which had been accepted by the others (Mk xii. 18; Acts xxiii. 8). Much more, however, cannot be said about them. Without strong motives and powers of their own, they present a picture of "churchliness" which has become lifeless and is satisfied with its inherited position and cultic activities, and which, as so often happens, was only too prone to laxity and to making concessions to the current régime and pagan surroundings. The tradition by which they lived was, however, too weighty, and their flexibility even with regard to an ever strengthening Pharisaism too great for them to lose their official position. Together with the Pharisees and the lay aristocracy called the "elders" of the people,[19] their representatives form, under the chairmanship of the acting high priest, the senate in Jerusalem (High Court, Sanhedrin), the highest religious and legal authority of the Jews which retained, as we saw earlier, its own disciplinary powers up to the catastrophe of the year 70.

Apart from this official Judaism, there are still to be found in Jesus' day, in a diversity no longer possible for us to ascertain in detail, heretical Jewish groups. The Gospels especially show how the old enmity between the Jews and the inhabitants of Samaria, which went back in its origin to the split between the Northern Kingdom of Israel and the Southern Kingdom of Judah after Solomon's death, had grown to an extreme degree—an enmity which had finally come to a head with the reorganisation of the Jewish community after the exile. This enmity is a national as well as a religious one. The Samaritans are looked upon by the Jews as religiously unclean, because of their intermarriage with pagans, but more so as followers of a satanic heresy (Jn. viii. 48). Only the Mosaic Pentateuch[20] is valued by them as Holy Scripture; and the legitimate place of worship, hallowed by the ancient tradition of the patriarchs, is in their view the mountain Gerizim, in the heart of their country (Jn. iv. 20 f.; cf. also Lk. ix. 51 ff.). In other ways too the Samaritans differ in their religious customs and in their expectation of the Messiah from the Judaism of Jerusalem. Their religious vitality was already broken in the days of Jesus. The temple on their holy mountain was long since destroyed (128 B.C.), even though their own cultic observances continued. Land and people are hated and avoided by the Jews. And so they lead a separate existence as a sect, sparse remnants of which have survived right up to our day.

It is a mixed race, incidentally, which also lives in Galilee, the home of Jesus. That part of the population from which Jesus' family is descended (see pages 53 f.) belongs, however, to the Jewish religious community. Of religious peculiarities of the Galileans we know nothing. It is, however, easily understood that through the physical separation from the temple, the synagogue became here the centre of Judaism. This explains also how, in this remote country which was separated from Judaea by the notorious Samaria, and which in Jesus' day differed also in its political constitution from the genuinely Jewish country, popular religious movements were more likely to develop freely and unnoticed than in Judaea.

As one of the movements which splintered off from the official Jewish religion, the Essenes should be mentioned. Until recently we knew them only through the Jewish writers Philo and Josephus. Only in recent times have they attracted increased interest, after the discovery in 1947, in caves by the Dead Sea, of a large number of highly important original texts of this sect, which go back to the first century before Christ. The deciphering and publication of the manuscripts and their scientific discussion are not yet completed. There has, however, been no doubt for some time that they offer most important material for research into contemporary Judaism, and therefore into the environment of Jesus and the early Christian Church.[21] Also the origin of the order of the Essenes or, if we wish to give them their own self-designation, the "Congregation of the Covenant", goes back apparently to the period of the Maccabees. Priesthood and hierarchy are characteristic of the strict organisation of their community. No less typical, however, are a rigorous adherence to the law, apocalyptic hopes and the claim to be the true people of God. They are therefore in many ways like the Pharisees, and yet they differ from them mainly by their radical break with official

Judaism and their sectarian seclusion, but also by their adherence to the traditions of priesthood.[22] And so they live as a religious order, having everything in common, in their own settlements, with carefully regulated conditions of admission and a novitiate, with a minutely graded order of the various offices, strictest discipline, painstaking regulations for cleanliness, regular washing and common sacred meals, as the "children of light" in opposition to the "children of darkness". Several elements of their theology and piety point beyond the limits of Judaism. We may note especially the radical dualism of their religious ideas, which has been traced back quite legitimately to Iranian-Persian influences: their rejection of the sacrificing of animals; their sacramental rites; and the secretiveness concerning their doctrines and holy books to protect them against all desecration.

In spite of their aloofness, or perhaps just because of it, we have no records of any hostility towards the Essenes on the part of the leaders of the nation. On the contrary, they are said to be, at least according to the accounts of Philo and Josephus, patterns of piety, although it should be noted that the former was an Alexandrian Jew of the Diaspora and the latter says he had belonged to them himself for a period.

There have been earlier attempts to prove a close connection between the Essenes and Jesus himself and his message,[23] and one can indeed establish a few scattered parallels. Taken on the whole, however, the points of contact are few, and Jesus' attitude to the law, especially to the law of the Sabbath, his criticism of the cleansing rites, his own in no way ascetic bearing (Mt. xi. 19), above all, however, his concern about the people and his behaviour towards tax collectors and sinners which was offensive to all pious Jews, prove that he stands in complete contrast to these separate circles of the "righteous", as well as to the representatives of official Judaism. If anything is significant it is the fact that Jesus' message and activity were not directed towards gathering the "righteous" and the "pious", nor towards the organisation of the "holy remnant".[24] Neither is there anything in the Gospels which betrays any immediate contact between Jesus and Essene circles. Unquestionably, however, their theological views and the forms of their communal discipline had a considerable, though in detail still a disputed, influence on the theology, the celebration of the sacraments and the ecclesiastical order of the original Palestinian Church. This applies above all to those Jewish Christians who, once again strictly adhering to the law, were soon expelled by the Church at large as heretics. In all probability the last remnant of the Essenes merged with them after the year 70.[25]

In a completely different category are the Messianic rebel movements, which were mentioned before and of which we have already heard under the name of Zealots (see page 33). The chain of such plots and revolts extends from the time of the first Herod to the Jewish war, indeed up to the reign of Hadrian, when Barcochba fanned once again the extinct flame of rebellion (132 to 135). At the head of these (admittedly not always political) movements stands a great number of "prophets", many of them even claiming to be the promised Messiah. According to Josephus, these leaders are "seducers and deceivers who, under the guise of having been inspired by God, work towards rebellion and revolt, and who by their words turn the people's heads and tempt them into the desert as if God would reveal to them there the miracles of their liberation" (Bell. Jud., II, 13, 4). The Book of the Acts also gives some of their names (v. 34 ff.).

Jesus' message has nothing in common with these religious and political slogans. The fact, however, that such great numbers of persons and movements belonged to the history of that time helps us understand the suspicion cast on Jesus and his condemnation by the Romans. Only one of the Messianic prophets of that time has the closest connection with Jesus. It is John the Baptist and the movement which he brought to life.

4. JOHN THE BAPTIST

According to all the Gospels, the appearance and activity of John the Baptist[26] precede the history of Jesus. For the original Christian tradition, this fact means more than a historical memory. It gives a report of John the Baptist and his movement, not to reveal the background of contemporary history and the origins of Jesus' work, as might a biographer of Luther, who at first treats the work and teaching of the precursors of the Reformation and then proceeds to tell the history of his particular subject. Rather

John the Baptist, according to the tradition, stands right from the beginning in the light of God's redemptive plan. He himself is part of the Gospel of Jesus Christ (Mk. i. 1). His description is given wholly from the point of view of the believing community. To this corresponds the manner of presentation. Suddenly, abruptly, he stands there. No story of his being called precedes his appearance. The recorders do not linger for a moment on details of his biography; at least not Mark, Matthew and John. Only Luke (Ch. i) fills this gap by giving his earlier history. He also gives valuable information about the year of his appearance, the fifteenth of the reign of the Emperor Tiberius. This is the period between October 27 and September 28 (perhaps 28/29). In the bright light which the promise of the Old Testament throws on John, we catch sight of only those contours of his person, his message, his baptism and his violent death which are of the utmost importance for the story of him who is to come.

John too, like Jesus, is the prophet of the coming kingdom of God. He has nothing in common with the political revolutionaries and with those who pretend to be the Messiah. His ascetic clothing, the skins and leather belt, and his scanty food, remind us rather of the prophet Elijah. Significant also is the place of his appearance, the Jordan steppes in the wide valley on the southern reaches of the river. Since ancient times the desert is the place with which Israel's expectations of the end were associated; for it is an ancient belief that the end shall be as the beginning. Far away from the places of worldliness, but far also from the sacred places of worship, Israel as of old shall prepare for the final revelation of God. Thus John calls to repentance, and this call applies to all. For no claim of an inherited membership in God's chosen people will be of any account before the coming judge of the world. "You brood of vipers! Who warned you to flee from the wrath to come? Bear fruit that befits repentance, and do not presume to say to yourselves, 'We have Abraham as our father'; for I tell you, God is able from these stones to raise up children to Abraham. Even now the axe is laid to the root of the trees; every tree therefore that does not bear good fruit is cut down and thrown into the fire" (Mt. iii. 7-10). The time before the final judgment is as short as that between the laying bare of the root and the blow which

smites the tree. Of small avail is it to count on the guarantees which
have been given to God's own people, or even to those who think
of themselves as the "righteous". Here is a penetrating, sharp call
to battle against all presumptuous reliance on the merits of their
forefathers, especially on Abraham, who, according to the Jewish
faith, will save his children from the fate of hell. Let it be noted:
the idea of a chosen people is not being abandoned, the promise of
God is not being done away with. What is being destroyed is the
assumption that God's chosen people and the visible Israel here on
earth are one and the same thing. For God does not stand under
the compulsion of history, under a "must" which a presumptuous
faith casts up at him. He is free, and in his freedom stands by his
promise.

John's call to repentance renews the message of the Old Testament prophets of judgment. What makes it different is the urgent
nearness of the time of God's kingdom, and the disturbing
"Already" of the present hour in the world's course. Repentance
has here nothing to do with religious rites of repentance. But neither
does our definition as a "change of mind" exhaust its meaning, as
it does not make it clear that this conversion means not only a
change of mind but also of actions. It conceals the direction in
which it points; namely the turning away from an old godless past
and the turning towards God and his coming reign. The horizon
which opens up in the challenge of John the Baptist, as afterwards
in the message of Jesus, extends further and comprises more than
the individual renewal of man in his inner life. About face! That
means: make room here in our present existence for the coming
world change.

The Messiah whom John the Baptist announces is the judge of
the world; not the fulfiller of political expectations but he who
gathers in the last harvest—"His winnowing fork is in his hand,
and he will clear his threshing floor, and gather his wheat into the
granary, but the chaff he will burn with unquenchable fire" (Mt.
iii. 12). The same saying of John the Baptist uses a different picture
in calling the work of the "One to come" a baptism of the holy
Spirit and of fire, for the salvation of the true people of God and for
the destruction of those who are not prepared to repent (Mt. iii.
11).[27]

The Baptist stands in the service of him who is to come, as the one who is not worthy to loose the shoes of the stronger (Mk. i. 7). His baptism as well is to be understood in the light of the end of the world and the judgment. Baptism is characteristic of John to such an extent that he received from it his second name "the Baptist".[28] Clearly, this baptism has the meaning of an eschatological sacrament, not, however, acting as magic without regard to the preparedness of the baptised, but, as a "baptism of repentance" (Mk. i. 4), it is the last preparation and sealing of the baptised for the coming "baptism" of the Messiah, and preserves them from the day of wrath to come.[29]

The Christian Church has taken over this baptism of John, but has given it a new meaning. Other associations with the history of religion can no longer be established with certainty. Some scholars have connected the baptism of John with the Jewish baptism of proselytes,[30] which was performed in Judaism in connection with the circumcision of pagans joining the Jewish community. This is attested, however, only in slightly later times, and this derivation is unlikely. For apart from the question of the age of this Jewish rite, it would then appear that John had deprived it of its character as a religious ceremony and—what is all too paradoxical—had treated the Jews like pagans. Much more convincing is the reference to the various rites of baptism which we know from isolated Jewish sects in Palestine and Syria in the first few centuries.[31] The Essenes also belong to these.[32] But all these "baptisms", through which the baptised became a member of such a community, are at best initial baptisms, aiming at a continued repetition of ritual cleansings, and not happening once for all as with John. In the movement which John the Baptist called to life, the custom and interpretation of baptism can only have changed later, when John's disciples had themselves become a separate sect. Already the New Testament confirms that they became such a community, which rivalled the Christian community.[33] We probably have a last remnant of the Jewish baptismal sects of Palestine in the gnostic community of the Mandaeans, which, however, cannot be conclusively proved to be a remnant of John's sect. We know the Mandaeans from extensive original sources which, it is true, took final form and were collected only later. In their teachings and baptismal rites the Baptist and the Jordan still play a considerable part.[34]

The passages on John the Baptist from the Q source, which Matthew and Luke used and to which we owe the best information on John, do not yet show any trace of a separate individual sect, but only the strong influence of John on the people as a whole. The historical credibility of the tradition concerning the preaching and baptism of John the Baptist, clearly though the viewpoint of Christian faith is discerned in it, is confirmed by the fact that the Christian message no longer presented the work of the coming judge of the world in terms of a baptism of the Spirit and of fire, and that a strong tension exists between its presentation of Christ and the picture of the Messiah as announced by John. We get an impression of this tension from the short conversation with which Matthew introduces the story of Jesus' baptism (Mt. iii. 14 ff.). Here John asks Jesus, who comes to him to be baptised, "I need to be baptised by you, and do you come to me?" This is more than an expression of mere modesty, just as Jesus' answer: "Let it be so now: for thus it is fitting for us to fulfil all righteousness" is more than an utterance only of personal humility. The text also betrays no indication of wanting to give an answer to the question why the sinless Christ had come to receive a baptism of repentance. This theme is only found in apocryphal tradition (the Gospel of the Hebrews). It has since then survived tenaciously in the interpretation of the story of the baptism in Matthew. In reality this conversation is to be understood against the background of the announcement just made concerning the Messianic judge of the world and his baptism. Only thus can the question of John and Jesus' answer be understood: The time of my baptism is over, now has come the time of your baptism with the Spirit and with fire. What then does the following mean? the Messianic baptiser is one to be baptised, the judge of the world is among the sinners. Jesus' reply is at first mysterious: This is as it should be! It is under the "must" of God, the will of God—all righteousness shall be fulfilled.

It is clear that Christian reflection is expressed in these verses, passed on only by Matthew, which looks back in faith on the person and life of Jesus as a whole. It is equally clear, however, that it was precisely this strange contrast between the message of John the Baptist and the nature of Jesus Christ which was the cause of this reflection.

We should like to have more reliable information on what John thought of Jesus. Did he recognise in him the promised Messiah? Did this knowledge dawn on him later? The Christian tradition does indeed represent it so. Our judgment, however, will have to be a critical one here, in spite of our long familiarity with this point of view. Even the picture of the Messiah in John's preaching does not, as we have just seen, tally with the person of Jesus. The message of John speaks of the heavenly judge of the world, not of a human being here on earth. A continued existence of the movement of John could not be understood and could only be explained as an open rejection of Jesus' Messiahship and of his Church—and this in opposition to John's own words. Therefore we must allow for the fact that it was the Christian tradition which first made John, the prophet of the coming Judge of the world, into a witness for Jesus as the Messiah. Just how active this tendency was in the Christian tradition is most clearly noticeable in the Gospel according to John, which makes John the Baptist refuse emphatically all those Messianic attributes which people wanted to ascribe to him, and puts into his mouth the Christian kerygma as his testimony: "Behold the Lamb of God who takes away the sin of the world" (Jn. i. 29, 36).[35]

We may judge with greater confidence the other question of what Jesus himself thought about John, although his words too, in the tradition, are interwoven with statements which express the retrospective testimony of the later Church. The fact that Jesus let himself be baptised by John belongs to the data of his life which cannot be doubted. Nor can the fact that the meeting with John was and continued to be of the highest importance for his own understanding of his mission. Jesus of course did not begin his own work as a disciple of John, and did not directly continue John's work (cf. Ch. III). Nevertheless, he never opposes him. On the contrary, he acknowledged John and relates his own vocation with that of the Baptist. Thus, when questioned by the high priests, scribes and elders as to his own authority (Mk. xi. 27-33), he answers with this surprising question in return: "Was the baptism of John from heaven (i.e. from God) or from men?" And he declares to his opponents, who do not dare to answer lest they jeopardise their position: "Neither will I tell you by what authority I do these things" (v. 33). Their silence is answered with silence. Unmistakably this is his "Yes" which he pronounces on John and his baptism, and the meaning of this "Yes" is: The decision concerning John and his baptism of repentance, is also the decision concerning Jesus and his mission. This is expressed quite frankly in this passage: "All the people that heard him (John), and the tax collectors, justified God, having been baptised with the baptism of John; but the Pharisees and the lawyers rejected the purpose of God for themselves, not having been baptised by him" (Lk. vii. 29 f.; Mt. xxi. 32). In a different passage Jesus compares the people with children playing in the market place, to whom one may play a tune for dancing, or to whom one may sing a song of mourning (so as to play at "funerals" with them), and yet in their stubbornness and sulkiness they cannot be made to do anything. "For John came neither eating nor drinking and they say: 'He has a demon'; the Son of man came eating and drinking and they say: 'Behold a glutton and a drunkard, a friend of tax collectors and sinners!'" (Mt. xi. 18 f.) The Baptist was too gloomy for them, an eccentric ascetic, Jesus too worldly—not even giving due regard to the difference between the righteous and sinners; John and Jesus— extremes which are to be avoided. Of course, the meaning of this word is not to put a choice as between the "pessimistic" attitude of John and the "optimistic" one of Jesus before the people, but to link each up with the other, John sent by God in the time of preparation for the end, and Jesus the bringer of the time of rejoicing (cf. also Mk. ii. 18 ff). Task and destiny unite them both.

And so the person and message of John have an important place in Jesus' preaching, just as they do in the tradition of the Church.[36] This is also shown in the words of Matthew xi. 7 ff., where Jesus asks his audience what had drawn them to John: "What did you go out into the wilderness to behold? A reed shaken by the wind?"— that is to say, an insignificant natural phenomenon or, better, taking it symbolically: a changeable man who agrees with everybody. "Why then did you go out? To see a man clothed in soft raiment?

Behold, those who wear soft raiment are in kings' houses." One is as absurd as the other. They know it themselves. They have gone out to a prophet and were right in doing so. "Yes, I tell you and more than a prophet. . . . Among those born of women there has risen no one greater than John the Baptist" (Mt. xi. 7-11). It is, however, perhaps the following passage which expresses in the clearest terms how Jesus understood John and his own mission, that strangely dark saying which has puzzled many up to the present time: "From the days of John the Baptist until now the kingdom of heaven suffered violence, and men of violence take it by force" (xi. 12). Since the days of John the Baptist, therefore, the kingdom of God is on the way, although it is still being held up and opposed. But its hour has struck, although in affliction and concealment. John is herewith raised above all the prophets before him. "For all the prophets and the law prophesied until John" (xi. 13). He is no longer the herald of the future only, but already belongs himself to the time in which the promise is being fulfilled. This constitutes his greatness, and yet at the same time through this he is over-shadowed by Jesus himself, in whose words and work the kingdom of God, hidden therein, has begun.[37] Here lies, according to Jesus himself, the reason for the view of the Christian tradition which gives to John, with increasing emphasis, only the role of the forerunner. From then on he signifies for the Christian Church, in the terms of later Jewish apocalypticism, the returned Elijah who was to prepare the people of God for the coming of the Messiah. Far from merely assigning to him a temporal and now accomplished task, it recognised him to be the one who will be for ever prepar-ing the way for Christ and who, so to speak, stands guard at the frontier of the aeons. The way to Christ and into the kingdom of God did not merely at one time—in a moment of past history—lead through John the Baptist, but it leads once and for all only along that path of repentance shown by him. Faith in Jesus Christ is only there where the believer, for himself and within himself, lets the shift of the aeons take place in his own life.

The insoluble interconnection between Jesus and John has found diverse expressions in the tradition. Most distinctly perhaps in Matthew. He summarises the message of John and the message of Jesus in the same words: "Repent, for the kingdom of heaven is at hand" (iii. 2; iv. 17). And yet he differentiates between the two. For this reason the evangelist attaches the word of promise from the Old Testament (Is. xl. 3) to the saying when spoken by John (Mt. iii. 3): "The voice of one crying in the wilderness: Prepare the way of the Lord, make his paths straight." But when the message comes from Jesus' own lips (iv. 17), it is preceded in the Gospel by the prophetic word of fulfilment (Is. ix. 1 f.). "The people who sat in darkness *have* seen a great light; and for those who sat in the region and shadow of death light *has* dawned" (Mt. iv. 16).[38]

Chapter III

JESUS OF NAZARETH

THE nature of the sources does not permit us to paint a biographical picture of the life of Jesus against the background of the history of his people and his age. Nevertheless, what these sources do yield as regards the historical facts concerning the personality and career of Jesus is not negligible, and demands careful attention. We shall, therefore, try first of all to compile the main historically indisputable traits, and to present the rough outlines of Jesus' person and history. In doing this, we must, of course, desist from rash combinations of the biographical data and must use the greatest critical caution in order to be able really to focus those facts which are prior to any pious interpretation and which manifest themselves as undistorted and primary.

The childhood and adolescence of Jesus are obscure for us from the historical point of view. The birth narratives in Matthew and Luke, which differ from one another not inconsiderably, are too much overgrown[1] by legends and by Jewish as well as Christian messianic conceptions to be used for historical assertions. The importance and meaning of these texts lie in a different area. The home of Jesus is the semi-pagan, despised Galilee. His native town is Nazareth. His family certainly belonged to the Jewish part of the population which, since the times of the Maccabees, had reattached themselves to the temple cult in Jerusalem and the legal practices of Judaism. Only a criticism blinded by racial ideologies could deny the Jewish origin of Jesus.[2] Jesus' father was a carpenter, and possibly he himself was too.[3] We know the names of his parents, Joseph and Mary, and those of his brothers,[4] James, Joses, Judas and Simon (Mk. vi. 3). His brothers—as well as his mother—were originally unbelievers (Mk. iii. 21, 31; Jn. vii. 5), but later belonged to the Church and to its missionaries (Acts i. 14; I Cor.

ix. 5). The tradition occasionally also mentions Jesus' sisters (Mk. vi. 3; Mt. xiii. 56). Jesus' mother tongue is the Aramaic of Galilee, the same dialect by which the servants of the high priest recognise Peter when he denies his Master in Jerusalem (Mt. xxvi. 73). Hebrew was at that time no longer a spoken language, but rather only the language of religion and of scholars (somewhat comparable to the ecclesiastical Slavonic of the Orthodox Church). As a Jewish rabbi he must have been able to understand the ancient language of the Bible. On the other hand, we do not know to what extent he and his disciples knew Greek, widely used in administration and commerce. At any rate we find in Jesus no trace of the influence of Greek philosophy or of the Greek manner of living, just as nothing is known of activity on his part in the Hellenistic towns of the country. Rather we hear of his activity in the smaller hamlets and villages—Bethsaida, Chorazin, Capernaum—in the hill country and round the Sea of Galilee.

According to an isolated note in Luke, Jesus' public ministry begins, following the work of John the Baptist, at about his thirtieth year (Lk. iii. 23). His own baptism by John is one of the most certainly verified occurrences of his life. Tradition, however, has altogether transformed the story into a testimony to the Christ, so that we cannot gather from it what baptism meant for Jesus himself, for his decisions and for his inner development. But that this event was of far-reaching importance nobody will deny. It is all the more important that Jesus, without ever questioning the mission and the authority of the Baptist, nevertheless does not continue the work of the Baptist and his followers in the Jordan valley, but starts his own work in Galilee—like John, as a prophet of the coming kingdom of God. The instrument of his activity, however, is no longer baptism, but his spoken word and helping hand. We can no longer say with certainty how long Jesus' activity lasted. The first three Gospels create the impression that it lasted but a year. But they do not give a reliable chronology. We learn a great deal about his preaching, the conflict with his opponents, his healing and the additional help he granted the suffering, and the powerful influence which went forth from him. The people flock to him. Disciples follow him, but his enemies also arise and increase. All this will have to occupy us later. Here we are only concerned with the rough outlines of his life and his work. The last decisive turning point in his life is the resolution to go to Jerusalem with his disciples in order to confront the people there with his message in face of the coming kingdom of God. At the end of this road is his death on the cross. These meagre, indisputable facts comprise a very great deal. There is little enough in this enumeration, and yet it contains most important information about the life story of Jesus and its stages.

Much remains hidden in the obscurity of history. Tradition does not yield a logical and detailed account of the course of Jesus' life. Nevertheless, the Gospels furnish much more material as regards the outlines of his historical person seen in the setting of his own world. We shall, therefore, recall the picture of that world in which he appeared.

As we saw, time and history, the past and the future, determine in a unique way the thought, experience and hopes of the Jewish people. This people finds its God and itself in the past, in which its life and character were given to it; and in the future, in which its life and its character are to be restored to it. It knows no other security, even in a present which reveals nothing of this certainty and seems to mock this people's claim. It knows its sole task as that of guarding faithfully this past and this future. Thus the world in which Jesus appears is a world between past and future; it is so strongly identified with the one and with the other that, according to the Jewish faith, the immediate present is practically non-existent. The whole of life is caught in a network of sacred traditions. Everyone has his place within a structure determined and ordered by the law and promise of God. Whoever lives up to this divine system can claim eternal salvation; whoever does not is rejected. All time is time between, and as such it is a time of stewardship, founded in God's decisions of the past and looking forward to God's decisions in the future, which mean salvation or destruction for each one. We can now understand the strange picture presented by the historical milieu in which Jesus lived. It is comparable to a soil hardened and barren through its age-long history and tradition, yet a volcanic, eruptive ground, out of whose cracks and crevices breaks forth again and again the fire of a burning expectation. However, both, torpidity and convulsion, petrifaction and blazing eruption have, at bottom, the same origin: they are the outcome and expression of a faith in a God who is beyond the world and history.

This world comes alive and is immediately present in the story of Jesus, as told by the writers of the Gospels. All the characters who encounter Jesus bear the stamp of this world: the priest and the scribe, the Pharisee and the publican, the rich and the poor, the healthy and the sick, the righteous and the sinner. They appear in the story in a matter-of-fact and simple fashion, chosen at random and of great variety, and appearing in no particular order. Yet all the characters, however great their diversity, present a very human appearance. In their encounter with Jesus—whatever they experience in this encounter and whatever their attitude towards it—they come to this amazing event, their meeting with Jesus, as fully real people.

Jesus belongs to this world. Yet in the midst of it he is of unmistakable otherness. This is the secret of his influence and his rejection. Faith has given manifold expression to this secret. But even he who, prior to any interpretation, keeps his eyes fixed upon the historical appearance of Jesus, upon the manner of his words and works, even he meets with this his insoluble mystery. We become aware of the fact when we try to fit this figure into any of the descriptions and categories then prevalent in Judaism. He is a prophet of the coming kingdom of God. Indeed the title of prophet is occasionally used by the tradition (Mk. viii. 28; Mt. xxi. 11, 46, etc.). Yet he is in no way completely contained in this category, and differs from the customary ways of a prophet. A prophet has to produce his credentials, somewhat as did the prophets of the old covenant in telling the story of their calling and in accompanying their message with the sacred prophetic saying: ". . . says the Lord . . ." (Amos vi. 8, 14; Hos. ii. 16; xi. 11; Is. i. 24; and elsewhere). Jesus, on the other hand, never speaks of his calling, and nowhere does he use the ancient, prophetic formula. Even less do we find any trace of that self-justification typical of the apocalyptic visionaries of later Judaism, who claim the authority of ecstatic states of mind and visions, secret revelations of the next world, and miraculous insight into God's decrees. Jesus refuses to justify himself and his message in this way. But those who listen to him have to accept the saying: "And blessed is he who takes no offence at me" (Mt. xi. 6).

The prophet of the coming kingdom of God is at the same time a rabbi, who proclaims the divine law, who teaches in synagogues, who gathers disciples, and who debates with other scribes in the manner of their profession and under the same authority of scripture. The forms and laws of scribal tradition are to be found abundantly in his sayings. Prophet and rabbi—how does this go together? How does the message of the kingdom of God agree with the proclamation of the divine will? And what is the meaning of becoming a follower, and of the discipleship for which he calls, in view of this unity of prophet and rabbi? All these questions will concern us later.

This rabbi differs considerably from the other members of his class. Even external facts reveal this difference. Jesus does not only teach in the synagogues, but also in the open field, on the shores of the lake, during his wanderings. And his followers are a strange crowd. Even those people are amongst them whom an official rabbi would do his best to avoid: women and children, tax collectors and sinners. Above all, his manner of teaching differs profoundly from that of the other rabbis. A rabbi is an interpreter of Scripture. This lends authority to his office, an authority which has to prove itself from the given letter of Scripture and the not less authoritative exegesis of the "Fathers". Their authority is thus always a derived authority. Jesus' teaching, on the other hand, never consists merely in the interpretation of an authoritatively given sacred text, not even when words from Scripture are quoted. The reality of God and the authority of his will are always directly present, and are fulfilled in him. There is nothing in contemporary Judaism which corresponds to the immediacy with which he teaches. This is true to such a degree that he even dares to confront the literal text of the law with the immediately present will of God. (See Ch. V, 1.)

We shall meet this feature again in his similes and parables, no less than in the words of wisdom which speak with manifest relevance and utmost simplicity: for example, that "a city set on an hill cannot be hid" (Mt. v. 14); that "men do not light a lamp

and put it under a bushel" (Mt. v. 15); that "no one can add one
cubit to his span of life" (Mt. vi. 27); that one should "let the day's
own trouble be sufficient for the day" (Mt. vi. 34); etc. In all these
utterances Jesus draws into the service of his message the world of
nature and the life of man, and those everyday experiences which
everyone knows and shares, without using the established structure
of sacred traditions and texts. The listener is never obliged to look
for premises which would give meaning to Jesus' teaching, or to
recall the theory about doctrines and traditions which he would be
supposed to know beforehand. For Jesus never talks 'over' God, the
world and man, the past and the future, from any particular
"point of view".

This directness, if anything, is part of the picture of the historical Jesus. He bears the stamp of this directness right from the
very beginning. The immediate present is the hallmark of all the
words of Jesus, of his appearance and his actions, in a world which,
as we said, had lost the present, because it lived between the past
and the future, between traditions and promises or threats, in
security or anxiety, conscious of its own rights or under sentence
for its own lawlessness.

What the Gospels report on numerous individual occasions about
Jesus' attitude to and influence on the different people he encounters
is important in this context. We are not concerned here with the
question whether all these scenes can claim historical reliability,
how far we have to consider in them the influence of legends, and
to what extent typical stylistic devices are used which are to be
found elsewhere in the presentation of teaching and disputes, of
healings and the performance of various miracles. We have left no
doubt that these factors do play a considerable part. Nevertheless,
tradition has caught an essential feature of the historical Jesus, a
feature which accords exactly with what we have said about his
way of teaching.

Every one of the scenes described in the Gospels reveals Jesus'
astounding sovereignty in dealing with situations according to
the kind of people he encounters. This is apparent in the numerous
teaching and conflict passages, in which he sees through his opponents, disarms their objections, answers their questions, or forces
them to answer them for themselves. He can make his opponent

open his mouth or he can put him to silence (Mt. xxii. 34). The same can be seen when he encounters those who seek help: miraculous powers proceed from him, the sick flock around him, their relatives and friends seek his help. Often he fulfils their request, but he can also refuse, or keep the petitioners waiting and put them to the test. Not infrequently he withdraws himself (Mk. i. 35 ff.), but, on the other hand, he is often ready and on the spot sooner than the sufferers dare hope (Mt. viii. 5 ff.; Lk. xix. 1 ff.), and he freely breaks through the strict boundaries which traditions and prejudices had set up. Similar characteristics can be seen in his dealings with his disciples. He calls them with the command of the master (Mk. i. 16 ff.), but he also warns and discourages them from their discipleship (Lk. ix. 57 ff.; xiv. 28 ff.). Again and again his behaviour and method are in sharp contrast to what people expect of him and what, from their own point of view, they hope for. He withdraws from the people, as John reports, when he is to be made king (Jn. vi. 15). In his encounters with others we see time and again that he knows men and uncovers their thoughts, a feature which the Gospels have frequently elaborated to the point of the miraculous.[5] The two sons of Zebedee meet with this quality when Jesus turns down their ambitious desires (Mk. x. 35 ff.). Peter experiences it when, in answer to his confession of the Messiah, he is given Jesus' words about the suffering of the Son of man, and when, wanting to make Jesus forsake his path, he receives the sharp retort: "Get behind me, Satan! For you are not on the side of God, but of men" (Mk. viii. 27-33). The same is expressed by the scenes which describe Peter's denial (Mk. xiv. 29 ff.), and the betrayal of Judas (Mk. xiv. 17 ff.).[6] It would be possible to go on quoting other tales at random, even if they belong to the traditional store of legends. The important point is that in all of them the same feature recurs, by which the historical Jesus can be recognised. We need recall only two more stories from the synoptic Gospels. The first is the scene where Jesus is the guest of Simon the Pharisee, and a woman, known throughout the town as a sinner, enters, wets Jesus' feet with her tears, dries them with her hair and anoints them with ointment. When the Pharisee is secretly indignant at the awkward scene, he said to himself: "If this man were a prophet, he would have known who and what sort of woman this is who is touching him." Jesus gives him this answer: "Simon, I have something to say to you", and tells him the parable of the unequal debtors, to one of whom the creditor forgave a large sum and to the other a small one. "Which of them will love him more?" (Lk. vii. 36-50). A most illuminating illustration of Jesus' insight into the character of his interlocutors is the story of the rich man who asks him about eternal life. Jesus points him to the ten commandments (which shows that the right way has long since been made evident and does not need any specific new revelation), and the rich man professes that he has kept them all since his youth. The story ends, "And Jesus, looking upon him, loved him, and said to him: You lack one thing. Go sell what you have and give to the poor, and you will have treasure in heaven; and come, follow me." This is a demand on which the rich man founders (Mk. x. 17-22). The passages in the Gospels which deal with Jesus' perception and penetrating insight ought to be assembled without fear that this would be a merely sentimental undertaking. In reality we are here concerned with a most characteristic trait in the historical Jesus, one which quite accurately is confirmed by the nature of his preaching.

The Gospels call this patent immediacy of Jesus' sovereign power his "authority". They apply this word to his teaching: "They were astonished at his teaching, for he taught them as one who had authority, and not as the scribes" (Mk. i. 22; Mt. vii. 29). They also use it for the power of his healing word (Mt. viii. 5 ff.). The word "authority" certainly contains already the mystery of Jesus' personality and influence, as understood by faith. It therefore transcends the merely "historical" sphere. Yet it denotes a reality which appertains to the historical Jesus and is prior to any interpretation. In his encounters with the most different people, Jesus' "authority" is always immediately and authentically present. But the people to whom he talks and with whom he deals are also there, undisguised and real. They all contribute something towards the encounter with him. The righteous contribute their righteousness, the scribes the weight of their doctrine and arguments, the tax collectors and sinners their guilt, the needy their sickness, the demoniacs the fetters of their obsession and the poor the burden of their poverty. All this is not eradicated or irrelevant, but it does not count in this encounter. This encounter compels everyone to step out of his customary background. This bringing to light of men as they really are takes place in all stories about Jesus. It happens each time, however, simply and as a matter of course, without in any way being forced, without that awkward compulsion towards self-disclosure which is well known from a certain type of later Christian sermon.

Jesus' aid bears, therefore, the stamp of a genuine involvement and a passionate tackling of the situation, when he is wrathful over the power of disease (Mk. i. 41)[7] and commands the demons (Mk. i. 25); but also in the blessing when he calls the children to himself and lays his hands upon them or upon the sick (Mk. x. 13 ff.; vii. 31 ff., etc.).

Many of the texts mentioned will concern us later. We are here only concerned with that prevailing feature of Jesus' authority, equally recognisable in his words and in his deeds. It also characterises Jesus' way, the consistency with which he sticks at it and keeps on it to the very end; both when he takes up a certain position, contends and helps, and when he withdraws and withholds himself, not only from his opponents, but also from his followers.

The Gospels give us the right to discuss all this in a very human manner, without immediately using interpretations with which faith has invested the mystery of his person as far back as the early Christian tradition. We have, therefore, not begun straight away with the question of Jesus' "messianic consciousness", and we will not enter upon it until the end of the book (cf. Ch. VIII). For, however it may be answered, so much is certain: it is not a separate or prevailing theme in his preaching to which everything else is subordinated. He certainly does not make it the condition for the understanding of his message and actions. The very nature of his teaching and his actions, so vulnerable, so open to controversy and yet so direct and matter of fact, doom to failure any attempt to raise his Messiahship into a system of dogma through which his preaching, his actions and his history would receive their meaning.

We shall have to guard against any rash attempt to fit these features which we have tried to describe in rough and most incomplete outline into the usual categories of the religious genius, the person of great originality, and particularly into the picture of the pastor *par excellence*. What is essential is the indissoluble connection between what has been said here and Jesus' message about the reality of God, his kingdom and his will. This alone lends to Jesus' history and person the character of unmediated presence, gives the force of an actual event to his preaching, and makes his words and deeds so incomparably compelling. To make the reality of God present: this is the essential mystery of Jesus. This making-present of the reality of God signifies the end of the world in which it takes place. This is why the scribes and Pharisees rebel, because they see Jesus' teaching as a revolutionary attack upon law and tradition. This is why the demons cry out, because they sense an inroad upon their sphere of power "before the time" (Mt. viii. 29). This is why his own people think him mad (Mk. iii. 21). But this is also why the people marvel and the saved praise God.

The story told by the Gospels signifies the end of the world, although not, it is true, in the sense of an obvious drama and a visible catastrophe. On the contrary, it is not the world which ends here obviously and visibly; rather it is Jesus of Nazareth on the cross. And yet, in this story, the world reaches its end. The story breaks off, and the people who belong to it have to bear witness to what has happened, everyone in his own way. Pharisees, scribes and priests, as the guardians of law and tradition. The rejected, who, according to the prevailing standards of the same world, have no right and no place before God because of their guilt and fate, and who are now suddenly accepted as Jesus' boon companions. Those whom Jesus' word has freed from demonic powers. The sick who become healthy. But also the disciples, who leave everything and obey Jesus' call to "follow me". In each case a world has come to its end, be it for salvation or judgment. Its past is called in question. Its future is no longer secure—that future towards which it has been moving, according to all those traditions and laws which had been valid until then. In this sense its "time" has ended. In the encounter with Jesus, time is left to no one: the past whence he comes is no longer confirmed, and the future he dreams of no longer assured. But this is precisely why every individual is granted his own new present. For life, world and the existence of every individual, now stand in the sudden flash of light of the coming God, in the light of his reality and presence. This is the theme which Jesus proclaims.

Chapter IV

THE DAWN OF THE KINGDOM OF GOD

1. THE HOUR OF SALVATION

"Now after John was arrested, Jesus came into Galilee, preaching the gospel of God, and saying: 'The time is fulfilled, and the kingdom of God is at hand; repent and believe in the gospel' " (Mk. i. 14 ff.). "From that time Jesus began to preach saying, 'Repent, for the kingdom of heaven is at hand' " (Mt. iv. 17). With these words the first two evangelists sum up the whole message of Jesus. Each does so in his own language: Mark clearly in the language of the first Christian mission,[1] Matthew in the language of the first Jewish-Christian community, which shuns the name of God, saying "kingdom of heaven" instead of "kingdom of God".[2] There is no difference in substance: God's kingdom is near! That is the core of Jesus' message.

But what is meant by the "kingdom of God"? To Jesus' first hearers the word rule, or kingdom, of God was not, as it is for most people today, a vague or empty term. Yahweh's kingdom is praised in the Psalms:

"All thy works shall give thanks to thee, O Lord; and all thy saints shall bless thee!
They shall speak of the glory of thy kingdom and tell of thy power,
to make known to the sons of men thy mighty deeds, and the glorious splendour of thy kingdom.
Thy kingdom is an everlasting kingdom, and thy dominion endures throughout all generations" (Ps. cxlv. 10-13).

"The Lord has established his throne in the heavens; and his kingdom rules over all" (Ps. ciii. 19).

Every year the ancient Israelites celebrated in their worship Yahweh's enthronement, his ascending to be king of all nations, his victory over all his enemies (Ps. xlvii, xciii, xcvi, etc.). The prophet, too, gives the same picture of the moving moment when after a terrible time of suffering those who have remained amidst the ruins of Jerusalem eagerly await the return of the exiles, till the watchmen at their posts break out into cries of joy: "How beautiful upon the mountains are the feet of him who brings good tidings, who publishes peace, who brings good tidings of good, who publishes salvation; who says to Zion, 'Your God reigns'" (Is. lii. 7).

While in ancient ritual and prophecy the acknowledgment of Yahweh's reign is not merely an acknowledgment for the present, but at the same time an expression of hope, this applies even more in later Jewish thought. The revelation of the kingdom of God is the very essence of the hope, which will find its fulfilment only at the end of time. It is still hidden, still held back, the powers of evil—tribulation, sin and death—are still in control, but the hope of the appearing of God's kingdom holds firmly and unerringly to a belief in his victory and to the certainty of his promise. Therefore it can already be said of a man who becomes converted to Judaism and obeys its laws, and of the believer who in his prayer utters his confession to Israel's God: he takes the "yoke of the kingdom of heaven upon himself".[3]

Whatever political dreams or indeed whatever fantastic expectations of the destruction or rebirth of the world were bound up with the hopes of the Jews, it is a fundamental part of these hopes that the spirit of resignation which banishes God to a misty place beyond our ideals and which accepts the idea that no change is possible in this world, is totally strange to it. Even in its most distorted form their hope cannot be written off merely as a sudden reversion of feeling due to disappointment in the present, nor as a picture of the future sketched in glowing colours to offset the distress and despair of the present. Nietzsche's "resentment" theory does not apply here, however deeply such traits are inscribed in the hopes of the Jews. Upon this hope is built the certainty that God is the Lord of this puzzling world, and will not always remain afar off, but will reveal himself and vindicate his word. It is this certainty which makes the present lack of fulfilment the real difficulty for Jewish faith, and invests the hope of the coming of God's kingdom with its extreme tension.

Jesus' message lives by this same certainty. For him, too, God's kingdom means God's future and victory, overcoming the powers of the devil, a shift from this aeon to the next.

"Blessed are you poor: for yours is the kingdom of God.
Blessed are you that hunger now: for you shall be satisfied.
Blessed are you that weep now: for you shall laugh" (Lk. vi. 20 f.).

Immediately, however, the striking thing about his preaching in contrast to the hopes of the Jews emerges. Not a word does he say either to confirm or renew the national hopes of his people. He would assuredly come across such hopes in his dealings with the people and even among his disciples. The cries of the people as he rode into Jerusalem speak of it: "Blessed be the kingdom of our father David, that is coming" (Mk. xi. 10). The inscription on the cross speaks of it: "King of the Jews" (Mk. xv. 26), and shows that Pontius Pilate had him executed as one of the many Messianic pretenders to the crown, whom the Romans simply counted as rebels. Even the disciples on the Emmaus road say: "But we had hoped that he was the one to redeem Israel" (Lk. xxiv. 21; cf. also xix. 11), and elsewhere the disciples ask: "Lord, will you at this time restore the kingdom to Israel?" (Acts i. 6). But Jesus disappoints this expectation. Not once does he speak of the restoration of the kingdom of David in power and majesty, and of the Messiah who will destroy his enemies (Ps. Sol. xvii. 21 ff., 30 ff.). Perhaps the obscure words "From the days of John the Baptist until now the kingdom of heaven has suffered violence and men of violence take it by force" (Mt. xi. 12), involve a sharp, express refusal to have anything to do with the political Messianic movement of the Zealots.[4]

On the other hand, his message is much more closely allied to the apocalyptic, cosmic expectations of his day. Jesus, too, speaks of the day of judgment, soon to dawn violently, of the end of this world and the tribulations it must undergo comparable to the time of the flood (Lk. xvii. 26 f.; xxi. 34 f., etc.), of the coming of the

Son of man, Judge of the World (Mk. viii. 38; xiii. 24 ff.), of the great harvest of the world (Mk. iv. 26 ff.; Mt. xiii. 24 ff.), but also of the joy of the heavenly feast (Mt. viii. 11). And yet here, too, the contrast between his message and late Jewish apocalypticism is deep and fundamental. In comparison with the pictures painted by the latter, with extravagant flights of fancy and with its endless attempts to answer the ancient question of prophets and good men: "How long, O Lord?" (Ps. lxxx. 4; lxxiv. 10, cf. Dan. ix. 4-19), by means of observation of cosmic and historical events, or by fantastic calculations and arrangement of epochs, Jesus' gospel is remarkable for a distinct reticence. It is not given to any man to know the day and the hour. That is why he says: "Therefore you also must be ready; for the Son of man is coming at an hour you do not expect" (Mt. xxiv. 44). And that is why he refuses, in such a striking and emphatic way compared with the contemporary apocalypses, to depict in detail the future world, with its terrors and its joys. All the conceptions and pictures in Jesus' message are directed with concentrated force on one thing only, and are contained in that one thing—that God will reign.[5]

This is the first peculiarity of his message. But that is not all. Its real individuality lies in the directness—in New Testament language: the authority—with which Jesus proclaims that the kingdom of God is near and calls for conversion. This is precisely what seems to link him with John the Baptist. Did he not also preach: "Already the axe is laid to the root of the trees?" And yet, between these two and their preaching there is a difference like that between the eleventh and the twelfth hours. For Jesus calls: the shift in the aeons is here, the kingdom of God is already dawning. Now is the hour of which the prophets' promise told: "The blind receive their sight and the lame walk, lepers are cleansed and the deaf hear, the dead are raised up and the poor have good news preached to them" (Mt. xi. 5; cf. Is. xxxv. 5, etc.).

It is happening now in Jesus' words and deeds. Therefore the saying ends thus: "And blessed is he who takes no offence at me" (Mt. xi. 6). Therefore the blessing upon the eyewitnesses who understand the meaning of this hour: "Blessed are the eyes which see what you see! For I tell you that many prophets and kings desired to see what you see, and did not see it; and to hear what you hear, and did not hear it" (Lk. x. 23 f.). His saying to his disciples: "I saw Satan fall like lightning from heaven" (Lk. x. 18), sounds like the words of a visionary. But nowhere else does Jesus speak as an apocalyptic seer, who is carried off to heaven and allowed to behold the fall of demonic powers and the dawning of the Messianic splendour, and to whom the secrets of the final drama of the world are revealed by one of the heavenly spirits. What distinguishes Jesus from these seers is that he himself enters the battlefield; God's victory over Satan takes place in his words and deeds, and it is in them that the signs of this victory are erected. In Jesus himself is to be found the stronger man who puts an end to the rule of Satan and takes his booty from him (Mk. iii. 27). "But if it is by the finger of God that I cast out demons, then the kingdom of God has come upon you" (Lk. xi. 20). This is why he answers the Pharisees' question as to when the kingdom of God would come, as follows: "The kingdom of God is not coming with signs to be observed; nor will they say, 'Lo here it is!' or, 'there!' for behold, the kingdom of God is in the midst of you" (Lk. xvii. 20 f.).[6] In this way, in both word and action, Jesus fastens upon today, this present moment in which are contained the decisions of the ultimate future.

But while much importance is given to these words about the coming of God's kingdom, words which expressly point at once to Jesus himself, his preaching and his works, they are nevertheless found only here and there, and do not yet express an open claim to the dignity of the Messiah. The Jesus of the synoptic Gospels—and we may here say with certainty the historical Jesus—speaks in a characteristically different way from the Jesus of John's Gospel, who is seen entirely with the eyes of post-Easter faith. The great "I am" sayings of the fourth gospel (light, way, truth, resurrection, life) have no parallels in the synoptic Gospels. There is a profound reason for this. Jesus' preaching and works are the signs and announcement of the coming kingdom of God. Indeed he himself is the sign, just as the prophet Jonah in his day with his call to repentance was the only sign granted to the people of Nineveh. Whoever fails to see or hear it will wait in vain for a special miraculous cosmic sign to be given him by God (Lk. xi.

29-31).[7] But the sign is not the thing itself. He himself in his own person neither replaces nor excludes the kingdom of God, which remains the one theme of his message.

2. THE HIDDENNESS OF GOD'S REIGN

God's reign is hidden from us, and must be believed and understood in its hiddenness. Not in the way the apocalypticists thought, beyond the heavens, in the bosom of a mysterious future, but here, hidden in the everyday world of the present time, where no one is aware of what is already taking place. Of this Jesus speaks in his parables of the kingdom of God.

Jesus' Parables

It is not fortuitous that Jesus chooses precisely this method of teaching, the parable, when he speaks of the coming of God's reign. So we must here first consider the meaning of this form of teaching, and how Jesus has used it and moulded it to his purpose. The rabbis also relate parables[8] in abundance, to clarify a point in their teaching and explain the sense of a written passage, but always as an aid to the teaching and an instrument in the exegesis of an authoritatively prescribed text. But that is just what they are not in the mouth of Jesus, although they often come very close to those of the Jewish teachers in their content, and though Jesus makes free use of traditional and familiar topics. Here the parables are the preaching itself and are not merely serving the purpose of a lesson which is quite independent of them. Jesus' parables—and not only those which in the narrower sense treat of the kingdom of God—aim, as all parables do, at making things clear. They make use of the familiar world, a comprehensible world, with all that goes on in the life of nature and of man, with all the manifold aspects of his experience, his acts and his sufferings. Every spring and autumn the sower goes over his field, every year wheat and weeds grow together, daily the fishermen catch good and bad fish in their nets. Often, to be sure, the events are such as do not, thank God, happen every day: the breaking-in of thieves in the night; the faithlessness and criminal craftiness of a steward; the lack of consideration with which a man disturbs his neighbour in his night's sleep to ask him for a loaf for his unexpected guest; the brutality of a servant who in his distress is forgiven a huge debt by his master, and who yet manages cruelly to extract from his fellow servant a paltry sum; indeed even the experience of the father of the pro-digal son with the younger and elder brother is not an everyday affair.

By preference and with great art, Jesus' parables tell just such stories, which are not by any means a regular feature of daily life. Yet they always remain within the realm of what every man under-stands, what is a daily or at least a possible experience. It is just this way that things happen! That is the first reaction to each parable. It is never, as it were, a study in advanced mathematics. The parables are never equations with two or more unknowns. Many of the metaphors and parables of Jesus begin, therefore, with the disturbing question, a question which grips one right away, without any preliminaries: "Which of you . . .?"—a form of parable for which, remarkably enough, there is not a single parallel in rabbinic lore.[9] It is always a question aimed straight at the hearer himself, which neither demands from him knowledge or theoretical judgment, nor presupposes his goodness or education. The only presumption which is made in Jesus' parables is man, the hearer himself, man indeed in the plain, unadorned reality of his world, which is neither put to rights according to high moral standards nor deplored with righteous indignation. Thus the hearer is gripped just where he really is, and the strongest appeal made to his understanding.

And yet, of course, all this does not make the parables what they are. They become parable and preaching only by the fact that the kingdom of God, which is by no means familiar and commonplace, is related thereby to everyday life. Not everyone, of course, can recognise this, even those who are well acquainted with the affairs of the everyday world. But that most assuredly does not mean that great skill in interpretation is required, as the contemporary scribes practised in their allegorical expositions, in order to recognise a deeper meaning behind every single expression and every letter. Often enough Jesus' parables, too, have been inter-preted, since the earliest days of the Church, as such deep allegories, and thereby deprived of their real, simple meaning. Originally they have nothing to do with allegories.[10]

The Mystery of the Kingdom of God

And yet in the parable a mystery lies hidden. The Gospels, in a saying which in its present form certainly does not go back to the historical Jesus, call it the "mystery of the Kingdom of God", which is given to the disciples to recognise, but not to those "outside" (Mk. iv. 10-13).[11] Unquestionably the thought is here distorted by dogma, for the saying maintains that Jesus spoke in parables to the people, in contrast to his way of speaking to the disciples, with the specific intention of not being understood by the people. But this interpretation of the parables as designed to alienate, breaks down in every parable of Jesus, and conflicts with the evangelist's own words at the end of his chapter of parables, a statement which alone fits the case: "With many such parables he spoke the word to them (the people) as they were able to hear it" (Mk. iv. 33). Notwithstanding, a fundamental truth about the parables of Jesus is preserved in the original saying under consideration. They do indeed contain a mystery. But this mystery is nothing but the hidden dawn of the kingdom of God itself amidst a world which to human eyes gives no sign of it. And this must surely be heard, believed and understood—not against a background of tradition or theory, but by the hearer in his actual world.

This is what is spoken of in the two parables of the mustard seed and the leaven (Mt. xiii. 31-33). The mustard seed, which is put in the ground, is supposed in Palestine to be the smallest of all seeds, proverbial for the least significant of all things. And yet a tree grows from it, and the birds of the air seek shelter in it and nest in it. The peasant-woman puts only a little leaven in the dough, and yet it is sufficient to leaven three measures of meal, which makes a meal for over one hundred and fifty hungry mouths. The greatest of all, hidden in the least significant of all, but effective even in the smallest thing. So the smallest contains this within itself. What a contrast between the beginning and the end! More recent interpreters have rightly found the real point of these parables in this very aspect and, not without reason, named them "contrast-parables".[12] Thereby the very common interpretation, that these parables express the idea of a natural development, is ruled out. This is a modern idea and quite unbiblical. They tell of something which man indeed experiences daily, and which yet does not cease to be an incomprehensible miracle. Yet the idea of contrast contains only half the truth,[13] and it would be quite inadmissible to carry the paradox of beginning and end to absurd lengths. Just for this reason the hearer is directed to the world of his daily experience, to the seed and the fruit, the sowing and the reaping, the fig tree and the vineyard, the farmer and the house-wife. Of course he knows, when he so much as lifts his eyes, that the small beginning holds promise of a magnificent ending. For beginning and end, however wonderful and incomprehensible the end may be, stand in a very definite relationship, one to another. The end comes from the beginning, the fruit from the seed, the harvest from the sowing, the whole leavened loaf from the leaven. Thus our task is to understand the present, in which the coming event already finds its beginning, the present in its apparent insignificance; and from it we are to demand no other signs of the splendour to come. For God's kingdom comes in concealment, indeed even in spite of failure. A sower goes out to sow, and his seed falls by the wayside, among thorns, on stony ground, but "other seeds fell into good soil and brought forth grain, growing up and increasing and yielding thirtyfold and sixtyfold and a hundredfold" (Mk. iv. 3-8). This great assurance has the last word in the parable, an assurance of which the prophet says: "My word shall not return to me empty, but it shall accomplish that which I purpose, and prosper in the thing for which I sent it" (Is. lv. 11). The assurance has, however, the first word too, for "a sower goes out to sow— nothing more; and that means God's new world" (Schniewind).[14]

All these parables have obviously a very definite and contemporary reference.[15] We can no longer determine with any certainty their setting in the life of Jesus in every case, for the Christian community has, as tradition shows, applied these words often to their own case, to their tasks and needs.[16] But we can accept as a very real probability that parables of seed and leaven are an answer to the headshaking and the questions which have been posed hundreds of times, right from the first days: An unknown rabbi of Nazareth in a remote corner of Palestine? A handful of disciples, who, when it came to the show-down, left him in the lurch? A doubtful mob following him—publicans, loose women, sinners, and a few women and children and folk who got help from him? On his cross the sport of passers-by? Is this the kingdom of God? The shift in the ages? Why doesn't he authenticate himself in a different way? And these are not just modern ideas that we put forward. Questions and protests such as these are behind the demands for signs that are made by Jesus' opponents and the story of his temptation by the devil (Mt. iv. 1 ff.), who enjoins him when hungry to perform the miracle of turning stones into bread, who challenges him who trusts in God to give objective and empirical proof of this trust, and finally offers him all the kingdoms of the world if he will bow the knee to him—this story gives the conclusive answer which sums up Jesus' way and works.

The little parable of the seed which grows of itself also belongs to the "parables of growth" which clearly contain a very definite contemporary reference: "The kingdom of God is as if a man should scatter seed upon the ground, and should sleep and rise night and day, and the seed should sprout and grow up, he knows not how. The earth produces of itself, first the blade, then the ear, then the full grain in the ear. But when the grain is ripe, at once he (the master of the field) puts in the sickle, because the harvest has come" (Mk. iv. 26 ff.). Here, too, it is essential to keep clearly before us the point of comparison. It is not the natural comprehensible process of development, and certainly not the thought that man's work and effort are to bring about the kingdom of God—an interpretation which still has serious consequences right up to our day.[17] It is notable that the farmer's work is described with the minimum of words and comes to an end at the decisive point. No, just as the earth "of itself" brings forth fruit, so the kingdom of God comes by its own power alone, a miracle for man, which he can only await with patience. This parable is obviously an answer to the passionate striving of those who want to force the coming of the kingdom of God (Mt. xi. 12). Compare, too, the parable of the tares among the wheat, which shall grow together till the harvest (Mt. xiii. 24 ff.)—a reproof to that pious zeal which tries to gather the righteous together now and to set them apart from the ungodly.[18]

We are always brought back to this same feature: the hidden-ness, the insignificance of the beginning, in which the promise of what is to come is nevertheless imbedded. No one is to think that he can or should help out the small beginning, and no one should think that he can discover visible signs of what is to come. So the beginning of the kingdom of God is an insignificant event *in* this time and world. *Within* this time and world it sets an end to both. For the new world of God is already at work.

This would admittedly be completely misunderstood, if it were taken merely as an extremely paradoxical teaching as to the coming of God's kingdom, which destroys the whole structure of traditional hopes and ideas. Actually Jesus' message means no less than this—and yet, if we read only this in the parables of Jesus, we have not apprehended their clear and urgent appeal to the under-standing of the hearers. They are told in order to deny to the hearer the attitude of spectator. Not by chance does the parable of the sower end with the words: "He who has ears to hear, let him hear" (Mk. iv. 9). And very properly the later meaning of the parable (iv. 13 ff.) shows that the role of spectator does not suit the hearer in this story. He is not the spectator who, as it were, can watch the sower at his work from the edge of the field or the boundary path; quite otherwise, he is part of the story himself: he is the ground on which the seed falls. Thus the parable speaks with full confidence of the fate of the word of God, and no less clearly of the fact that this word is the fate of the hearers for time and eternity. We understand now Jesus' sharp word against foolish speculation, which tries to reckon the beginning of the kingdom of God from cosmic signs, as the farmer tries to forecast the rain from the rising cloud and the heat of the next day from the south wind (Lk. xii. 54 ff.). This is more than a condemnation of the boldness which ventures with an air of wisdom to deal with questions sur-passing the powers of man. Hence it is something quite different from the expression of resignation: as much as to say, who could get anything certain out of these matters! "You hypocrites! You know how to interpret the appearance of earth and sky; but why do you not know how to interpret the present time? And why do you not judge for yourselves what is right?" (Lk. xii. 56). That is to say: He who looks forth to find the kingdom of God as he would look at the weather or any other event which can be observed, and who says with the false prophets: "Look here—look there!" (Lk. xvii. 20; Mk. xiii. 21), not only wants to know too much, but is fundamentally in error about God and himself. He is running away from God's call, here and now; he is losing himself and at the same time has lost the future of God by this very attempt to possess it.

Blessed are the Poor

In one of the first collections of sayings of the Lord, presented to us by Matthew in his Sermon on the Mount and Luke in his Sermon in the Plain, the Beatitudes come at the beginning. Beatitudes occur frequently elsewhere in Jewish and Greek literature, but characteristically and chiefly in their wisdom sayings. In this literature people are called blessed to whom a virtuous wife, well-behaved children, success and a happy lot are granted; the dead who have safely reached the end of the road are called blessed on inscriptions on tombs.[19] Jesus' Beatitudes, however, are not wisdom sayings but, like the word of a prophet, they are a summons and a promise.[20] Who are those that are addressed? The first Beatitude names them and includes in itself all that follows: "Blessed are you poor, for yours is the kingdom of God" (Lk. vi. 20; Mt. v. 3).[21] The old prophetic message, and the comfort of which many psalms speak, are heard again in these words. "For thus says the high and lofty One who inhabits eternity, whose name is Holy: 'I dwell in the high and holy place, and also with him who is of a contrite and humble spirit, to revive the spirit of the humble, and to revive the heart of the contrite'" (Is. lvii. 15; cf. xlix. 13). "Who is like the Lord our God, who is seated on high, who looks far down on the heavens and the earth? He raises the poor from the dust, and lifts the needy from the ash heap . . ." (Ps. cxiii. 5 ff.). The evangelist Luke has expressly set down the relevant word of the prophet as the governing text of all Jesus' works. "The spirit of the Lord is upon me, because he has anointed me to preach good news to the poor. He has sent me to proclaim release to the captives, and recovering of sight to the blind, to set at liberty those who are oppressed, to proclaim the acceptable year of the Lord" (Lk. iv. 17 ff.; Is. lxi. 1 f.). It is the text of the first sermon of Jesus in Nazareth; and its interpretation is provided by this one saying, "Today this scripture is fulfilled in your hearing."

Since the days of the prophets and the psalms, "poverty" and "mourning" have had their place in the history of Jewish piety.[22] One group after another claimed them for their own, to distinguish themselves from the impious and to make sure of God's goodwill towards themselves. Even in a non-canonical collection of psalms, taken from Pharisaic circles, these religious titles of honour are to be found.[23]

Yet there is nothing which permits us to look upon those to whom Jesus' beatitudes are addressed as members of such a religious group or social stratum, where one quite clearly made a virtue of necessity and used the renunciation of one's claims as an even higher claim. As Jesus uses the words, poverty and humility have their original meaning. The poor and they that mourn are those who have nothing to expect from the world, but who expect everything from God. They look towards God, and also cast themselves upon God; in their lives and in their attitude they are beggars before God. What unites those addressed in the beatitudes and pronounced blessed, is this, that they are driven to the very end of the world and its possibilities: the poor, who do not fit in to the structure of the world and therefore are rejected by the world; the mourner, for whom the world holds no consolation; the humble, who no longer extract recognition from the world; the hungry and thirsty, who cannot live without the righteousness that God alone can promise and provide in this world. But also the merciful, who without asking about rights, open their hearts to another; the peacemakers, who overcome might and power by reconciliation; the righteous, who are not equal to the evil ways of the world; and finally, the persecuted, who with scorn and pains of death, are cast bodily out of the world.[24]

Not that the situation at the limit of human existence is here glorified in itself. Misery and poverty mean distress and torture, just as do blindness, lameness, leprosy and the certainty of death (Mt. xi. 5 f.). But God waits beyond the limit, or rather he no longer waits, but comes to those who wait for him. Though his kingdom be in the future, yet it breaks even now like a ray of light upon the darkness of the oppressed, with this oft-repeated "Blessed are you". For while Jesus does not call present poverty blessedness for its own sake, neither does he bring comfort with the hope of a better "beyond". Blessed are you! does not mean: you are entering heaven, nor: you are already in heaven, if you understand it aright; rather it means: God's kingdom comes to you.

All the beatitudes are directed towards the coming kingdom of God and are embraced in one idea, that God wills to be present with us and will be with us all, in as manifold and individual a way as our needs are manifold and individual. With special clarity, therefore, these very words of Jesus show that the kingdom of God cannot be described as can an earthly thing or a distant wonderland —every attempt to "define" it can thus only come to grief—for it is a happening, an event, the gracious action of God.[25] God will comfort them; God will satisfy them, be merciful to them, call them his children. He will give them the earth for their inheritance, will allow them to see his face; for their good he will administer his kingdom. This, his kingdom, is near! Therefore this is a time of joy, and the time for mourning is past. Who will fast now that the time of the wedding has come? (Mk. ii. 19).

Just as the "today" and "now" of the beginning of the kingdom of God which Jesus proclaims and promises no longer fits into any Jewish conception of hopes for the future, so the band of those to whom his call applies cannot be limited by the standards of traditional belief. The ancient conviction that the people of Israel were the sole object of the choice and promise had been questioned in late Judaism for some time. It still exists—even up to the time of the growth of the Christian Church. But the recognition that Israel as an earthly nation cannot simply be equated with the real Israel had long been aroused. Just for this reason many such groups as the "Pious", the "Separate" (Pharisees), the "Children of the Light", the "Congregation of the Covenant", all sharply divided from one another, had gathered in the late period and tried to form the "holy remnant", in the sense of the old saying of the prophet about the stump which was to remain when the tree was felled (Is. vi. 13), and to assemble the righteous in special communities.[26] Only against the background of such tendencies can we judge the significance of the fact that Jesus' preaching betrays not a trace of all this. He does not gather together the holy and the good, but he is "a friend of tax collectors and sinners" (Mt. xi. 19). To be sure he too knows he is sent to Israel, and his first answer to the Syro-phoenician woman is: "Let the children first be fed, for it is not right to take the children's bread and throw it to the dogs" (Mk. vii. 27). But his mission is to "the *lost* sheep of the house of Israel" (Mt. xv. 24). And in spite of priests, Pharisees and scribes, in spite of ritual and law, indeed just because of them, he looks upon these as the exhausted flock pushed down to the ground without a shepherd (Mt. ix. 35 ff.).

Up till now, then, Jesus' words and works are confined to Israel, just as those sent out on the first mission recognise his command: "Go nowhere among the Gentiles and enter no town of the Samaritans, but go rather to the lost sheep of the house of Israel" (Mt. x. 5 f.).[27] It can be seen from words like these that Jesus has by no means substituted the idea of a kingdom of God embracing all men for the hope of the coming of the kingdom of God to Israel alone. But it is no less clear that through Jesus' words and attitude the illusion of the inalienable, as it were, legal rights of Israel and its fathers is attacked at the root and shaken to pieces. Countless words, parables and stories express this very thing; for example, the words which Matthew has inserted in the tale of the heathen centurion of Capernaum. "Many will come from east and west and sit at the table with Abraham, Isaac, and Jacob, in the kingdom of heaven, while the sons of the kingdom will be thrown into the outer darkness; there men will weep and gnash their teeth" (Mt. viii. 11 f.). Similarly, the parable of the great supper, when the guests originally invited make excuses, so that in anger the Lord of the feast finally shuts them out and tells his servants to bring in the poor, the maimed, the blind and lame from the lanes, and at last those who are outside in the highways (Lk. xiv. 16-24).[28] Thus the coming of the kingdom of God means the complete shaking and abolition of the standards and limitations that were sacred to pious believers. The last become first and the first last (Mt. xx. 16). The tax collector despised by every Jew as the classic example of a traitor and turncoat is justified, and the Pharisee goes empty away (Lk. xviii. 9-14). The no less hated Samaritan, considered unclean by every Jew, wins God's favour and shames priest and Levite (Lk. x. 30-37).

To understand how all these words of Jesus must have affected the Jews, offending and revolting them—but also how they brought freedom and joy—we should try to hear them as it were with the ears of people in the Germany of the Third Reich, and recall the talk prevalent at that time, laden as it was with hatred and snobbism; only that here the Jew was himself the hated one. But such a transposition is no doubt unnecessary and, being the speech of yesterday, it would perhaps fail to have any effect on our fast-moving and forgetful generation. In fact, however, only the language alters, and the means of that self-assertion which thrives on condemnation of other people still remains, especially where morals, religion and church are being upheld and defended. Whenever it comes to speaking of God, the good man wants to be approved by God—and for this purpose he will appropriate even the tax collector's prayer, if he must—and the godless must be condemned. Hence one reaches an understanding of the incisive words of Jesus to the righteous: "Truly, I say to you, the tax collectors and the harlots go into the kingdom of God—but not you" (Mt. xxi. 31).[11]

The people who receive help from Jesus are therefore throughout, as the Gospels show, people on the fringe of society, men who because of fate, guilt or prevailing prejudice are looked upon as marked men, as outcasts: sick people who, according to the current doctrine of retribution, must bear their disease as a punishment for some sin committed; demoniacs, that is to say, those possessed of demons; those attacked by leprosy, "the first-born of death", to whom life in companionship with others is denied; Gentiles, who have no share in the privileges of Israel; women and children who do not count for anything in the community; and really bad people, the guilty, whom the good man assiduously holds at a distance. At the same time we may look in vain in Jesus' behaviour for any trace of a romantic predilection for the "underworld", or a sentimentality which confuses the boundaries of good and evil, excuses guilt and caricatures virtue. Neither is the prodigal son idealised, nor is the behaviour of the elder brother called in question. ("Lo these many years I have served you, and

I never disobeyed your command" (Lk. xv. 29). The same is true of the proofs of piety which the Pharisee enumerates in the temple (Lk. xviii. 9 ff.), and of the words of the rich young man when he answers the enumeration of the commandments with "All these I have observed" (Mt. xix. 20). Indeed Jesus does not even deny outright the hidden connection between fate and guilt (Mk. ii. 1 ff.; Lk. xiii. 1 ff.), although he firmly declines to weigh the one against the other in a particular case (Jn. ix. 1 ff.), and the problem of theodicy, a vexed question then as now, has only the smallest place among his sayings. Thus Jesus' attitude and message can in no way be interpreted as a "reversal of all values", or a systematic revolution in the realm of moral and social standards. The sentence which justifies his attitude and his works is all the more simple and basic: "Those who are well have no need of a physician, but those who are sick. I came not to call the righteous, but sinners" (Mk. ii. 17). His freedom displays itself not in an abstract criticism of accepted standards, but in the way in which he, as a matter of course, makes himself accessible to those who need him, ignoring conventional limitations, and thus according such outcasts proper recognition.

This is the light in which Jesus' sitting at table with tax collectors and sinners must be seen, which called forth the mocking and derisive words: "Behold, a glutton and a drunkard, a friend of tax collectors and sinners" (Mt. xi. 19). Eating with others is for the Jew the closest form of intimacy. There is a natural connection here with questions of honour. That is why the question of whom one invites, to whom therefore one shows this honour, and how one places the guests at table (Lk. xiv. 7-14) is so important; likewise who is to be absolutely excluded from such an invitation. We hear that Jesus does not dissociate himself from such an ordering of society, and that he accepts the honour which now and then a Pharisee does him, just as he honours the host by his presence (Lk. xiv. 1 ff.; vii. 36 ff.). But in just the same way he sits as a guest in a tax collector's house (Lk. xix. 1-10), and sitting at meat with sinners is really the astonishing thing at which his enemies murmur: "This man receives sinners and eats with them" (Lk. xv. 2).

Now what does this sitting at table with others mean? Is it only an act and expression of a human attitude which is not denied even to the outlaw, leaving convention and prejudice far behind? Jesus' parables show that the fellowship of the table is, as it has been from ancient times, a symbol of the closest fellowship with God, and a picture of that joyful age brought by the Messiah (Mt. viii. 11; Mk. ii. 15 ff.; Lk. xiv. 16 ff.; Mt. xxii. 1 ff.).[30] So there can be no doubt that Jesus' earthly fellowship with tax collectors and sinners has also a strong connection with his preaching of the coming of the kingdom of God. We must not be too quick to seek too close a relationship between this connection and a Messianic doctrine which the texts do not express and which, where such expressions do appear, point clearly to the belief of the later Church.[31] And yet the gospel tradition has given apt expression to the unity of words in Jesus' preaching and attitude, by choosing significantly and not fortuitously the scene of a feast for many of the sayings of the lord. That is the case not only for the parable of the great supper (Lk. xiv), but especially in the three parables of the lost—the lost sheep, the lost coin and the prodigal son (Lk. xv). Of course there is no historical importance in their setting.[32] And yet the frame is not unimportant, a true and un-mistakable indication that what the parables say actually happens in Jesus' fellowship with other people. If it were otherwise, we could find the meaning of the parables as has so often been done, in the timeless idea of a loving, forgiving Father in heaven. In fact, however, the parables tell of this love becoming a reality in Jesus' deeds and words. In the story of the healing of the paralytic Jesus says to the sick man: "My son, your sins are forgiven" (Mk. ii. 5). Why are his opponents enraged at this? Not because he expresses the idea of the love of God and the hope of his mercy, but because he is doing what is God's prerogative. "Why does this man speak thus? It is blasphemy! Who can forgive sins but God alone?" (Mk. ii. 7). This infuriates his opponents, even as it makes harlots and tax collectors participants in his joy. "Today salvation has come to this house!" can also be cited from the story of Jesus' visit to Zacchaeus the tax collector (Lk. xix. 9).

3. REPENTANCE AND READINESS
The Call of the Hour

Judaism, too, knows of the necessity and promise of repentance.[33] There are numerous words among the sayings of the rabbis which tell of the duty lying upon all, even upon the righteous, to repent, especially in the face of death. They tell also of the power of repentance to make atonement, of God's pardoning goodness, of the outward expression of repentance in sackcloth and ashes, in remorse and tears, in prayer and fasting. They speak also of the importance of a true repentance, which shows itself in the renouncing of former sins and in making good any wrongs committed. Nor is there any lack of words warning people against taking things too lightly, against an attitude which presumes on grace and simply counts on it while continuing in sin. "He who says: I will sin and repent, sin and repent—is granted (by God) no opportunity for repentance."[34] Therefore in the Gospels both John the Baptist and Jesus call for fruits meet for repentance (Mt. iii. 8; xii. 41, etc.).

And yet Jesus' call to repentance opens up quite a new horizon. It is heard in view of the dawning of the kingdom of God. This gives it its reason and its ultimate urgency. Jesus' message here comes very close to John the Baptist's. "Repent, for the kingdom of heaven is at hand" (Mt. iii. 2; iv. 17). This comprises the preaching of both. Both do away with the presumptuously asserted distinction between the supposedly righteous and the notorious sinners. For both of them, repentance ceases to be an exercise of piety by means of which the righteous man can show himself to be such. Both put an end to the hypocritical play with repentance. But even in comparison with that of John the Baptist, Jesus' call to repentance has a new meaning; just as the idea that now is the dawn of the kingdom of God, the hour of salvation, is different from the fiery day of the last judgment proclaimed by John.

Repentance now means: to lay hold on the salvation which is already at hand, and to give up everything for it. "The kingdom of heaven is like treasure hidden in a field, which a man found and covered up; then in his joy he goes and sells all that he has and buys that field. Again, the kingdom of heaven is like a merchant in search of fine pearls, who, on finding one pearl of great value, went and sold all that he had and bought it" (Mt. xiii. 44-46). Repentance now means: no longer to make excuses with a thousand otherwise cogent reasons, like the guests who were first invited to the supper; but to accept the invitation, to set out, to come (Lk. xiv. 16 ff.; Mt. xxii. 1 ff.). This very call to repentance speaks, too, of a decision and an action on God's part first, which comes before all action and decision on the part of men. The very placing of the beatitudes before everything else shows just this. Certainly they are followed by the inexorable demand for a new and sincere obedience which goes as far as to say: "You, therefore, must be perfect, as your heavenly Father is perfect" (Mt. v. 48). One might imagine for a moment that the words about obedience and a new righteousness came first, and the beatitudes followed as a reward and a promise for those who fulfil God's commands. But in doing this we would be making Jesus a Jewish rabbi like any other. But God's action and decision come on the stage earlier than any decision of man.

To accept the invitation, to rise up, to come—that means, of course, renunciation, giving up all that by which man in the ordinary way tries to make and maintain his living. Yes, renunciation of himself, offering up his life: "Whoever seeks to gain his life will lose it, but whoever loses his life will preserve it" (Lk. xvii. 33). Yet surrender and sacrifice for the sake of life: "If your hand or foot causes you to sin, cut it off and throw it from you; it is better for you to enter life maimed or lame, rather than with two hands or two feet to be thrown into the eternal fire. And if your eye causes you to sin, pluck it out and throw it from you; it is better for you to enter life with one eye than with two eyes to be thrown into the hell of fire" (Mt. xviii. 8 f.; v. 29 f.). An obedience which in this sense is not ready for action is no real obedience.

Salvation and repentance have, however, now changed places. While to the Jewish ways of thinking repentance is the first thing, the condition which affords the sinner the hope of grace, it is now the case that repentance comes by means of grace. Those who sit at the table of the rich lord are the poor, the cripples, the blind and the lame, not those who are already half-cured. The tax collectors and sinners with whom Jesus sits at meat are not asked first about the state of their moral improvement, any more than is the prodigal when he returns home. The extent to which all talk of the conditions which man must fulfil before grace is accorded him is here silenced, is shown by the parables of the lost sheep and the lost coin, which tell only of the finding of what was lost, and in this very manner describe the joy in heaven "over one sinner who repents" (Lk. xv. 7, 10). So little is repentance a human action preparing the way for grace, that it can be placed on the same level as being found.

In the mounting light of this grace, however, it can be seen that the first become last and the last first, the lost become the saved and the righteous the lost. Repentance means, therefore: humbling oneself before God, "For everyone who exalts himself will be humbled; and he who humbles himself shall be exalted" (Lk. xiv. 11). "Truly I say to you, whoever does not receive the kingdom of God like a child shall not enter it" (Mk. x. 15; Lk. xvii. 17). It is clear that the supposed innocence of the child is not what is set up here as the ideal, as these words are often understood by a sentimental romanticism. The smallness of the child, his real dependence on aid, his incapacity to get on in life by himself, this is the fundamental idea of these words. How radically they are meant to be understood and how foreign to the natural man, is shown by Nicodemus in the Gospel of John. There Jesus' words appear in a slightly altered form: "Unless one is born anew, he cannot see the kingdom of God" (Jn. iii. 3). Nicodemus, a "master of Israel", can only ask: "How can a man be born when he is old? Can he enter a second time into his mother's womb and be born?" But God's kingdom brings and demands this change.

Joyful Living

In his joy the man who has found the treasure in the field goes and sells everything he has and buys the field (Mt. xiii. 44). If Jesus' call to salvation is at the same time a call to repentance, the call to repentance is at the same time a call to rejoice. That is why, when speaking of fasting, the time-honoured practice of repentance, Jesus says to the disciples: "And when you fast, do not look dismal, like the hypocrites, for they disfigure their faces that their fasting may be seen by men. Truly, I say to you, they have their reward. But when you fast, anoint your head and wash your face" (as for a festival), "that your fasting may not be seen by men but by your Father who is in secret: and your Father who sees in secret will reward you" (Mt. vi. 16-18). Again and again in the Gospels the deep gloom which hangs over the righteousness of the "good" becomes apparent; in the grumbling of the Pharisees and scribes over Jesus' eating with sinners; in the indignation with which they hear the words of forgiveness that he speaks to the sick of the palsy (Mk. ii. 6 f.); in the anger they show when they call him a "glutton and a drunkard" (Mt. xi. 19); in the wrath aroused in them by the cries of joy that greet Jesus as he rides into Jerusalem (Mt. xxi. 15 f.). This joylessness can be heard in the prayer of thanks offered up by the Pharisee as he sets out all his pious words before God as in a shop-window (Lk. xviii. 9 ff.), and in his righteousness profits by the guilt of others. It is heard in the parable of the prodigal son, in the words addressed to the father by the elder son, when he remains outside and refuses to take part in the feast: "You never gave me a kid, that I might make merry with my friends" (Lk. xv. 29); and again in the complaint of the first labourers to be hired in the parable of the labourers in the vine-yard (Mt. xx. 1 ff.), that those who were hired last received the same reward from the master. But this is the very thing which decides who will finally be lost, who in the end are the first and who the last. "Or do you begrudge my generosity?" is the lord's last word to the grumblers in the parable of the labourers. "It was fitting to make merry and be glad; for this your brother was dead, and is alive; he was lost and is found", were the last words of the father to the elder brother. The joy is the joy of deliverance from death. It is a matter of nothing less than this. For this reason the last words in both parables, far from sounding a note of reproach and fault-finding, have a note of questioning and of urgent per-suasion. What becomes of the prodigal son, we know; but what will become of the elder brother?

What it means not to live in this joy is shown by the parable of the wicked servant. "Therefore the kingdom of heaven may be compared to a king, who wished to settle accounts with his servants. When he began the reckoning, one was brought to him, who owed him ten thousand talents; and as he could not pay, his lord ordered him to be sold, with his wife and children and all that he had, and payment to be made. So the servant fell on his knees, imploring him, 'Lord, have patience with me, and I will pay you everything.' And out of pity for him the lord of that servant released him and forgave him the debt. But that same servant, as he went out, came upon one of his fellow servants who owed him a hundred denarii; and seizing him by the throat he said, 'Pay me what you owe.' So his fellow servant fell down and besought him, 'Have patience with me, and I will pay you.' He refused and went and put him in prison till he should pay the debt. When his fellow servants saw what had taken place, they were greatly distressed, and they went and reported to their lord all that had taken place. Then his lord summoned him and said to him, 'You wicked servant! I forgave you all that debt because you besought me; and should not you have had mercy on your fellow servant, as I had mercy on you?' And in anger his lord delivered him to the jailers, till he should pay all his debt" (Mt. xviii. 23-34).

Jewish ways of life no longer provide the clue to the meaning of this parable.[35] Nor is there any penal law which has as a punishment the sale of wife and children, or torture. Here we are concerned with other, Oriental tyrannies: a great king and his satrap, boundless mercy and boundless anger, unlimited by any law. For everything in this parable is beyond measure and limit; the first debt is measureless, and in the face of it the servant's offer, as everyone realises, is only a futile promise; measureless, too, is the compassion which the master shows him. "He released him and forgave him the debt." But also the disparity between the first debt, which was forgiven, and the second, which was not, is inconceivable.[36] Measureless and quite inconceivable is the first servant's insistence on his right when he meets the second—"Pay what you owe"—and the cruelty with which he tries to collect his debt. Awful and terrible, finally, is the lord's last judgment of the first servant. But can there be any other ending here? There remains no room for astonishment, but only for simple acceptance on the part of the hearer. "So also my heavenly Father will do to everyone of you, if you do not forgive your brother from your heart" (Mt. xviii. 35).

Wisdom and Watching

"Why do you not know how to interpret the present time?" Jesus asks his hearers (Lk. xii. 56). To interpret the present time means: to lay hold on the hour of salvation. But it also means to recognise and use the last hour, before the catastrophe of God's judgment breaks forth. People come to Jesus with stirring news: Pilate has cruelly massacred some Galileans, at the very moment when they were slaying their animals for sacrifice in the court of the temple. Another event moves them: eighteen men have had a fatal accident at the pool of Siloam in Jerusalem probably while building an aqueduct.[37] The question which Jesus is asked is the ancient one about the correlation between fate and guilt. This question looks back and tries to find order and meaning in world events and in the lives of men, and to fathom God's justice. But Jesus replies: "Do you think that these Galileans were worse sinners than all the other Galileans because they suffered thus? I tell you, No; but unless you repent you will all likewise perish" (Lk. xiii. 1-5). Thus he puts an end to the question of God's justice in relation to this catastrophe and that, and turns it into a new question to his questioners, facing them with themselves and the future of God. It is not a miracle that these have been struck down, but that you have escaped. What does this miracle mean? This is immediately followed by the parable of the unfruitful fig-tree, which year after year has borne no fruit and well deserves to be cut down now. But the gardener, ready once more to take all possible trouble with it, begs the master of the vineyard for one last chance: "Let it alone, sir, this year also" (Lk. xiii. 6-9). The miracle is therefore God's undeserved patience, passing all comprehension. The master is right when he says: "Why should it use up the ground?" Yet God's patience too has its limit: "this year also."

Jesus' parable of the unjust steward (Lk. xvi. 1-8) gives a very drastic picture of a man who has no illusions about the future, and seizes his last chance. There are many occasions when Jesus speaks as strongly, even as provocatively, as he does here. The deception of a steward is reported to his master. He has squandered his master's possessions. Now he is in a tight corner. He will lose his post and be thrown out. Then he reflects on the last remaining possibilities. The work of a labourer is beyond his strength. He is ashamed to beg. So the cunning idea comes to him to induce the dealers who owe his master oil and wheat to falsify their bills. One good turn deserves another. If he has not left them in the lurch, no more will they abandon him, when he is in trouble. "The master" (that is to say, Jesus)[38] "commended the dishonest steward for his prudence; for the sons of this world are wiser in their own generation than the sons of light" (Lk. xvi. 8). With this the parable ends.[39] Not a word of moral indignation at the action of the rascal, who heaps one deception upon another. Consequently the average pious reader of the Bible, even today, gives this parable a wide berth. But it is, as no other, a model of how Jesus goes about things. Does this rouse your indignation? Open your eyes! Here you see what it means to make use of the present moment in view of a relentless future: not to suppose that the future will not be so bad, and that better times will come again, nor on the other hand to sit resigned with hands folded. Wisdom consists not in being indignant but in being prepared.

The folly that does not comprehend this is depicted just as drastically in the illustration of the rich farmer who gathers in his harvest with contentment and satisfaction and wants to build bigger barns for it, and yet is disgraced before God: "Fool! This night your soul is required of you; and the things you have prepared, whose will they be?" (Lk. xii. 16-20). It is very significant that Jesus speaks of the folly of this farmer—as of the wisdom of the steward—without calling up any apocalyptic pictures, indeed in the style of the wisdom literature, which appeals to the natural understanding. Does not man know that he must die? Does he not understand the folly of his cares, which devour body and soul instead of serving life? "Is not life more than food, and the body more than clothing?" (Mt. vi. 25). Does he not grasp the paradox, that in some cases he survives his earthly treasures which moth and rust consume or thieves steal (Mt. vi. 19 f.), and that in some cases his wealth outlives him? Indeed the proverbs of all nations speak of this—whether with calm cheerfulness or sad resignation—in the sense of the well-known *memento mori*. In Jesus' message, however, all these words refer to the coming of the kingdom of God. "Instead, seek his kingdom and these things shall be yours as well" (Lk. xii. 31).

He who understands the hour as he awaits God's future, holds himself in readiness, as the servants watch and wait for their master (Mk. xiii. 33 ff.; Mt. xxiv. 45 ff.; Lk. xii. 35 ff.).[40] The servant who waits in wisdom and faithfulness takes, one might say, no time for himself, and in contrast to the world, is the very man who has time. It is characteristic of those who do not hear God's call, from the time of the flood to the last judgment, that they have no time. "They ate, they drank, they bought, they sold, they planted, they built . . . marrying and given in marriage" (Lk. xvii. 28; Mt. xxiv. 38). Nor have they any time in their supposed piety, which neglects nothing among the ordinances and commandments, and yet loses sight of mercy in the welter of their works and achievements (Mt. xxiii. 9, 13; xii. 7). The sharpest of Jesus' utterances about these are the Woes over the Pharisees: they have hopelessly reversed the inner and the outward things; blind guides, who strain out a gnat and swallow a camel (Mt. xxiii. 24 ff.). But the same inversion of values threatens the disciples too. Thus at any rate did Matthew understand the "Lord, Lord" saying, which was no doubt originally addressed to the people, but which he has applied to the Church (Mt. vii. 21 ff., as opposed to Lk. vi. 46).[41] They come before the judge of the world with their confession and the account of all their marvellous deeds and achievements done in his name, and yet he rejects them, because they have not realised that when all is said and done they themselves were called to do the will of God.

Before God, however, the wise and faithful servant is at the same time the one who has no time, who is faithful to his task, faithful in the management and increased of the estate entrusted to him (Mt. xxv. 14 ff.), and faithful in his love towards the least of Jesus' brethren (Mt. xxv. 31 ff.), constantly ready for action, with his torch alight (Lk. xii. 35). His waiting is not for the nothingness of the unknown, not for the silence of death, but for the Lord who has met and will meet his disciples. Even in Jesus' future the servant will be the same: "He will gird himself and have them sit at table, and he will come and serve them" (Lk. xii. 37).[42]

4. FUTURE AND PRESENT

There is a remarkable tension, it would seem, between such sayings of Jesus as speak of the kingdom of God as a future happening, and such as announce its arrival now, in the present. "Thy kingdom come" is the second petition in the Lord's Prayer (Mt. vi. 10). "I shall not drink again of the fruit of the vine until that day when I drink it new in the kingdom of God", says Jesus to the disciples at the Last Supper (Mk. xiv. 25; Mt. xxvi. 29). A whole chain of such sayings is found in another place: "For as the lightning flashes and lights up the sky from one side to the other so will the Son of man be in his day. . . . On that day, let him who is on the housetop, with his goods in the house, not come down to take them away; likewise let him who is in the field not turn back. Remember Lot's wife. . . . I tell you, in that night there will be two men in one bed; one will be taken and the other left. There will be two women grinding together; one will be taken and the other left. And they said to him, 'Where, Lord?' He said to them, 'Where the body is, there the eagles will be gathered together' " (Lk. xvii. 24-37). God's kingdom is future. That is why it is a question of "entering into the kingdom of God", into "life", into "joy". Sayings of this kind pervade all the Gospels. What is their relationship to the others, which announce the dawn, indeed the presence of God's kingdom today and now: "But if it is by the finger of God that I cast out demons, then the kingdom of God has come upon you" (Lk. xi. 20); "I saw Satan fall like lightning from heaven" (Lk. x. 18)? What is their relationship to the blessing of the eye-witnesses (Lk. x. 23 f.), to the proclamation of the time of rejoicing (Mt. xi. 5 f.; Mk. ii. 18 f., etc.)?

The attempts of the commentators to deal with this question are numerous. They have sought the aid of psychological explanations, and thought they observed various "moods" in Jesus himself. His prevailing mood, according to some, was one of expectation of the coming of the kingdom; but in the elation of enthusiasm and joy he could, in bold anticipation of the fulfilment, consider the present as the dawn of the kingdom. "There no longer exists for him any gulf between present and future; present and future, the ideal and reality are wedded together" (Bousset).[43] According to the others, this apparent contradiction is explained by the psyche of the prophet, who sees the future at one moment as present with us, and at another as stretching far ahead into distant time.[44] But such attempts at explanation bring to the texts a point of view against which the texts themselves, without exception, rebel. They tear asunder what ought to hang together. For quite obviously the problem lies not in the fact that these pronouncements appear side by side, but that they are, paradoxical though it seem to us, closely interwoven.

Not much better are biographical explanations which try to divide contradictory pronouncements into different periods in the thought and teaching of Jesus. Some would place those concerning the approach and presence of the kingdom in the latter part of his work;[45] or, conversely, they would put them at the beginning and try to explain the actual sayings about the future on the basis of disappointment in this expectation, and the indefinite postponement of the final consummation.[46] But this attempt, too, leads only to fantastic combinations and constructions which are not borne out by the texts.

Others, again, turn to differences in the transmission of Jesus' sayings, and acknowledge Jesus as the author of the sayings which deal with the presence of the kingdom of God and its development from a small beginning to magnificent completion, and say it was only the later Church, obviously reviving Jewish apocalyptic pictures and representations, which distorted the original message of Jesus.[47] It is clear that this theory, too, can be reversed. Actually we ourselves observe again and again that we do have to reckon with such a process. Indeed it can be shown in the so-called synoptic apocalypse in Mark xiii (see also pages 93 f.), that Jesus' own message is overlaid in no small degree by the later apocalyptic tradition of the Church. And yet, against this attempt, it must be said that in any case these criteria for making a distinction do not fit the facts. Just as we do not ascribe to Jesus merely the preaching of a "realised eschatology" (C. H. Dodd), we should not make him an apocalypticist who merely renews the old expectations of late Jewish hopes in a more vivid form, and ascribe in either case the other view to the Church. Nor will it do to distinguish in the sayings of Jesus between real pronouncements and those of only "symbolic" importance, and understand the sayings about the future merely as metaphors for the "timeless" and "eternal".[48]

None of these attempts at a solution leads to the goal. The reason for this failure might well lie in the wrong kind of question. We have seen already what decisive importance for the understanding of the kingdom of God in Jesus' preaching lies in these words: "The kingdom of God is not coming with signs to be observed" (Lk. xvii. 20). Therefore he who asks questions like these: What is "happening" now and what will "happen" later? How much is taking place now? What will develop from these beginnings? What is the consummation like?—he who asks such questions has from the very start yielded to the temptation of making the kingdom of God something like a world phenomenon which can be observed and reckoned up. To be sure, no one can deny that Jesus' eschatological sayings, as far as they speak in the language and imagery of his time, about a definite happening now and in the future, are open to such an interpretation. And indeed there are people who set themselves to arrange the individual sayings of Jesus into conceptions comparable to our this-worldly mathematical calculations, and to make a sequence of this-worldly facts out of this, regardless of the usually grotesque result, and apparently justified by the large number of references which they can produce for every sentence. Yet nothing is gained here by a mere biblicism, and the elementary misunderstanding of Jesus' message is only too clear.

We must not separate the statements about future and present, as is already apparent from the fact that in Jesus' preaching they are related in the closest fashion. The present dawn of the kingdom of God is always spoken of so as to show that the present reveals the future as salvation and judgment, and therefore does not anticipate it. Again, the future is always spoken of as unlocking and lighting up the present, and therefore revealing today as the day of decision. It is therefore more than a superficial difference, more than one of degree, concerned, so to speak, only with the quantity of colour employed by the apocalyptic painter, when one notes that Jesus' eschatological sayings do not describe the future as a state of heavenly bliss nor indulge in broad descriptions of the terrors of the judgment. Hence in Jesus' preaching, speaking of the present means speaking of the future, and vice versa.

The future of God is *salvation* to the man who apprehends the present as God's present, and as the hour of salvation. The future of God is *judgment* for the man who does not accept the "now" of God but clings to his own present, his own past and also to his own dreams of the future. We might say with Schiller: "What we have denied the moment, eternity will never give back." Only here it applies in a new and fulfilled sense. In this acceptance of the present as the present of God, as we have tried to make clear, pardon and conversion are one in the works of Jesus.

God's future is God's call to the present, and the present is the time of decision in the light of God's future. This is the direction of Jesus' message. Over and over again, therefore, we hear the exhortation: "Take heed, watch" (Mk. xiii. 33-37; cf. 5, 9, 23, etc.). This "take heed to yourselves" (Mk. xiii. 9) stands in marked contrast to all curious questioning. Therefore, those very words of Jesus which refer to the future are not meant to be understood as apocalyptic instruction, but rather as eschatological promise, as W. G. Kümmel has pertinently observed.[49]

Certainly, in what has come down to us in the Gospels, there is no lack of sayings of an apocalyptic nature. They are gathered together in the thirteenth chapter of Mark's Gospel, taken up by Matthew and Luke and, especially by the latter, considerably remodelled. This so-called "synoptic apocalypse" is, however, a very complex composition. Undoubtedly traditional matter which has its origin in late Jewish apocalypticism has been taken over during the transmission of the synoptic material and set down as sayings of Jesus (sayings about war and rebellions, earthquakes and famines, darkness and falling stars, the laying waste of Judaea and the desecration of the temple).[50] Other sayings tell clearly of experiences of a later time (persecutions, false doctrines, seduction and so on). Unquestionably, too, genuine sayings of Jesus are interwoven with both. All this clearly has the intention of putting some chronological order into the sequence of the final events, and of making clear the "signs of the time" which give the hearer and reader a glimpse of the course of the world and its end.[51] The whole chapter is therefore permeated with indications of time:

"The end is not yet . . . this is but the beginnings of sorrows . . . in those days . . . then . . . then . . ." This is not the place to determine which words of this apocalypse are to be ascribed to Jesus himself, a topic concerning which there is considerable disagreement on specific points. But it is clear that the speech as a whole is an apocalyptic composition, which even betrays itself as a literary production by the sentence "let the reader understand" (Mk. xiii. 14). Above all, we see from Luke, who in Chapter xxi. 20 (as also occasionally elsewhere) has read into the existing text the events of the Jewish war in the sixties in some detail, that the more and more detailed interpretation of just such speeches during their transmission was especially common. It is therefore difficult to refrain from giving a critical judgment on the obvious tendency to set up as it were a "calendar" of the final events, in view of Jesus' own words which forbid such apocalyptic speculation. The quite varying history of the identification of the individual motifs of this "apocalypse" with ever new historical figures and events shows how questionable these assertions are. This is already seen by the time of the writing of the Gospels, but especially throughout the history of the Church up to our own times. In this way, for example, the apocalyptic utterance about the "desolating sacrilege" (Mk. xiii. 14, from Dan. ix. 27; xii. 11)—a mysterious symbol for the Antichrist who will penetrate into God's sanctuary and desecrate the temple—is applied in turn to Antiochus IV Epiphanes, through Caligula, Domitian and many names of the Middle Ages, on down to Napoleon and Hitler. Hence, the enlightened assertion that such explanations are typical manifestations, products of an excited apocalyptic fancy obsessed with the idea of the end of the world, seems to be very near the mark. One cannot dispute the relative validity of such a view, when one considers all the fanatical attempts to give, as it were, historical names to the stages which must be gone through as the world moves towards its end. But it is all too clear that even that enlightened standpoint proves itself, in the light of the message of Jesus, somewhat audacious. It attempts to look out at history as a whole from the higher watchtower of the observer; here, of course, in the opposite sense to apocalypticism, in that it denies any relation whatsoever of history and the present to God's future.

Thus we are brought back again to the "Take heed, watch!", which noticeably pervades even this "apocalypse" of the Gospels. Jesus' message demands that we reckon with the future lay hold on the hour, do not calculate the times. Those who wait in the right way are therefore called to fulfil the will of God now with all their might.

Chapter V

THE WILL OF GOD

1. JESUS AND THE LAW

JESUS enters on the scene like a scribe. He teaches in the synagogue and discusses with his opponents. He is asked questions concerning the meaning and application of the commandments, concerning the correct teaching as to the resurrection of the dead (Mk. xii. 18 ff.); indeed his judgment is sought in legal disputes (Lk. xii. 13 f.). Thus it corresponds with the picture of the Jewish rabbi, who is theologian and jurist at the same time. However, we never hear of him "studying" in the school of a famous rabbi; indeed his adversaries call him frankly "unlearned" (Jn. vii. 15; cf. Mk. vi. 2). Meanwhile we must not without further examination read back into Jesus' times the strict regulations of later rabbinical literature for study and ordination of the scribes. Certainly the respectful title "Rabbi" with which he is addressed is applied rightly. Nothing entitles us to assume that Jesus, from a given moment onwards, perhaps under the influence of John and his movement, took off the scholar's gown to become a prophet, although he was thought by many of his hearers to be a prophet, and although his own saying concerning the prophet who counts for nothing in his own city (Mk. vi. 4) confirms this. Nevertheless, he does not cease to be a rabbi. This corresponds, too, with the exposition of the Gospels in general. Luke's story of Jesus at the age of twelve, in the temple, shows the boy in the midst of the scribes (Lk. ii. 41 ff.). Jesus sends the healed leper to the priests so that he may be declared ritually clean, and tells him to offer up the sacrifice which Moses has commanded for the cleansing (Mk. i. 44). Even the long twenty-third chapter of Matthew, which contains the sharpest attacks on the Pharisees, calls the scribes and Pharisees, without irony, those who sit on the throne of Moses (Mt. xxiii. 2). Jesus' attitude to them therefore is not to be interpreted as out and out repudiation of any communion with them, as the schematic arrangement of the scenes of conflict in the Gospels might tempt us to believe. Repeatedly he is a guest in the house of a Pharisee (Lk. vii. 36; xi. 37; xiv. 1). Indeed, Pharisees come and warn him against the plots of Herod: "Get away from here, for Herod wants to kill you" (Lk. xiii. 31). It is not even true to say that Jesus attacked the contemporary method of expounding the tradition of the law as such, which claimed the same authority for Torah, its exposition and its application.[1] Jesus, too, not only quotes the letter of scripture, but adds immediately in the accustomed way the interpretation applicable (Mt. v. 21, 43). Not the method of interpretation but the content is attacked. This is what is meant by the saying: "So, for the sake of your tradition, you have made void the word of God" (Mt. xv. 6; Mk. vii. 13).

Nevertheless, he never claims for himself the authority of the fathers, as was the general custom of the rabbi. The scripture passages he uses in his arguments are not like mere texts followed by exposition, but are post facto explanation and justification of his message and conduct. We have drawn attention to this rather essential feature before (see above, pages 57 f.). Also in his daily life, as we have seen, Jesus moved about with an informality which does not fit the picture and customs of a rabbi, at least as we know them from later texts: among his followers are women: children are allowed to approach him; he sits down at table with tax collectors, sinners, and prostitutes (Lk. vii. 39).

Significant above all, however, is the open conflict with the law which causes the mounting antagonism of the Pharisees and scribes. Not infrequently the formal authority of the latter is in their favour at that. Jesus' attitude is described in the many disputes about the Sabbath (Mk. iii. 1 ff.; Lk. xiii. 10 ff.; xiv. 1 ff.; Jn. v. 1), which show him healing the sick and his disciples plucking the ears of corn on their way through a cornfield (Mk. ii. 23 ff.). This is no open offence against the scriptures themselves, but only against that Sabbath casuistry developed in Judaism to the greatest degree of pedantry. For the governing principle of his argument is: "The Sabbath was made for man, not man for the Sabbath" (Mk. ii. 27). For this to come from the lips of an ordinary rabbi is quite without parallel.[2]

The scriptures themselves, however, as is especially clear in two passages in the Gospels, have to submit to Jesus' criticism. The first concerns Jesus' attitude to the regulations for cleanness (Mk. vii. 14-23). When one considers the significance which was attached to the commandment for ritual cleanness[3]—for it is with this that such regulations are concerned, and not with commandments of hygiene and conduct—already in the Old Testament and not only in contemporary Jewish practice, one learns to appreciate the revolutionary meaning of the saying: "There is nothing outside a man which by going into him can defile him; but the things which come out of a man are what defile him" (Mk. vii. 15). Some ancient manuscripts were still aware that there is more here than an expression of rationalistic enlightenment, and therefore added the saying: "If any man has ears to hear, let him hear." It not only puts in question the exegesis of the scribes and Jewish practice. "Whoever contests that what enters a man can defile him challenges the presuppositions and the letter of the Torah and the authority of Moses himself. Beyond that he challenges the presuppositions of the whole cultic ritual of antiquity with its practices of sacrifice and atonement. In other words, he abolishes the difference, basic for all the ancient world, between the temenos, the sacred area, and the profane world, and is therefore free to keep company with sinners" (E. Käsemann).[4] One may with some justification point out that these words of Jesus concerning the clean and the unclean have been paralleled, or might have been, by other philosophers and religious thinkers. They undoubtedly fit into an era in which things originally meant in a cultic, ritualistic sense are being spiritualised and moralised—a process which affected the thinking especially of Hellenistic Judaism. But here we are not concerned with establishing the first occurrence of such thoughts in the history of thought, but rather with the presuppositions on which they are based, the radical way in which they were pronounced, and the consequences to which they lead both teacher and hearer.

Whether this first word was already meant as an attack by Jesus on the letter of the Torah may perhaps be doubted. In the case of the second reference, however, which concerns the question of divorce, there is an openly declared criticism of the law of Moses (Mk. x. 1 ff.). Jesus forbids divorce, although the law of Moses permits the possibility of a legal settlement (Deut. xxiv), and calls the permission given by Moses a concession to the hardness of the human heart. "For your hardness of heart he wrote you this commandment. But from the beginning of creation, 'God made them male and female.' For this reason a man shall leave his father and mother and be joined to his wife, and they two shall become one flesh. So they are no longer two but one. What therefore God has joined together let not man put asunder" (Mk. x. 5-9). It is significant that the Jewish-Christian Matthew has qualified this sharp criticism of the Mosaic Torah, and has turned this basic conflict into the same dispute which was being discussed in contemporary Judaism by the leading schools of Hillel and Schammai, namely that of a sufficient cause for divorce (Mt. xix. 3). Nevertheless, he too has retained the remark about the law of Moses having regard to the hardness of their hearts (xix. 8). Yet the Jesus of his pericope represents in this matter only the stricter point of view of the disciples of Schammai in opposition to the dubiously lax ideas of the school of Hillel, by forbidding divorce but permitting it in the case of adultery (Mt. xix. 9; v. 32). The parallel texts in the Gospels according to Mark and Luke show that this is a weakening of the original word of Jesus (Mk. x. 11 f.; Lk. xvi. 18; cf. also I Cor. vii. 10).[5]

The freedom of Jesus over against the law which is revealed in these two passages is without parallel as far as a rabbi is concerned. Even a prophet could not have gone against the authority of Moses without being called a false prophet.[6] We understand now why his "But I say to you" from the Sermon on the Mount cannot have its equivalent in the literature of the rabbis. Also the "Amen" which meets us, so unexpectedly, at the beginning of so many of Jesus' commands and prophecies must be understood in this connection.[7] The Gospels have taken it over, like a few other sayings of Jesus, without translating it from the Aramaic into the Greek. Originally it is the response with which the congregation replies to the prayer uttered in their presence, and with which they make it their own. Here, however, it is as good as a confirmation by oath, which with the greatest and most immediate certainty points to the validity of the words which are to follow.

In saying this we must not, of course, forget for one moment that Jesus does not intend to abolish the scriptures and the law, and

to replace them by his own message. They are and remain th
proclamation of God's will. For Jesus, however, the will of God i
present in such immediate fashion that the letter of the law may b
gauged by it, as the examples show. It is no coincidence that jus
for this reason the question as to the first and greatest command
ment plays such a decisive part in his preaching. Again we have t
realise that this is in no way a natural question for the Jew to ask
Admittedly it appears here and there in Judaism and can, i
principle (as shown in Lk. x. 27), also be answered by a Jew in th
sense of the twofold commandment of love; the love of God an
the love of our neighbour. There is no lack, however, of Jewisl
utterances forbidding emphatically any such differentiation be
tween things of greater or lesser importance, because the law i
"made law" by God and any discrimination must appear as humai
presumption. In Jesus' preaching, however, this discrimination i
exercised, thoroughly and without inhibition, although not from
the point of view of a purely rational criticism, but because of the
immediate presence of the divine will, which also demands the
immediate assent of our understanding. This means at the same
time, *for the sake of the law, not against the law*: "I desire mercy, and
not sacrifice" (Mt. ix. 13; xii. 7), "And you shall love the Lord
your God with all your heart, and with all your soul, and with all
your mind, and with all your strength" (Mk. xii. 30).

2. THE NEW RIGHTEOUSNESS

Jesus' proclamation of the divine will, concisely and impressively
put together by Matthew in the sayings of the Sermon on the
Mount (Chaps. 5-7, cf. App. II), has two fronts which appear to be
opposed to each other.[8] The first is found in the word: "Think not
that I have come to abolish the law and the prophets: I have not
come to abolish them but to fulfil them" (Mt. v. 17). The second
is contained in the saying: "For I tell you, unless your righteousness exceeds that of the scribes and Pharisees, you will never enter
the kingdom of heaven" (Mt. v. 20). The second is also evident in
the antithesis proclaimed anew again and again: "You have heard
that it was said to the men of old. . . . But I say to you" (Mt. v.
21-48). All these sayings of the Sermon on the Mount are a fundamentally new message, as also are the Beatitudes which follow

them. It cannot be combined with the old. This would mean sewing a piece of new cloth on an old garment and putting new wine into old bottles; for the new will only endanger the old (Mk. ii. 21 f.), and would, intermingled with the old, only perish with it. What then is this incompatible New?

Jesus' sayings are directed to two different fronts, which are as relevant today as they were in the days of Jesus and the early Church. The first is the front of the fanatics who wish to claim Jesus for their own as the great revolutionary, as the prophet of a new world order, as the bringer of a new era, to which must be sacrificed all that is gone before, the word of God in the law and the prophets. They are obsessed by a picture of the future of the world; and for them the will of God which has ever summoned and bound us is a burdensome chain which must be discarded. This picture of the future of the world is now made the only valid law. To compel this future, to proclaim it and to bring about its realisation, is the command of the hour.

This movement rushes towards a dreamed-of future, right past the law of God and heedless of it. We have met this tendency in many different forms in the course of a long and changing history. More than that! Its threat is still with us. In Marxism and Bolshevism we have today, although greatly changed, an example of its historical reality. For there is no longer any doubt that this movement in world politics, in spite of being trimmed with scientific theories, must be understood as a secularised eschatological doctrine of salvation, as a doctrine of the kingdom of God without God.[9] A wealth of individual features reveals it as a kind of new world religion. The unshakable faith in the coming fulfilment of the meaning of history, which will become reality *within* this history as the kingdom of man; the doctrine of a central crisis in world history when there occurs the dawn of the new day (in the awakening and the rising of the proletariat); the doctrine of radical evil in the shape of exploitation, which is the "original sin" of this present era; the doctrine of the redemption of man from his "estrangement", of a redeemer[10] who is at the same time the "redeemed" (the proletariat); the expectation of a coming world situation in which the inexhaustible life-streams of paradise are opened up, and where man is the lord and new creator of the whole of nature. The surrounding of technology with a strange myth, the self-assured way of speaking, the dogmatic intransigence of its teaching, the demand for the total submission of man[11] which, logically enough, must prove itself ever anew in confessions of conversion or, in certain cases, in confessions of sin, and which has to be maintained in a relentless preparedness for battle and in an asceticism undertaken for the sake of the battle's aim—all this speaks one unmistakable language. "He who wants the future must not enquire into the past" goes a saying of Stalin's, which reminds us immediately of a word of Jesus': "No one who puts his hand to the plough and looks back is fit for the kingdom of God" (Lk. ix. 62).

This similarly is not a coincidence, but originates in the fact that Jesus' word and Bolshevism today are both concerned with the future, that future which transcends all our history. Both wish to open up this future, a future which is not somewhere in heaven but which shall become real here on earth. Nevertheless, the difference is fundamental, and these revolutionaries, when they wanted to claim Jesus as an ally in the struggle for a new world or social order, have had to learn again and again that they could not rely long on this ally, and that the kingdom of God which he proclaimed would not square with their own expectation. It is, therefore, not surprising that today this alliance, often enough attempted in the revolutionary movements of the West, has apparently been definitely renounced, and that this completely secularised Marxist doctrine of salvation has replaced that of Jesus.

We need hardly say that these features and problems which have been mentioned as pressing us at the present moment are only mentioned as examples or explanations, and not in the interests of an always very questionable inclination to identify the devil, so to speak, with one individual person in history. The modern analogy is given merely to indicate the contemporary relevance of the first thrust of Jesus' preaching mentioned above.

"I have not come to abolish the law and the prophets but to fulfil." This summarises Jesus' disapproval of all fanatical disregard for the law and his basic approval of the law. If we ask for the reason for that disapproval and that approval, the answer can only be: because for Jesus the true future does not demand the sacrifice of man. We do not mean here the sacrifice which has the promise: "Whoever shall lose his life (for my sake) shall find it", but that fatal and yet so alluring kind of sacrifice, by which man loses himself to a phantom, a mere dream of the future. To put it differently, he becomes an anonymous cog in a world machine, and therefore has ceased to be an individual, called by God and responsible to God at every moment and with his whole life. We might also say, because the God whom Jesus preaches cannot be exchanged for an idea, and the man to whom his word applies is a responsible being, hence his disapproval of that fanaticism which rejects the law, and hence his approval of God's law.

But the Sermon on the Mount has yet another direction, which becomes evident in the words with which Jesus compares his interpretation of God's will to that which was "said to the men of old". It is the commandment not only to avoid murder, but also not to indulge even in thinking about it, or in bursting out with words of rage towards one's brother; not only to avoid adultery, but not even to give way to lustful looks or thoughts and to preserve marriage inviolate; Jesus' call to unqualified truthfulness, and therefore to the renunciation of oath and swearing; his call to the renunciation of the right of retaliation even where one has received injusice, and also his commandment not to resist evil; and finally his call to a love which embraces not only the neighbour but also the enemy (Mt. v. 21-48). This is the "righteousness which exceeds that of the scribes and Pharisees", without which no one may enter the kingdom of God (Mt. v. 20).

All these antitheses contain one sustained theme which may be summarised in these few words: "Not only—but even . . ." Even wrath, even the lustful look, even the "legal" divorce, even the mere oath (by which *one* word is singled out above others as true), even the kind of retaliation which remains within the limits prescribed by the law, even the kind of love which yet excludes the enemy, are against God's will.

One may not simply claim that the radical interpretation of the divine demand which is expressed in these words of Jesus is absolutely foreign to the Jewish understanding of the law. There are not a few sayings of rabbis which are akin to some of the words of Jesus, and are at pains to penetrate within the wording of the law to the underlying will of God. It is, however, typical for the Jews, as we see exemplified in the teaching and attitude of the scribes and Pharisees, that God's will and law are understood in the sense of a legal statute with which one may not argue. A legal statute which fences life in on all sides has also this implication: there are as many gaps in the fence as there are posts. It is, therefore, no coincidence that the rabbinic tradition is interwoven with minute discussions and regulations which stipulate precisely to which situations of the daily life the individual commandments and prohibitions may be applied, and where they have no claim to be observed. Hence the minutest explanations as to the question of what in the sight of the law constitutes breaking the Sabbath or committing adultery, or any other offence against a cultic commandment; which formula of swearing an oath is permissible and which not; where a measure of retaliation is in accordance with the law and where not, etc.

Yet where the law of God is being dealt with in such a way, its authority is necessarily formalised, and a corresponding formalisation of the obedience which man owes it is the inevitable result. Obedience becomes something measurable, something that can be demonstrated, deeds become works, works are accumulated into capital. The great reckoning with God begins: reckoning and counter-reckoning; merit and debt; reward and punishment; the actions of men being bartered in transaction with God. Hence the words of the Pharisee in the temple (Lk. xviii. 9 ff.) who has augmented the obligatory tasks by additional ones assuring him special rewards, achievements which he now enumerates in his "prayer of thanksgiving".

What does this conception of the law reveal? Evidently this: the law has become separated from God and has become man's real authority. It no longer leads to a meeting with God, but rather frustrates it. Correspondingly man has retreated behind his deeds and achievements—as well as behind his guilt. God is concealed behind the law and man behind his achievements and works. Law and performance are the two sides of the protecting wall, behind which man takes up his own position and asserts himself before God.

Jesus' word penetrates this supposedly protecting wall and makes thrusts directly towards that area which, in the reversal of God's will, has become a network of laws and religious and moral traditions. He liberates the will of God from its petrifaction in tables of stone, and reaches for the heart of man which seeks seclusion and safety behind the stronghold of observance of the law. He detaches the law of God from the "traditions of men" and sets it free, and makes man in a new sense a captive—man who deludes himself that his life is in order under the existing régime.

Of set purpose Jesus does not do this through general theological discussions or with the proclamation of theological and moral principles, but with a call to concrete obedience: "Be reconciled to your brother!" "If your eye causes you to sin, pluck it out!" "Let what you say be simply 'Yes' or 'No'; anything more than this comes from evil." "But if any one strikes you on the right cheek, turn to him the other also; and if any one would sue you and take your coat, let him have your cloak as well; and if anyone forces you to go one mile, go with him two miles. Give to him who begs from you, and do not refuse him who would borrow from you. Love your enemies and pray for those who persecute you." His word is always specific, where as a rule we cannot get beyond commonplaces or a casuistic righteousness. This is why his teaching hits the mark in its incomparable way. Here is the secret of the conciseness and vividness, the cutting edge and the healing power of his words. Nowhere is to be seen in them the neutralising and isolating layer of conventionalism so frequently found, especially in religious speech. They always convey the original freshness of real spontaneity. Never is there the correct, the all too correct preaching *about* God. God is always present and so is man, in unmistakable reality.

This makes it clear that the words of Jesus in their concreteness have nothing to do with the casuistry of Jewish legalism. Characteristic of this legalism is its endeavour to enmesh man's whole life ever more tightly. With each new mesh, however, it forms a new hole, and in its zeal to become really specific it in reality fails to capture the human heart. This "heartlessness" is characteristic for all casuistry. The concrete directions of Jesus, however, reach through the gaps and holes for the heart of man and hit their mark where his existence in relation to his neighbour and to his God is really at issue.

This is pointed out particularly clearly in the antitheses of the Sermon on the Mount. God's claim becomes in them extremely simple. *What* man does becomes strangely relative, and the *How* of his actions is given the real importance. This does not mean by any means that we are no longer concerned about actions, but that what counts is only the "motive". This distinction between action and motive which has become so general in modern ethics is entirely foreign to Jesus' teaching. Particularly these antitheses show that Jesus counts the very state of mind as action: they aim at obedience right in the heart of the actual deed itself. "He who hears my words and does them . . . !" The "relativisation" of the action means rather that it is being considered in the light of what man *really* is and wants to do. It is now no longer simply a work behind which, so to speak, man can take refuge; just as the law is no longer a statute standing between God and man.

The simplicity of Jesus' interpretation of the divine will is proved also in the fact that it contains nothing impossible to understand. We have repeatedly drawn attention to the significance of the "wisdom sayings" in Jesus' preaching. Their characteristic is this, that they appeal immediately to the knowledge, experience and understanding of man, and reject all necessity for outside proof, whether it be from the prescribed sphere of authority found in the scriptures or in the recognised interpretation of the fathers, or whether it be from the network of apocalyptic doctrines. "A city set on an hill cannot be hid" (Mt. v. 14). "And do not swear by your head, for you cannot make one hair white or black" (Mt. v. 36)—i.e. by your oath you pledge something which it is not in your power to pledge! "Which of you by being anxious can add one cubit to his span of life?" (Mt. vi. 27). "The eye is the lamp of the body. So, if your eye is sound, your whole body will be full of light. But if your eye is not sound, your whole body will be full of darkness. If then the light in you is darkness, how great is the darkness!" (Mt. vi. 22 f.). These and innumerable other passages confirm what has been said: the immediate obviousness of Jesus' words, which leaves no room for an "if" or "but", and which requires no justification from outside.

This transparency is typical for the claims of the Sermon on the Mount as a whole. No one can honestly say that he could not understand all this. For how can God accept and let pass what is here judged—a divided heart and a partial obedience? Innumerable objections and questions occur to us, where the application of the Sermon on the Mount in political and legal life, or even only in the everyday contacts of our life in the community, are concerned. Questions like: Where shall we land, if we try to govern and fashion the world with these directions? What happens to my inalienable rights? Shall evil not triumph? But all these questions become of secondary importance before the recognition that what is said here is true. The first thing required of the hearer of the Sermon on the Mount is not the questioning of the possibility of its fulfilment, but rather the acknowledgment of the reality of God's will. This is the other revolutionary challenge of the Sermon on the Mount, directed towards those who merely live by "What has been said to the men of old", and who understand the will of God to be the protection and guarantee of sacred religious and moral traditions.

What has been said above makes it clear that the righteousness which exceeds that of the scribes and Pharisees is in no way something like a higher grade of Pharisaism, more rigorous and more painstaking even than that of Jesus' adversaries. Such a conception can, it appears, refer to the expression "exceed" and to the question concerning "more than others" which we meet in the last series of sayings about loving our enemy. This certain "extra" is to distinguish the actions of the disciples from that of the Gentiles and tax collectors. "And if you salute only your brethren, what more are you doing than others? Do not even the Gentiles do the same?" (Mt. v. 47). There is, however, no doubt that the "righteousness which exceeds" is not a quantitative difference, even though Jewish-Christian traditions present Jesus' demand as a precise and strict obedience to the jot and tittle of the letter of the law (Mt. v. 18 f.). Some of the antitheses immediately following this (divorce, retaliation, love of our enemies) are in point of fact a rather violent onslaught against jot and tittle, in so far as they not only give the established law a radical interpretation, but abolish it. And so the antitheses even compel us in retrospect to adopt a metaphorical and spiritual understanding of what the Gospel-writer wished to say with this Jewish idiom about obscuring every jot and tittle.

The truth is that the new righteousness is qualitatively a new and different attitude. In accordance with the biblical idiom elsewhere, neither the concept "righteousness" nor that of "perfection" could be exceeded. "You, therefore, must be perfect, as your heavenly Father is perfect" (Mt. v. 48). This is not an ideal which may be achieved step by step, but means "wholeness" in comparison with all dividedness and brokenness; a state of being, a stance whose reality is in God. In the demand which he makes upon them, Jesus points the disciples, with the greatest emphasis, to God—the God who will come and is already present and active. To live on the basis of God's presence and in expectation of his future, this is what Jesus aims at in his commandment: "That you may be the children of your Father who is in Heaven!"

This is where Jesus' message of the approach of the kingdom of heaven and his preaching of the will of God become completely one. Both show forth the pure and unveiled will of God. Both witness to his reign, and both are the judgment upon a life which exists solely on an earthly diet and its supposed realities and standards. There exists, therefore, no gulf which cannot be bridged between the Beatitudes and the demands of the Sermon on the Mount. To live in the presence of God and in the expectation of his future is the blessing which Jesus' Beatitudes promise, which is no less the blessing of his commandments. The door which Jesus opens with the Beatitudes is not closed by him again like the angel with the sword of fire.

The oneness of Beatitudes and demand is, however, a *hidden* one. It has become customary for theologians to engage in many-sided reflections on Christ's saving work, in order to make the connection between the two intelligible.[12] It is significant, however, that Jesus in all these passages never mentions himself.[13] To be sure we are not to forget by whom they are spoken, for we must recall the difference between Beatitudes and wisdom sayings (page 75). Yet it is equally clear that Jesus is present in the sayings in no other way than in his words, completely one with his words. No "Christology", no matter how true to the scriptures and to the faith, can or should diminish the pressure placed upon those who hear the Sermon on the Mount. They have to meet it defence-lessly as those who are still chained to this world and who enquire and must enquire after the world's demands.

The conflict between God's reign (and will) and existence on earth must therefore be endured. It is only in this way that the decisive thing happens to those who are called and those who hear. They are placed where the world and its possibilities end, and the future of God begins. Like the "Christology" of the Sermon on the Mount, so is its "eschatology" a *concealed* one. This means that the claims of Jesus carry in themselves "the last things", without having to borrow validity and urgency from the blaze of the fire in apocalyptic scenes. They themselves lead to the boundaries of the world, but do not paint a picture of its end.[14]

Those called to the new righteousness are liberated from the world, and yet put into the world again in a new way: "You are the salt of the earth, You are the light of the world" (Mt. v. 13 f.). As the liberated among a world which is doomed to die of its own evil and of its own good, of its enthusiasm for the future as well as of its worship of traditions, of its own law as well as of its own lawlessness—we may add here: in the East as in the West—in such a world the disciples have been called to raise high the symbols of the new righteousness,[15] and in obedience to reckon with God's power and possibilities. Certainly the Sermon on the Mount has no programme for the shaping of the world and for legislative and social reforms,[16] little though we may deny its effect on history in this respect. No one can deny that again and again it has quickened man's conscience. But none the less this also applies, that just because it leads so often to a hopeless tension between God's will and man's ability, it also wakens the hunger and thirst after righteousness which receives Jesus' promise (Mt. v. 6).

3. THE COMMANDMENT OF LOVE

One of the scribes asks Jesus: "Which is the great command-ment in the law?" and receives the reply, "You shall love the Lord your God with all your heart, and with all your soul, and with all your mind. This is the great and first commandment. And a second is like it, you shall love your neighbour as yourself. On these two commandments depend all the law and the prophets"

(Mt. xxii. 34-40).[17] This twofold commandment of love is the fulfilment and essence of the entire law (Mt. v. 17; vii. 12). All other commandments are included in this first and foremost one.

It is therefore essential to understand the meaning of this two-fold commandment. What is the relationship between these two commandments and how do they become one? Are the love of God and the love of our neighbour one and the same thing? Surely not. That would mean eliminating the barrier between God and man which is in fact immovable. Whoever considers both command-ments in this sense to be identical knows nothing of God's sovereign rights, and will very soon make God into a mere term and cipher, which one will soon manage to do without. In Jesus' preaching, love for God consistently takes precedence. This is made abundantly clear in the entire teaching on the reign of God, and in the call to obedience to his sovereign will. "No one can serve two masters" (Mt. vi. 24)—this law cannot be repealed, not even by our duty to our neighbour.

Although the love of God does not simply merge with the love of our neighbour, Jesus does not on the other hand remove the confrontation with another person involved in our love of our neighbour. He does not simply make it into a means to the love of God. A love which in this sense does not really love the other person for his own sake but only for the sake of God is not real love. An example is the love of his neighbour in the story of the Good Samaritan (Lk. x. 30 ff.). The help the Samaritan renders to him who has fallen among the thieves is given solely in response to the other's need. This is told with the greatest care: he binds up his wounds, he alleviates his pain, sets the sick man on his beast, brings him to the inn, puts him into the inn-keeper's care the next day, pays the initial expenses and promises to be responsible for any further expenses incurred when he comes again. Note how simply and without sentimentality the Samaritan is described: the shrewd merchant, practical and careful with his means and money, who does nothing that is not necessary at the time. In all this there is no parade at all of "religion". What he does is aimed at the sufferer without side glances at God. This is expressed incom-parably well in the words of the judge of the world, who at the end of time judges those on his right and on his left according to what

THE WILL OF GOD

they have done unto the least of his brethren, and in complete
ignorance as to their action's significance (Mt. xxv. 31 ff.). Those
on his right, the blessed of the Father, are those who can only ask:
"Lord, when did we see thee hungry, and feed thee, or thirsty and
gave thee drink? When did we see thee a stranger and welcome thee,
or naked and clothe thee? And when did we see thee sick or in
prison and visit thee?" Their actions were evidently not meant for
him, but only for those in trouble. But just because of this they are
accepted. "Truly, I say to you, as you did it to one of the least of
these my brethren you did it to me." The cursed, however, who
put the same astonished question, are those who want to make
their ignorance an excuse for their neglect and thereby prove that
they would have been prepared to love their neighbour only if in
meeting him they had quite unmistakably met Christ himself.
Love of our neighbour can never be merely an indirect love,
achieved by the detour via a supposed love of God.

What then is the meaning of this double commandment of love,
if these two possibilities, to dissolve the love of God into the love
of our neighbour and the love of our neighbour into the love of God,
are not to be valid? Clearly the inseparable unity into which Jesus
brings them has its reason and meaning not in the similarity of
those towards whom this love is directed, but in the nature of this
love itself. It is in Jesus' own words the renunciation of self-love,
the willingness for and the act of surrender there where you actually
are, or, which is the same, where your neighbour is, who is waiting
for you. In this way and no other God's call comes to us, and in
this way the love of God and the love of our neighbour become one.
Surrender to God now no longer means a retreat of the soul into
a paradise of spirituality and the dissolution of selfhood in adora-
tion and meditation, but a waiting and preparedness for the call
of God, who calls to us in the person of our neighbour. In this
sense the love of our neighbour is the test of our love of God.

The one question which decides everything is therefore the
question who our neighbour is. In Jesus' conversation with the scribe
concerning the greatest commandment, which precedes the story
of the Good Samaritan in the Gospel according to Luke, the
scribe puts this truly urgent question, to which the story itself is
the answer. The story makes it impossible for the scribe to pose

his question "at a distance", to treat it as a general theoretical problem which could be solved by a neat definition of what the meaning of "our neighbour" is and is not, and by fixing definite conditions and religious performances. As if a law could ever define where we are called upon and where not. Jewish thought, and also the natural man in general, are both concerned with this problem. "Who then is my neighbour?" means in the language of the Jew: Who is my "friend"? The Jew has no doubt about the answer. His "neighbour" is his kinsman in comparison with the foreigner. An essential part of this way of thought is that it moves, so to speak, in concentric circles.[18] It begins in the closest circle and grades the claims made upon us in the order: our nearest neighbour, our neighbour, our not so near neighbour, until we come to those towards whom we have no further obligation, indeed whom we have a right or even an obligation to hate (Mt. v. 43 ff.). Jesus puts an end to this way of thinking. He puts the other person in the centre, not, however, as the representative of mankind in general, but as an encounter with one as incalculably real to me as the miserable man on the Samaritan's way. Just as we cannot put our neighbour "at a distance", so we cannot put the question "Who then is my neighbour?" at a distance either. What Kierkegaard says applies here: "Indeed, everyone has a distant knowledge of his neighbour, but God only knows how many really know him from close at hand. And yet, at a distance, our neighbour is a mere phantasy: he whose very name means being near, the man at hand, indeed every man. At a distance our neighbour is only a shadow which passes through our mind like a phantom. The fact, however, that the person we just passed at that same moment was in actual fact our neighbour, we may unfortunately never discover."[19]

It is therefore of great importance from whose point of view the story of the Good Samaritan is told. It might be told by the priest and Levite who passed by on the other side, or from the point of view of the Samaritan. But the story begins with the man who fell among the thieves, and forces the hearer to put himself in his place. Put into his position, the hearer experiences the approach and the passing by of the first two, and we all feel how little it matters to the miserable man whether they may have good reasons for their hastening past him, and whether their attitude can be excused or justified. Placed in the position of the wounded, the hearer experiences also the approach of the Samaritan, from whom the Jew here by the wayside may not expect anything according to current thought. But to his astonishment he is seized with compassion and helps him. And he, who has made the enquiry as to who his neighbour is, is himself all of a sudden asked in return: "Which now of these three, do you think, proved neighbour to the man who fell among robbers?" The question: Who is my neighbour? has been changed into another: To whom am I neighbour?

Thus the questioner, in being asked to make his neighbour's position his own, finds himself directed to himself, and learns what it means to love one's neighbour as oneself. For we are most skilled in the love of ourselves; whether in selfish passion or in cool reflection, whether prompted by blind instinct or by some ideal, we desire our own self. Knowing this, however, we know what we owe the other person. On completely reversing our natural will which is directed towards our own self, the question need no longer be asked. The significance of this turning point has again been formulated most impressively by Kierkegaard: "If we are to love our neighbour *as ourselves*, then this commandment opens, as with a master-key, the lock of our self-love and snatches it away from us. Should the commandment to love our neighbour be formulated in another way than by the expression *as thyself*, which can be handled so easily and yet has the tension of all eternity, the commandment could not master our self-love so effectively. The meaning of *as thyself* cannot be twisted and turned; judging man with the insight of eternity, it penetrates the innermost part of his soul, where his egoism resides. It does not allow our egoism to make the least excuse, nor to evade it in any way. What a wonderful thing! One might have made longer penetrating speeches about the way man should love his neighbour, but again and again our egoism would have managed to produce excuses and evasions, because the matter would not have been completely exhausted, a certain aspect would have been passed over, a point not would have been described precisely enough or not would have been sufficiently binding in its expression. This *as thyself* however—truly, no wrestler could clasp his opponent more firmly or inextricably than this commandment clasps our egoism."[20]

As never before the story of the Good Samaritan makes it plain that true love cannot justify or spare a corner for self-love, and knows no reserve, not even towards an enemy. All too frequently our use of the expression "acting the Good Samaritan" arises from the acts of charity described in the tale. Originally, however, the statement of the man's nationality is intended to bring out the natural relationship of inborn arch-enmity between him and the Jew overtaken by misfortune. But this no longer applies. Love breaks through the boundaries—fortified as they are by age-old religious and social history and, to all appearances, impenetrable.

Jesus never bases this claim of love upon a universal idea of God, or upon an enlightened view of the national and religious questions at issue between Jews and Samaritans. Nor does he base it upon some such conception of man, say as is taught by the Stoics, to the effect that man as such is sacred (*homo res sacra homini*, Seneca Ep. 95, 33). Nor is his commandment to love our enemies concerned with achieving a pedagogical effect upon the other or with our own self-discipline. The ground of his command of love is simply because it is what God wills and what God does. That is the meaning of the passage: "So if you are offering your gift at the altar, and there remember that your brother has something against you, leave your gift there before the altar and go; first be reconciled to your brother, and then come and offer your gift" (Mt. v. 23). For God is prepared to wait, and does not want men to come to him alone, unreconciled. Reconciliation to him without a readiness to be reconciled to your brother is impossible. The fifth petition of the Lord's Prayer puts it similarly: "Forgive us our debts as we also have forgiven our debtors" (Mt. vi. 12). God makes no difference between friend and foe. "For he makes his sun to rise on the evil and on the good, and sends rain on the just and on the unjust" (Mt. v. 45). Therefore, the bridges between man and man, although they may appear to have been destroyed a thousand times through wrong-doing, denunciation and persecution, are never broken down in God's sight. Even the persecuted and the abused is not relieved of his duty: "Love your enemies; do good to those who hate you, bless those who curse you, pray for those who abuse you" (Lk. vi. 27 f.).

The fact that love has no limits does not imply the vague boundlessness of some concept of mankind. The natural divisions between friend and foe, between Jew and Samaritan, neighbour and stranger, Pharisee and tax collector, righteous and unrighteous, are certainly everywhere presupposed, and not ignored; but love penetrates these frontiers for God's sake and for our brother's sake, for whom I have a responsibility from which God does not release me. Hence Jesus' answer to Peter's question: "Lord, how often shall my brother sin against me, and I forgive him? As many as seven times?" "I do not say to you seven times, but seventy times seven" (Mt. xviii. 21 f.).[21]

Again and again the "love" (*agape*) which Jesus demands has been compared with the Greek word for "love" (i.e. *eros*), which is a different word and has a different meaning. It appears that Wilamowitz is right in saying: "Even if our modern language is so poor and in both cases calls it love, the two ideas have really nothing to do with each other."[22] The difference is indeed great, and it is no accident that the word "*eros*" never appears in the whole New Testament, just as, on the other hand, there is hardly any proof of the occurrence of "*agape*" in Greek literature. The verb "*agapān*" does, however, appear there, and yet in fluctuating meanings, and taken on the whole plays only the role of Cinderella. "*Eros*" (and the verb "*eran*") means the passionate love which desires the other person for itself. It signifies the passion which plunges man into pain and bliss, a frightful demon from whom no one is safe. It leads to the heights of ecstasy and thrusts down into the abyss of guilt (Sophocles, *Antigone*, 781 ff.). Thus, "eros" is the demon of blind sensuous passion, but also the desire for beauty, the creative driving power of the soul which reaches after the highest divine gifts. This is how, in Plato's *Symposium*, Diotima praises "Eros", "which never receives enough praise", the force which moves man in his helplessness and need, which overcomes him and powerfully rouses him, and yet at the same time is the power which brings him to himself. "A great daemon standing between the mortal and the immortal" (*Symp*. 202d), "the child of abundance and poverty" (203c).

It is understandable that theology has stressed again and again the radical contrast between *eros* and *agape*, and has felt that no better pair of ideas could be found to convey the difference between the Greek and the Christian attitude to life.[23] Christian thought as a rule cannot do enough to bring out the different implications of this antithesis: *eros*, the love which demands, *agape*, the love which is generous; one seeks what is in its own interest, the other what is in the interest of the other person, etc. In spite of the incontestable truth which can and must be asserted by this anti-thesis, it has, nevertheless, led in both directions to disastrous and far-reaching distortions. If this is true of the generally broken and negative attitude of the Christian faith to what the Greeks call "*Eros*", it holds true no less in the understanding of the biblical "*agape*". We should after all ask ourselves: Is it true that in the *concept* of "*agape*" as the heavenly love, the elementary traits of earthly love are cancelled out? Against this we have the simple fact that neither the Greek Old Testament (Septuagint) nor the New Testament are interested in such differentiation of the ideas of divine or human love We find "*agapān*" also used very freely in the case of the human love of father and mother towards their children, and above all of the love of a man towards his wife. In Jesus' saying Matthew v. 46 the same concept *agapān* is used, irrespective of whether it refers to the love of our enemies or to the love of a friend who loves us in return. It would be impossible to deny the aspect of a passionate longing in the love with which God loves man. Already in the Old Testament, the love of God towards his people is a great desire. "I spread out my hands all the day to a rebellious people" (Is. lxv. 2). The yearning love of a man for his faithless wife is an illustration used again and again by the prophets (especially Hosea) for God's love. God is a "jealous" God. These elementary traits of God's love in the message of Jesus should under no circumstances be taken away, as they are part of the very being of all love. It resembles the love of the father in the parable of the prodigal son, who has found again him for whom he has longed and whom he has missed. One cannot speak of love in too human, too "anthropomorphic" a way. Only then is the full wonder apparent, that God's longing becomes his self-giving.

We must therefore beware of a mere formal exhibition of the antithetic structure of the two conceptions. In practice this has meant a temptation to rob *"agape"* of its human aspects and to condemn *"eros"*. Jesus' commandment of love and that of the whole New Testament, in its promise as well as in its demand, never reduces man to a spectre, but calls him, as he really is, in the light of God's love, a love both past and present, into new being and into new activity.

Looked at from this angle we see once again why the question: "Who is my neighbour?" which the scribe put to Jesus is basically an impossible question. The scribe asks it so as to "justify himself"—i.e. to assert himself in face of the commandment. He tries to make a problem where there can be no problem of a theoretical nature. He is making a last effort to stand back from the request made of him with such urgent force—an effort which should never be made. "You shall love your neighbour as yourself"—he will never receive a different answer. In the meaning of these words, love is always self-explanatory. Again and again man can only be referred to what he knows already. Jesus never calls him to his ideal destiny, but lays hold of him in what he already is and does. Therefore, the simple golden rule: "So what you wish that men would do to you, do so to them" (Mt. vii. 12), can be called the essence of the whole law. What we should hear in obedience is simply this: "Do this and you will live!—Go and do likewise!" (Lk. x. 28, 37).

4. CREATION AND WORLD

The word creation hardly ever occurs in Jesus' teaching, nor does the word "Nature", which goes back to Greek thought. Yet everybody knows the direct, the natural and the memorable way in which Jesus points the hearer to the creation, how he makes it speak and preach about God. The parables show this, and many other words confirm it. One can certainly not talk about it in a simple enough way. Jesus develops no theory about the beginning of the world, nor does he present an interpretation of the first chapter of the Bible. Of course he can on one occasion make use of the language of the creation narrative (Mk. x. 6 f.), and he shares with every Jew the Old Testament faith in God the Creator and Lord, who called creation into being, cares for it and governs it. But creation does not become a topic of speculation for Jesus. Rather the creation itself is immediately present in his words, in the form in which we all have it before our eyes, there in front of us, in each individual creature. The fowls of the air who neither sow nor reap nor gather into barns; the lilies of the field so beautiful and carefree, who neither toil nor spin and yet are far more splendid than Solomon in all his glory (Mt. vi. 26 ff.); the fig-tree which when the sap rises into its branches in the spring, puts forth leaves and heralds summer (Mk. xiii. 28);[24] the seed, which grows and ripens till the harvest comes (Mk. iv. 3 ff.; 26 ff.; Mt. xiii. 24 ff. and others); the sparrows, so common that they are sold in the market for a penny (Mt. x. 29); sun and rain (Mt. v. 45); sunset and the south wind (Lk. xii. 55); the flash of the lightning (Mt. xxiv. 27). But also the wild dogs which licked Lazarus' sores (Lk. xvi. 21); moth and rust (Mt. vi. 19 f.); even the eagles who gather where there is a carcase (Mt. xxiv. 28); all are to be found in his preaching, just as are the wheat and the grapes, the thorns and the thistles. It is not a world transfigured by romance. Nowhere is there a hymn of praise for nature like the hymn to the sun by St. Francis. But even less is this whole world, so to speak, consumed in a fire of apocalyptic expectation. Everything stays and remains here in its own place, which it does not owe in the first instance to reflection upon any doctrine of creation and final consummation.

Jesus' manner of speaking of all this differs in no way from the manner in which he regards the life and deeds of man, undisguised, without embellishments, but also without moral anger or censure. This is what life is like: children sitting sulkily in the markets; their playfellows want to play at weddings, but they do not want to dance; they want to play at funerals with them, but they will not lament (Mt. xi. 16 f.). Who then would put a light under a bushel or under the bed instead of on a stand (Mt. v. 15)? Which father would be so unnaturally cruel as to give to his child a stone when he asks for bread, to give him a serpent instead of fish, or offer him a scorpion for an egg? (Lk. xi. 11; Mt. vii. 9 f.). Life goes on in the manner in which a woman bakes bread (Mt. xiii. 33), in which the shepherd goes after his one sheep which is lost (Lk. xv. 1 ff.), in which the farmer does his work (Mk. iv. 3), and then rests and sleeps (Mk. iv. 26 ff.). Life also goes on as when one person has a lawsuit against the other and they journey to the judge. It is not yet settled who is right. It is therefore more prudent for the adversaries to make peace in good time and while they are on their way together, lest one of them perchance should face the bitter reckoning (Mt. v. 25 f.).[25] It is as when a man returning from a journey into a far country reckons up with his servants (Mt. xxv. 14 ff.), or when the proprietor goes out into the market and hires labourers for his vineyard—early at six o'clock, at nine, at midday, and at three and five o'clock (Mt. xx. 1 ff.). It is as when someone builds a tower and does not have the money to finish the building, or when a king going to make war against an enemy stronger than himself does not negotiate peace in time; both may become a general laughing stock if they do not calculate the cost beforehand (Lk. xiv. 28 ff.). No wonder that he who builds his house upon sand and not upon rock experiences a great catastrophe when the rains and the floods and the storms beat upon the house (Mt. vii. 24 ff.). Life is also like the way things go on in the great nations of the world: "You know that the rulers of the Gentiles lord it over them, and their great men exercise authority over them!" (Mt. xx. 25).

Solid and matter of fact, the world is presented in its immovable reality, made neither better nor worse in the interests of a religious doctrine. Failing to see this, we shall fail to understand the gaiety which is so typical for so many of Jesus's sayings, a gaiety which gives authenticity to the earnestness of his words.

It is this very creation, this very world, which Jesus makes speak and which preaches to us about God. "He makes his sun to rise on the evil and on the good, and sends rain on the just and on the unjust" (Mt. v. 45)—even nature itself a witness for the love of our enemies, which knows no boundaries and penetrates all frontiers! Birds and lilies are witnesses of the divine care which makes a mockery of our worries. Not a sparrow falls to the ground without the will of your father. Seed, growth and harvest speak of God's promise; lightning, rain and storm of his judgment. Not that we might conclude from the creation and from the course of history that there is a God. On the contrary. The world is seen in the light of the rule and will of God. Thus it becomes a parable and manifests itself as creation. Again and again it is the undistorted place where man is, remote from all imaginations and dreams and especially from all religious phantoms, so that the listener can understand, in terms of the world as it is, God's nature, his actions and the significance of his reign.

In these sayings of Jesus this question frequently returns: "But if God so clothes the grass of the field, which today is and tomorrow is thrown into the oven, will he not much more clothe you, O men of little faith?" (Mt. vi. 30). Or: "You are of more value than many sparrows" (Mt. x. 31). Or: "If you then, who are evil, know how to give good gifts to your children, how much more will your father who is in heaven give good things to those who ask him!" (Mt. vii. 11). Thus creation points beyond itself to God the creator and God the coming Lord.

The famous answer which Jesus gave to his adversaries in reply to the question about the tribute to Caesar is certainly to be understood in this sense (Mk. xii. 13 ff.). It is the only scene in the Gospels where the problem of the power of the state is mentioned. This seems strange to us, who look back on a long history filled with the varying disputes between Church and State, the Christian and the world. Therefore the temptation is great to overtax the relatively few statements on this issue in the New Testament and especially in the Gospels, and to draw more out of them than they contain.

True, the fact that the problem of the state is mentioned in Jesus' message only on the margin is significant enough. What do we hear anyway in the Gospels of the great Roman Empire under whose rule and military power the Palestinian countries after all still lived? We therefore have no right at all to treat the Gospels under the pretentious general heading: Christ and the Caesars.[26] This state of affairs may be explained up to a point by the fact that Judaism had long since lost its position as a sovereign state (see also pages 29 ff.), except for a few remaining traces. And yet it is well known how discontented Palestine was in this period of Roman rule. Rome was and remained the hated pagan foreign ruler, and the ideal of a theocratic state had become in no way extinct in Judaism. We cannot speak of any relaxation or fading of political passion in Jesus' time. The Jewish people had certainly not become a non-political little people, but—and this is a special reason which may fan the political instincts and passions—a people deprived of its political existence.

Seen against this background, it is most astonishing and remarkable that political problems should take second place in Jesus' preaching. The reason for this is without any doubt the expectation of the approaching reign of God. And it is to this expectation that Jesus points the people, outraged, as we have seen, by the procurator's atrocious murder of the Galileans: "Unless you repent you will all likewise perish" (Lk. xiii. 5). With the utmost concentration Jesus preaches the coming kingdom of God. But let us remember at the same time that this kingdom is not a distant ideal for him, and that this actual world does not lose its contours in the glare of the last day. Thus it cannot be said that the question "Is it lawful to pay taxes to Caesar or not?" (Mk. xii. 14) does not concern him. To be sure, this question does not refer to payment of tax in general, or to the claims of political government as such, but to the per capita tax which the Caesar in Rome ordered in his provinces for the imperial fiscus. This custom was particularly painful and annoying to the Jews, as the imperial denarius bore the image of Caesar, and so in a special measure reminded them of the yoke of the foreign rule. The insidious question of his adversaries confronts Jesus with the choice between loyalty towards the powers that be, and his popularity among his own people.[27]

Jesus has the Roman silver denarius brought to him with the image and inscription of the emperor on it, and asks the Pharisees, "Whose likeness and inscription is this?" "They said to him: 'Caesar's.' Jesus said to them: 'Render to Caesar the things that are Caesar's, and to God the things that are God's.' " From the stamp on the coin he derives Caesar's rights and powers, which should not be contested. But this is what makes the answer really hit its mark, and what really puts the questioner to shame. Here is no theoretical discussion, but the opponents are referred to a decision which they have already made a long time ago. Gaily they conduct their business, unconcerned about the image and emblem of Caesar on these coins, so long as they can do business with them. Only when they come to pay their tax are their passions roused, and they feel called upon to make their "profession of faith".

But there is more than this in Jesus' answer. The point of view to which they have just been so energetically referred, confronts them with a question they have not considered before. A new horizon opens suddenly for the discussion. If it were really a matter of the question put by his opponents, the answer would only require to be: "Render to Caesar what belongs to Caesar." But then Jesus adds the important thing, the thing that really matters. "And render to God what belongs to God." This is the aim of his statement, and in view of its essential meaning the entire question of the opponents, along with the supposedly so pious sentiments and religious scruples, is silenced.

The simplicity of this decision must on no account be complicated, nor need we ascribe to this word "render" the underlying thought of "an obligation to give back".[28] Such reflections have, of course, already been raised by the Church Fathers. But the verb (apodidonai) is a technical expression for any payment of debt or tax. Certainly it would be best to take the simplest interpretation and not to read profound principles in, so that a "highly positive and imperative lesson" emerges. We do not have to do with the principle that the people of God should contribute to the upkeep of the empire, any more than the second proposition means (as it would according to such an interpretation) that the state should contribute to the temple tax. The meaning of Jesus' words would then have been clearly this, that Jesus has brought the rule of Caesar and the rule of God into a fundamental relationship to each other: "The imperium Caesaris is the way, the imperium Dei the goal of history" (Stauffer).[29] In such an interpretation the emphases of the double saying in Mark xii. 17 have obviously been significantly moved. Of course the saying has been constructed in form according to parallelismus membrorum. But there cannot be any serious doubt that it is a question of an "ironical parallelism" (A. Schweitzer, M. Dibelius).[30] In reality the second half has all the weight, and just because of this the first has its weight taken from it. This means that the question concerning the Caesar tax, taken so seriously and put so provocatively by his opponents, is put in the margin. It is certainly not declared unimportant or to be left to the whim of the individual, but it is, nevertheless, dismissed as a question which has been long ago decided. Not decided, however, is the question of the meaning of "Render to God the things that are God's". This means: the coin belongs to Caesar, but you to God. Probably it contains an even more specific thought: the coin which bears the image of Caesar, we owe to Caesar. We, however, as men who bear the image of God, owe ourselves to God.[31] This is not meant as a timeless general proposition, but is to be considered, like all Jesus' teaching, in the light of the coming kingdom of God, which is already present in Jesus' words and deeds and has begun to realise itself.[32] Through this interpretation of "Render unto God the things that are God's", the other part receives the meaning of a temporary, interim obligation, soon to end. For the reign of Caesar passes, but God's reign comes and does not pass away.

Already the oldest history of the exposition of our text shows how soon this main implication had been forgotten, and how the saying assumed very rapidly the meaning of an unconditional fulfilment of an obligation towards the powers of the state. And now the passage is quoted (e.g. by Justin, Apol. I, 17) to commend the Christians as the most loyal citizens of the state, and no other mention is made of that ultimate limitation of the power of the state.

Jesus' saying is therefore most decidedly not to be understood in the sense of a judgment of Solomon, which conclusively, fairly and neatly separates the realm of politics from the realm of religion. Such a distorted "doctrine of two realms" which, as is sufficiently known, has often enough led to a proclamation of the simple right of a state to be a law unto itself, and to a fatal confusion of the kingdom of God with a Civitas Platonica—a remote ideal state—has no right to base its arguments on Jesus.[33] It appears, therefore, that not much is said in Jesus' preaching on the problems of the state. Hence M. Dibelius remarks quite rightly that Mark xii. 17 is indeed a passage touching upon a political situation, but is not essentially a political passage. But the very fact that here the entire problem of the state is thus put in the margin, and that its fundamental problems are not allowed to come to the surface, is obviously a very important word on the whole matter. For this means that because God reigns, the hearer is set free from a basic concern as to this supposed problem. This question can only become a fundamentally disturbing one for us so long as we will not concede the challenge of the kingdom of God, and the temporary nature of this world. Herewith Jesus' word opposes all attempts, be they Jewish or Christian, reactionary or conservative-loyal, to improve the world with ideologies.

5. GOD THE FATHER AND HIS CHILDREN

We have to free ourselves from the assumption that Jesus was the first to call God Father in the history of religion. Nor is he the first to have made the idea of all men being children of God the centre of his message. The idea of the fatherhood of the deity is with very different variations common to numerous religions. We have the example of mythical religions, such as the Greek, where Zeus is the head of the family of gods. As is well known, his paternal authority in these myths of the gods is not infrequently put to a severe test. Enhanced by a philosophy, we meet this idea in Stoicism, where the deity is understood to be the father of the universe, and men are taken to be his children, related to him and sure of his care and providence. Thus we read in one of the most magnificent documents of Stoic piety, Cleanthes' Hymn to Zeus (b. 330 B.C.).

> But, Zeus, thou giver of every gift,
> Who dwellest within the dark clouds, wielding still
> The flashing stroke of lightning, save, we pray,
> Thy children from this boundless misery.
> Scatter, O Father, the darkness from their souls,
> Grant them to find true understanding—
> On which relying thou justly rulest all.[34]

"To have God as Creator, as a father and guardian, should this not deliver us from suffering and fear?" asks Epictetus (b. *circa* A.D. 60).[35]

God is called Father also in the Old Testament and in Jewish thought, but in a completely different sense. Here we have neither the thought of a physical descent of gods, demi-gods or heroes from a divine father, nor the idea of a divine kinship in which all men share, who, as reasonable beings in a reasonably governed universe, call God their father. The fatherhood of God in the Old Testament designates the exclusive relationship of the election of Israel by Yahweh. Thus the people of Israel are called the firstborn son of God (Ex. iv. 22 f.), and Yahweh is called the Father of Israel (Jer. xxx. 9). This can become a consolation which even outweighs what is otherwise so important in Old Testament-Jewish faith, namely the descent of the people from their earthly forbears: "For thou art our Father, though Abraham does not know us and Israel (i.e. Jacob, the ancestor) does not acknowledge us; thou, O Lord, art our Father, our Redeemer, from of old is thy name" (Is. lxiii. 16). In a very special sense the king of the people is regarded as God's son. As we read already in the ancient promise to Nathan, with a view to the future "shoot" of the house of David: "I will be his father, and he shall be my son" (II Sam. vii. 14; Ps. lxxxix. 27 ff.). So also in the passage which speaks of the king, which is quoted in many parts of the New Testament as indicating the promised Messiah: "You are my son, today I have begotten you" (Ps. ii. 7).[36] As usual the Old Testament meaning is not based on an idea of a miraculous birth here on earth, but on the investment of the king with the rights of a son. This is made quite clear in the 2nd Psalm, in that the ruler is informed of Yahweh's decree (v. 7) at the moment of his enthronement.

First in the Jewish period is this idea transferred to the relationship between the individual believer and God, but certainly not even here on the grounds of a general conception of man whose nature and being it is to be a child of God, but rather as a consolation and a promise for those who obey God's commandments: "Be like a father to the orphans and instead of a husband to their mother; you will then be like a son of the Most High, and he will love you more than does your mother" (Sirach iv. 10). Similarly runs the mockery of the faithful by the godless: "He boasts that God is his father. Let us see if his words are true, and let us test what will happen at the end of his life; for if the righteous man is God's son, he will help him, and will deliver him from the hand of his adversaries" (Wisdom of Solomon ii. 16 ff.). Despite the fact that the individual is here no longer looked upon only as a member of a nation, it would not be permissible to speak of an enlarging of the father-son conception beyond the national limits, to the point where it reaches universal significance for mankind. On the contrary, it is being narrowed down from the conception of the nation to that of the righteous among the nation. In this way it could certainly be applied anew to the people, but now no longer in the sense of an election which has already taken place, but as an ultimate hope which embraces once again the entire nation. "You shall follow after my commandments. And I shall be your Father and you shall be my children" (Book of Jubilees i. 24).

Jesus' use of the name "Father" for God cannot therefore be taken as the introduction of a new idea of God. It reveals peculiarities, however, which have the closest connection with Jesus' message as a whole. It is significant that the father-son relationship is nowhere applied to the nation, just as Jesus certainly never refers to the nation and its history as a guarantee of redemption. Neither is sonship the prerogative of the pious. God is father "to the evil and to the good, to the just and to the unjust" (Mt. v. 45; xxi. 28-32). This does not exclude, but rather explains the commandment: "Love your enemies and pray for those who persecute you, so that you may be sons of your father who is in heaven. . . . You, therefore, must be perfect, as your heavenly father is perfect" (Mt. v. 44 ff.).

Once again it is God's immediate presence, his presence with us now and his proof of being present, that gives significance to these words: "Not one sparrow will fall to the ground without your Father's will. But even the hairs of your head are all numbered" (Mt. x. 29 f.). "For your Father knows what you need before you ask him" (Mt. vi. 8). "For your heavenly Father knows that you need them all" (Mt. vi. 32). Especially, however, his goodness is evident in his attitude towards the lost. Jesus' story of the prodigal son speaks in unequalled terms of God's fatherhood (Lk. xv. 11 ff.). We must not allow our view to be dimmed with regard to the fact that the father is the principal figure in this parable, however much we are told about the fate of the two sons. It is the father who lets the younger son set out on his journey to freedom, when he demands his own portion of his goods, and treats the father as if he were already dead. It is the father who does not organise a search after his son nor run after him, but who, nevertheless, is present in his son's memory, when he in misery and hunger comes to himself amid his herd of swine. For it is not his remorse for the sins he has committed, but, to begin with, quite simply the realisation that he has come to the end of his tether, which makes the son turn back. Nevertheless, it is obviously not only this, but the memory of his father's house, where even the least of his hired servants has bread enough and to spare, and it is anticipation of his father's house, which make him start on the journey home. Admittedly it is a memory which reminds him not only of the good things he used to enjoy, but rather says to him: you have despised his goodness. And it is a hope which not only says to him: there lies the house of your father, but at the same time: you have forfeited your rights. Thus his decision comes about: "I will arise and go to my father." "Father I have sinned against heaven and before you; I am no longer worthy to be called your son; treat me as one of your hired servants." Confession and petition, awakened by the father's goodness, are cut short by the same goodness (cf. Lk. xv. 19, 21). For the father did not wait in his home, but saw the son when he was still a great way off. He has compassion on him and runs towards him and falls on his neck and kisses him. The reunion ends with the father's command, exclaimed with overwhelming words of joy, which do not seek the rendering of an account, which make no conditions, which set no time for probation: "Bring quickly the best robe, and put it on him; and put a ring on his hand and shoes on his feet; and bring the fatted calf and kill it, and let us eat and make merry; for this my son was dead and is alive again; he was lost and is found."

It is worth noting, that here, as in no other place, joy has been painted, so to speak, in the richest colours,[37] while just at this point artistic representation of our story fails badly as a rule. Only Rembrandt, who has made several etchings and paintings of this parable, is a true interpreter. On an etching of the year 1630, father and son are seen both facing the viewer to an equal extent, the son a figure of misery, fallen on his knees, and the father rushing towards him with long, hurrying steps, and embracing him. On a later oil-painting of the artist in the Leningrad Hermitage, however, the kneeling son is before him, and, with his back to the viewer, buries his face in his father's lap, held by his father's hands.

The main figure in the parable is the father right up to the last scene, his meeting with the older brother. Here, too, the father comes out, no less anxious for the older one, and entreating him, just as he had the younger one. Does the older one not know what has happened? He seems in the story to be the one who knows most. It is left to him to mention what has not been mentioned in the whole story so far, that the younger one, whom he refuses to call brother, has wasted his goods with prostitutes. The depth, however, of what has happened, only the father really knows: "This your brother was dead, and is alive; he was lost, and is found."

It becomes clear in this parable as nowhere else that the fatherhood of God can only be understood as a miracle, and as an event which now takes place. That is why the well-known piece by André Gide called "The Prodigal Son" seems to miss the essential part of the parable. The author here finishes with a conversation between the brother who returned and an imaginary third and youngest brother, who, enchanted by the adventures of the homecomer, will not allow his brother to dissuade him, but takes the same road. And so the parable has been turned into a poem of the eternally human. With that it has been robbed of its essential meaning: the message of the miracle of an ultimate event.

The nearness of God is the secret of Jesus' language about God as Father. This is also shown in the expression by which Jesus chooses to address God in prayer, an expression which would have appeared to any Jew too unceremonious and lacking in respect. Abba—Father, this is the word Jesus uses (Mk. xiv. 36), and which the Hellenistic Church has taken over in its original Aramaic form from the oldest records about Jesus (Rom. viii. 15; Gal. iv. 6). It is the child's familiar address to his father here on earth, completely uncommon in religious language. The nearness of the Father in his goodness certainly does not exclude the majesty of God, the demanding King (Mt. xii. 50), and the Judge to come (Mt. x, 33; xvi. 27). This corresponds with the address "Our father—who art in heaven" (Mt. vi. 9), in the prayer which Jesus teaches his disciples, and in which both trust and reverence are embraced.

One last feature should be taken notice of, so as to understand the use of the name of Father in Jesus' message. Although we find numerous passages where Jesus says "My Father (in heaven)" and "thy Father" or "your Father", there is nowhere a passage where he himself joins with his disciples in an "Our Father". We have

no reason to doubt that this usage was truly characteristic for
Jesus himself, and certainly as an expression of his mission. The
consistency with which the tradition has retained this particular
feature is at least an unmistakable proof that the believing community looked upon the secret of the fatherhood of God and the
secret of our being the children of this father as a miracle, not as a
natural fact. This is why Paul, in speaking of the "sons of God",
never makes mention of this except by speaking at the same time
of the sending of "the Son" (cf. Gal. iv. 1 ff.), and why the Church
calls God "the Father of our Lord Jesus Christ" (II Cor. i. 3 ; Eph.
i. 3, etc.). Not in the strength of their own nature, but by the
power of the "Spirit" who cries in their hearts, the believers cry:
"Abba! Father!" (Rom. viii. 15; Gal. iv. 6).

6. FAITH AND PRAYER

When the father of a sick child comes to Jesus and asks, "If you
can do anything, have pity on us and help us!" Jesus answers:
"(You say) if you can! All things are possible to him who believes!"
(Mk. ix. 22 f.). Another saying puts it similarly: "If you have
faith as a grain of mustard seed, you will say to this mountain,
'move hence to yonder place', and it will move" (Mt. xvii. 20).

What does this faith mean? Faith for Jesus has not yet acquired
the meaning of the obedient acceptance of a message of salvation,
nor the acceptance of the truth of a doctrine of the one almighty
God, and the coming of his Messiah. The people of whose faith
we hear in the Gospels do not look as if they would pass such an
"examination" of faith: the pagan centurion who beseeches him
for his servant's sake (Mt. viii. 5 ff.), the Syrophoenician woman
who appeals to Jesus for her sick daughter and who will not be
turned away (Mk. vii. 24 ff.; Mt. xv. 21 ff.), the father in the
story of the epileptic boy (Mk. ix. 21 ff.). We can say with certainty: wherever in the tradition the word "faith" refers to the
message of salvation and to Jesus as the Messiah, or where the
word "faith" is used in this sense absolutely without any addition,
we have to do with the usage of the later Church and her mission.
In numerous cases this can be confirmed by a comparison of the
synoptics.[38]

This first, negative statement, however, should not deceive us into assuming that the word faith in Jesus' teaching becomes on that account any more immediately comprehensible, or less foreign for modern man. It means something quite different from the mere attitude of a general trust in God, so typical, for example, of the Stoics, and seen in Epictetus and others. In the tradition of Jesus' sayings faith is always linked with power and miracle. As an example, this is very simply expressed in the words of the centurion of Capernaum, when Jesus agrees to come and help his servant: "Lord, I am not worthy to have you come under my roof; but only say the word, and my servant will be healed" (Mt. viii. 7).[39] He knows the power of the word in his military profession. Under the power of authority himself, he also exemplifies that power daily to his subordinates. The emperor in Rome issues an order, and the legions in the remotest parts of the empire move accordingly. And this applies also to the small area under the centurion's command. Thus he knows of the power of the word, but experiences at the same time its limitations at the sick bed of his servant. His faith is simply trust in Jesus' power to command, which has not reached here its limit. This is what surprises Jesus in this story: "When Jesus heard him, he marvelled, and said to those who followed him, 'Truly, I say to you, not even in Israel have I found such faith'" (Mt. viii. 10). The Syrophoenician woman, with the same trust in Jesus' power, appeals to Jesus for her daughter who is possessed of the devil, and traps him as he rejects her appeal with his own words: "And he said to her, 'Let the children first be fed, for it is not right to take the children's bread and to throw it to the dogs.' But she answered him, 'Yes, Lord; yet the dogs under the table eat the children's crumbs'" (Mk. vii. 27 f.).

All those who turn to him in faith count on the power of Jesus which knows no bounds, and on the miracle which he can work, where all human help fails. Thus the bearers who came bringing one sick of the palsy (Mk. ii. 1 ff.), the lepers (Mk. i. 40 ff., etc.), the blind by the wayside (Mt. ix. 27 ff.; xx. 29 ff.), the woman who was a sinner (Lk. vii. 36 ff.). The miracle stories in all the Gospels are meant to show that Jesus does not disappoint these expectations, and that he has been given this power. It would be difficult to doubt the physical healing powers which emanated from Jesus, just as he himself interpreted his casting out of demons as a sign of the dawning of the kingdom of God (Lk. xi. 20; Mt. xii. 28). There can be just as little doubt that precisely in this area of the tradition many stories have taken on legendary traits, and legends have been added. This applies particularly, though not exclusively, to the "nature miracles" in the narrower sense of the term.[40] We are driven to this critical judgment when we compare one with another the texts which have been handed down to us, when we see the growth of tradition already within the four Gospels, when we consider the style of the stories and the not infrequent parallels with non-Christian ancient literature. It is not important to establish here the historicity of this or that individual story in every particular; just as it is altogether absurd to consider recognition of their historicity as a proof of faith, and denial of their historicity as disbelief, although such an assumption is widespread among many "Christian" circles to this day.

At the same time there can be no doubt that the faith which Jesus demands, and which alone he recognises as such, has to do with power and with miracle. And this not in the general sense, that God is all-powerful and can work miracles, but in a very concrete sense: faith as very definitely counting on and trusting in God's power, that it is not at an end at the point where human possibilities are exhausted. This faith becomes real where strength and weakness meet. It is the opposite of all doubt (Mk. xi. 22 f.). That is why Jesus in the story of the epileptic boy rejects that very modest word of the father, so understandable after all his earlier experiences: "If you can do anything", and ascribes to faith a power which knows no bounds: "All things are possible to him who believes" (Mk. ix. 22 f.).[41] Does he demand too much of the petitioner and thus deprive him of his help? Not at all. Yet the further conversation with the father shows the only form his faith can take. "And the father of the child cried out: 'I believe; help my unbelief!' " (Mk. ix. 24). I believe!—here the petitioner has indeed exceeded his own ability, and confesses a faith greater than he really has. Help my unbelief!—here he who falls short of faith throws himself on the power and help of Jesus. In this paradox of faith and unbelief, as the story points out, faith becomes true and capable of receiving the miracle of God. Where Jesus does not find this faith, he cannot work a miracle (Mk. vi. 1-6). This certainly does not mean that faith itself is the power which works the miracle, although in the Christian view faith may be enabled to work miracles (Acts ii. 43; v. 12; Mk. vi. 7; I Cor. xiii. 2; II Cor. xii. 12). What matters here, however, is the readiness to receive the miracle. It is so indispensable for Jesus' work that he can say repeatedly to the cured and the saved—for both terms are implied by the word "salvation"—"Your faith has made you whole" (Mt. ix. 22; Mk. x. 52; Lk. xvii. 19).

Hence the paradox of which we have just heard in the father's request (I believe, help my unbelief) does not mean the destruction of faith. Neither is the father of the boy half believing, half un-believing. The nature of true faith is that it should be whole. That is why faith, be it only the size of a mustard seed, nevertheless receives the whole promise. Significantly enough, Luke understands this saying as Jesus' reply to the disciples' request, at first glance understandable and yet at the same time absurd: "Increase our faith" (Lk. xvii. 5 f.). It is certain that faith, as soon as it has withstood one temptation, is put to further tests. The Gospels speak of this in many different ways. Satan wants to bring faith to an end (Lk. xxii. 31 f.). Tribulation and persecution, the cares of the world, the deceitfulness of riches, the lusts of other things, choke it (Mk. iv. 14 ff.). Suddenly faith, when it comes to the point, is inadequate. Its resources prove insufficient. This is, in Jesus' words, to be "of little faith". It is entirely different from "mustard seed faith". We recognise this "little faith" under the testing conditions of worry (Mt. vi. 31), hunger (Mt. xvi. 8), or waves and storm (Mt. viii. 26; xiv. 31).

Does faith need miracle? This question is first asked openly in the Gospel of John, and decided here quite clearly. The faith which will not believe until it has seen a miracle is no real faith. This is why Jesus withdraws from the crowd who believe only because of the signs he works (Jn. ii. 23 ff.). Hence his first word to the noble-man who asks him to heal his son: "Unless you see signs and won-ders you will not believe" (iv. 48). For: "Blessed are those who have not seen and yet believe" (Jn. xx. 29). But the synoptic tradi-tion also reports that Jesus does not wish to be known as a "miracle-worker", that he withdraws from the people, and asks those he has healed to keep silence (Mk. i. 35 ff.; i. 44, etc.).

Above all, the refusal of a "sign", which the Pharisees demand of him (Mk. viii. 11 f., etc.), shows that Jesus will not allow miracles to be considered a proof of God's working and power, which could be demanded as the prerequisite to faith. Such a demand is a challenging of God. Trust and obedience have both been destroyed at the roots. This is already pointed out in the story of Jesus' temptation (Mt. iv. 1 ff.). The result of the first temptation shows Jesus, even in the midst of starvation from which there seems no escape, trusting still in God for the miracle, and therefore not performing it himself. For it is with the words of Deuteronomy viii. 3, that he retorts to the devil: "Man shall not live by bread alone, but by every word that proceeds from the mouth of God" (Mt. iv. 4). There is nothing here to make us suppose that the passage has a different meaning from the original text, which refers to the miracle of the provision of manna after the forty years of the people's wanderings in the desert.[42] Now the devil lays hold on Jesus through this very faith, following him right to the point where Jesus has taken his stand, and tries to tempt him who trusts in God to perform a miracle. He even goes so far as to quote from the same Scriptures to which Jesus has just referred. "He will give his angels charge of you to guard you in all your ways. On their hands they will bear you up, lest you dash your foot against a stone" (Ps. xci. 11 ff.; Mt. iv. 6). But Jesus repels the tempter once again with a word from Scripture. "You shall not tempt the Lord your God" (Deut. vi. 16; Mt. iv. 7).[43] To demand a miracle means to experiment with God.

Trust and obedience are according to Jesus' teaching a part of true "prayer". He therefore forbids the vain repetitions of the heathen, who "think they will be heard for their many words" (Mt. vi. 7). Repetitive prayer is an expression both of presumption and anxiety. It presumes to wear God down (*fatigare deos*),[44] and at the same time has the anxious thought that God must be briefed as to the need of those who pray. "Do not be like them, for your father knows what you need before you ask him" (Mt. vi. 8). But it is important to note that Jesus in this saying gives prayer its justification, and does not declare it unnecessary. In the piety of the Stoics the very opposite conclusion was drawn from the statement of the goodness and providence of God, and the prayer of petition was declared pointless, as it denies the divine omnipotence and omniscience.[45] Jesus, however, considers that the children of God have a right to the prayer of petition. The thought of God's omnipotence should never mean that man is to rise in contemplation to the higher level on which God dwells. Man rather remains within the limits of his own needs or, better, when he prays, he need not pretend to a status, a righteousness, which he does not possess. Just as man is given the freedom to pray, so Jesus gives him the definite promise of his prayers being heard: "Ask, and it will be given you; seek, and you will find; knock, and it will be opened to you. For everyone who asks receives, and he who seeks finds, and to him who knocks it will be opened" (Mt. vii. 7 f.; Lk. xi. 9 f.). It is worth noting how the same words of command and promise are repeated here, and hence the command and the encouragement to pray become one. In this sense it could almost be said with a rather bold use of the parable of the importunate friend (Lk. xi. 5-8), that God himself in Jesus' story appears, as it were, in the role of the importunate, and will not allow himself to be refused by man, who wants to be left in peace behind shut doors. Thus the imperatives beat and knock, as against a door which ought to open. It is instructive for us today to notice how different Jesus' outlook on prayer is from that of modern thought. The general opinion of modern man seems to be that prayer is a matter for someone who is no longer a seeker, but for one who has found, for someone who no longer stands knocking outside, but has crossed the threshold into the area of life in which there is an unbroken communication between God and the one who prays, and between him who prays and God. Jesus, however, does not see the position of the person who prays like this. Even Paul says of the prayer of a Christian who stands under the power of the divine Spirit: "For we do not know how to pray as we ought" (Rom. viii. 26). The petitioner, therefore, does not stand in a sphere of saintliness, but in unavoidable reality, in the worldliness of his existence and of his world.

This is why the parable of the importunate friend says with such refreshing worldliness: "I tell you, though he will not get up and give him anything because he is his friend, yet because of his importunity he will rise and give him whatever he needs" (Lk. xi.

8). We find the same meaning in the similar parable of the widow who asks to be avenged before the judge, who at length gives in to her for fear the woman might become violent in the end (Lk. xviii. 1-5). Both parables say that if this is what can happen on this earth, where he who is disturbed in the night and the unjust judge can be persuaded, how much more should God hear our prayer. With this promise, both parables are an encouragement and a challenge to untiring prayer.[46] Both parables appear to be opposed to Jesus' sayings about the heathens' use of vain repetition (Mt. vi. 7); in reality, however, they too are a challenge to unswerving trust.

Just as in all other parables (see on pages 69 ff.), so also here the hearer is challenged in the very secular reality of his life here in this world. He is arrested in the place where he actually is, and compelled to answer the question: "Who among you?" He who is thus addressed always stands in the place where God, in the interpretation of the parable, takes his stand.[47] This is the meaning of the sayings which Matthew and Luke similarly transmit in this context, concerning the father who would not give his child a stone for bread, or a snake for fish, or a scorpion for an egg (Mt. vii. 9 ff.; Lk. xi. 11 ff.).

Jesus speaks of prayer in this "unholy" way so as to dispel the mist of "pious" thoughts which has always surrounded prayer: in mysticism, which understands it as an exercise for purification and contemplation; in the piety of the Stoics, in which its only function is to become one in praise with the providence of God; in Jewish thought, where prayer is part of the works of the pious. The "fatherhood" of God means what it says. We can therefore not speak of him in a human enough way, if he is not to be removed to a distant nebulous sanctity and become a mere spectre. Jesus' teaching about prayer is the proclamation of the nearness of God.

We must of course always keep in mind that the God who is near us does not cease to be the holy, the heavenly father, the coming judge. His fatherhood, his nearness is the primary proof of his majesty. It is therefore hardly necessary to mention that Jesus' invitation to "unashamed" petition is not an invitation to "shameless" prayer. Jesus' preaching also treats of the latter. The prodigal son's demand: Give me, father, that portion of thy goods which is

mine! is such a one. Within this context also belongs the presumptuous claim that "God must . . . ," expressed by those whose faith
in election leads them to rely on their own works and their descent
from Abraham (Lk. xviii. 9 ff.); the same is true of those believers
who with their "Lord, Lord!" boast of their wonderful works before
the judge of the world (Mt. vii. 21 ff.). There are no visible differences between the "unashamed" prayer which Jesus has taught
us and the "shameless" prayer. There can be none, for the difference lies in the petitioner himself before God.

In surveying Jesus' teaching about prayer, we may notice that
the question of unanswered prayer, which is so frequently asked,
nowhere appears. Is it possible to answer it at all? One thing is
certain, that it cannot be put first, as is customary in modern
thought. If it confronts us when we have really heard the challenge
to pray, we become aware that the experience of unanswered
prayer, rather than leading us to silence, leads us to more earnest
prayer; always, however, asking, as Jesus did in Gethsemane: "Thy
will be done!" (Mk. xiv. 36), and as he teaches his disciples in the
Lord's Prayer: "Thy will be done, on earth as it is in heaven!"
(Mt. vi. 10). This petition applies everywhere and includes all the
praying of which Jesus speaks.

The Lord's Prayer which Jesus teaches his disciples might truly
be called the summary of all his sayings about prayer. But it is
more. It is no longer only a word *about* prayer and a call *to* prayer,
but is itself a prayer. It occurs twice in the Gospels, in a longer and
a shorter version (Mt. vi. 9 ff.; Lk. xi. 2 ff.), which shows how
little interest the Church had in preserving even these sayings of
Jesus as it were for the archives.[48] The text, if we are to follow
Matthew, speaks in the first three petitions of what is God's
("Thy . . ."); in the last four of matters concerning man ("us . . .",
"our debts. . .", etc.). For almost every petition we could find a
parallel in the treasury of Jewish prayers, above all in the prayer of
"Eighteen Petitions" (see page 38). In translating it back into the
Aramaic, we notice a kind of rhyme, in the uniform repetition of
the same final syllables (suffixes)—"Thy" (Petitions 1-3), "us",
"our" (Petitions 4-7)—a law of style which appears in many of
the later Jewish prayers.[49] There is here, however, a profound
difference. The first characteristic of the Lord's Prayer in contrast

to Jewish prayers is the great simplicity and plainness, and the absence of all pompous calling on God's name, all pompous homage. Most characteristic, however, is the completely different order of the petitions in the Lord's Prayer compared with the Prayer of Eighteen Petitions. This Jewish prayer is framed by praise, thanksgiving and benediction, and consists at its real centre of twelve petitions, which refer first of all to the life of the Jewish people now in the world. These are followed by petitions for the future, most specifically for the restoration of the political sovereignty of the nation, the ending of foreign rule, the return of the dispersed and the sending of a national Messiah. Jesus' prayer begins with eschatological petitions, making no reference at all to national expectations and apocalyptic embellishments. The opening petitions are three versions of one and the same idea, that God's name may be hallowed, that his kingdom may come, and that his will may be done. These first three petitions pray, as it were, for the revelation of God and his kingdom, while the following petitions pray for the deliverance from the troubles which beset and threaten the petitioner now: our bodily concerns,[50] guilt, temptation and the power of evil. Here, too, it is characteristic how simply and definitely the petitioner is left within the confined area of his own needs. The individual remains before God in his distress and in the perils of the world, and yet it is just in this way that the group of praying men and women is united into a fellowship which is founded on the Lord's Prayer alone.[51] Thus the prayer becomes a "*Summa laudis divinae*" (Bengel), the essence of all praise of God, and remains at the same time the petition of the "pilgrims and strugglers" who have not yet reached their goal.[52]

7. THE REWARD OF GOD

Jesus promises to those who do the will of God his reward in the kingdom of heaven. He ridicules the hypocrites who do their good works to be seen of men, who sound a trumpet before them when they do their alms, who love to observe the times of prayer in the most conspicuous parts of the synagogues or at the corners of the streets, and who keep their fast with sour faces so that they may be seen by others. "They have their reward." "Beware of practising your piety before men in order to be seen by them;

for then you will have no reward from your Father who is in heaven" (cf. Mt. vi. 1-18). "But lay up for yourselves treasures in heaven, where neither moth nor rust consumes and where thieves do not break in or steal. For where your treasure is, there will your heart be also" (Mt. vi. 20 f.). Innumerable sayings and parables contain this idea of reward as a matter of course and with the greatest emphasis.[53] It is not only characteristic of Jesus' teaching. For a long time the idea of a reward had played a decisive part in the Old Testament, and even more in later Judaism. All guilt calls for punishment, every good deed for its reward. Jesus and the faith of the early Church have not abandoned this idea, for it expresses a self-evident and simple, fundamental insight, which is also constantly at work in Jesus' message. It concerns man's position before God.

God is lord and man is his servant. Strictly speaking man's relationship to God as that of a servant to his master certainly excludes the thought of a reward, or at least limits it. For the servant is his master's own property, his slave whose body and life belong to him, and who has no special claim on a reward. Hence the saying: "So you also, when you have done all that is commanded you, say, 'We are unworthy servants, we have only done what was our duty' " (Lk. xvii. 10)[54]. The master is entitled to claim his servant completely. To "serve two masters" (Mt. vi. 24) is therefore an absurdity. The master can entrust his servant with money and goods, as he pleases (Mt. xxv. 14 ff.), and he can claim it back from him when he pleases (Mt. xviii. 23 ff.; Lk. xvi. 1 ff.). As far as the slave is concerned, however, the field to which he has been sent to work is not his own, the goods entrusted to him do not belong to him, and the services which he is obliged to render do not rest with him. He is therefore required to be faithful, faithful in the face of his master's strange, superior will ("to be faithful to oneself" is everywhere in the New Testament a possibility reserved for God and not for man; cf. II Tim. ii. 13). Hence in a strict sense the idea of a reward has nothing at all to do with the relationship between master and slave, for the latter has no property, but is his master's property. Different, however, is the legal position of the "labourers" who, as Jesus' parables show, are engaged as additional workers at harvest time by a farmer or the owner of a vineyard. Through a legal contract they enter for a limited time into a working relationship with the master which is regulated as regards work and reward, and are dismissed again after due payment of wages (Mt. xx. 1 ff.). They are no doubt entitled to make claims, but therefore do not stand in the same relationship of personal trust to their master as do the slaves. The master does not communicate with the labourers directly, but through his slaves (Mt. xx. 8; xxi. 33 ff.). These alone really belong to him and experience his strictness and his goodness (Lk. xii. 35 ff.; Mt. xviii. 23 ff.; xxv. 14 ff.), as they also suffer in their own bodies the insult done to their master (Mt. xxi. 33 ff.; xxii. 1 ff.). Thus it becomes understandable that in general the term 'slave' is used for the messengers of God, while the term 'worker' is seldom used, and only on occasions where the service to be rendered is concerned (Mt. ix. 38). Right from the start, therefore, the reward, which is nevertheless promised in Jesus' parables to the servants also, is seen in a different light. It loses the character of a payment which is owed, and becomes a mark of distinction with which the trusted servant is rewarded as a sign of even greater trust (*praemium*, not *pretium*). This is shown in the parables of the servants who wait for their lord (Lk. xii. 35 ff.), as in that of the talents (Mt. xxv. 14 ff.; Lk. xix. 11 ff.). "I will set you over much!" "Enter into the joy of your master." Herewith the servant is not paid and dismissed, but is received into the closest and most lasting relationship with the lord.

A second fundamental motif which expresses the idea of a reward is the expectation of the divine judgment. With all his decisions, his thoughts and deeds, man moves towards the everlasting decision of God. The things which for us are the past, and which we consider finished, are before God eternally present—even the most humble deed, a cup of water given even to the smallest (Mt. x. 42), and also every idle word that we speak (Mt. xii. 36). This expectation gives to all that we have done and left undone its importance for life and for death. The verdict of the coming God alone decides concerning our life and actions—how can we then still speak of any value which may be attached to the deed itself? This is the fundamental reality towards which man moves whether he knows it or not, whether he believes it or not.

How pompous and lamentable is the earthly life of the rich man at whose door Lazarus lay, when seen in the light of eternity, and how temporary and light was the tribulation which Lazarus had to bear (Lk. xvi. 19 ff.). How pitiful the goods of the foolish farmer who builds larger barns and who thinks, self-satisfied and prosperous, to have laid up a store of goods for many years, and who does not think of death (Lk. xii. 16 ff.). How questionable the wealth of the rich to whom Jesus' woe applies (Lk. vi. 24 ff.), how small the agony of the disciples who here become the victims of their persecutors, but hereafter are saved from him who is able to destroy both body and soul in hell (Mt. x. 28). Thus the idea of a reward is an inalienable part of the expectation of the last judgment. It places man as an individual before the heavenly judge, an expression of the abiding relevance of his temporary, earthly life to the eternal decision of God.

If we were to mention a third motif which is present in the idea of a reward, we might well say that the weakness of the creature before his creator finds clear and definite expression in it. This third is certainly only a variation of the first two fundamental propositions of which we spoke. Where man believes in the promise of God's reward and expects it, he recognises also that he did not make himself and that he cannot add one cubit to his span of life (Mt. vi. 27), that every moment of his life he is dependent on God the Creator and Father to give him what he needs, and not to deny him his true fulfilment. All this becomes unmistakably clear in Jesus' teaching about the reward of God.

The conception of a reward has without question come to him through the Jewish Old Testament tradition. But it is clear at once that we meet it there in a very different form. It has become, especially in later Judaism, painfully rigid, and had petrified into a doctrine of retribution meant to throw light on the riddle of history and the life of the individual. How is it that the good must suffer and the wicked prosper—this is the question which has been asked unceasingly since the days of the psalmists. Misfortune and suffering must be God's punishment, and can be traced back to man's wrongdoing. The Book of Job already shows that it does not work out this way (cf. also Psalm lxxiii). Hence Jewish doctrine teaches that only the life beyond will even things up. The righteous should therefore bear patiently the suffering inflicted by God here on earth, so as to diminish the measure of punishment which awaits them in the life beyond, and through good works store up a treasure in the other world, so that they may attain there the serene enjoyment of eternal bliss.

Jesus' teaching entirely removes the idea of a reward from the hopeless tangle of Jewish doctrine. In his message its origin and place are to be found neither in reflection upon God's justice in history—just as the perplexing problem of "theodicy" is altogether foreign to his thinking and teaching—nor in reflection upon the merits of those who have observed the law, and their reward in the life beyond. Instead, the idea of a reward has now been completely absorbed into the message of the coming kingdom of God which is dawning now. Indeed, the kingdom of God itself is now the "treasure in heaven" for which it is worth giving up all earthly ties. This is the final certainty which the psalms of the Old Testament reach, as they struggle with the problems of "theodicy": "God is the strength of my heart and my portion forever" (Ps. lxxiii. 26). In Jesus' message, too, this is the essence of all reward. The idea of a reward can have nothing to do with payment for services rendered. The reward which is promised to him who hears God's call and obeys his will is this, that God will be for them. He gives the persecuted a share in the glory of the world to come (Mt. v. 12); he will receive the trusted servants into his joy (Mt. xxv. 14 ff.). This is the reward the disciples may expect. Paul later called this reward "the reward of grace" in distinction to every reward of works to which men may lay claim (Rom. iv. 4), and has thereby brought out the proper meaning contained in Jesus' idea of a reward.

On this point Jewish thought has been quite rightly particularly repellent to modern man since Kant, from the moral as well as from the religious point of view. It makes reward the motive of moral action, and can think of reward only in relation to man's merit. By contrast Jesus detaches it completely from this entanglement. A base eudaemonism makes the decision as to what is good and evil dependent upon the outcome of our actions. In Jesus' teaching on the other hand reward and punishment never determine the content of the moral demand itself. What is good and evil is laid down in God's law, and is not dependent on the consequences of a good or evil deed. Mammon is not evil because it leads men to ruin, but because it enslaves its owner and turns him against God and thus brings him to hell.

Especially in the Sermon on the Mount Jesus has pointed out unmistakably the poisonous effect of the reward idea on all our doings, and particularly on our relations with others. "But love your enemies, and do good, and lend, expecting nothing in return; and your reward will be great, and you will be sons of the Most High" (Lk. vi. 35). At this very point is the parting of the ways between false and true love. The first calculates service and rewards, and is indeed a love which counts on being loved in return. The latter is a love which is not concerned with itself, but spends itself in helping others, indeed spends itself so completely that it no longer entertains thoughts of a reward. For real love is not only free from all thought of admiration and applause—it is even hidden from the person who possesses such love. He will never consider his own actions with pride: "But when you give alms, do not let your left hand know what your right hand is doing; so that your alms may be in secret; and your Father who sees in secret will reward you" (Mt. vi. 3 f.). So little can the divine reward establish the true obedience of love. We remember here once again the description of the judgment of the world in Matthew xxv. 31 ff., where the blessed of the Father can answer the judge of the world only with surprise, almost with a sense of self-accusation, as much as to say: You are mistaken! We did not recognise or mean you at all, but really only the person in need, and our deeds do not deserve to be mentioned now at the hour of judgment. The cursed, on the other hand, excuse themselves with the same answer: had we known what was at stake in our ordinary, everyday meetings, we would surely not have failed. And so these are rewarded just because they did not love for the sake of a reward, and the others are rejected because without the prospect of reward or punishment they could not be moved to do a deed of love.

The idea of the merit of good works and man's claim upon God is most clearly shaken and abolished in the parable of the labourers in the vineyard (Mt. xx. 1-16). Notice the careful description of the hiring of the labourers in the market place at the different hours of the day, at first exactly in accordance with the idea and legal arrangements then in force. This is followed by a contract in which the work to be done, the time and the wage are carefully laid down. All this, however, is only an effective setting for the astonishing conclusion of the parable: in the end the master gives everybody the same wages, and places those who were hired last on the same level as those who were hired first and who had worked hard in the heat the whole day long. This is an attitude which cuts through all the laws of civil order and justice. The scale of wages, at first so carefully described, receives a deadly blow through this conclusion of the story, against which those who were hired first can only register their amazed protest. This makes it abundantly clear, however, that this parable is meant to proclaim God's sovereignty, in contrast to all human conceptions of work and wages, of law and order. This sovereignty is seen in his goodness: "I choose to give to this last, as I give to you. Am I not allowed to do what I choose with what belongs to me? Or do you begrudge my generosity?" (Mt. xx. 14 ff.). This then is what constitutes God's kingship (xx. 1): God's mercy knows no limits. God's heart is here revealed. But also the heart of man, especially of man thinking in terms of "justice", who cannot rejoice in God's grace —who, like the older brother in the parable of the prodigal son, can only grumble against that goodness which is being bestowed upon the brother returned home (Lk. xv. 28 ff.; see page 85).

Thus the idea of reward has received a completely new meaning. Detached from deeds of merit and the claims of man, it has become an expression of divine justice and grace, to which man is directed, now more than ever called to effort and faithfulness, and on which he must lean.

Chapter VI

DISCIPLESHIP

THE Gospels give us a clear impression of the strong movement Jesus stirred up among the people, especially during the period of his Galilean ministry. Again and again we are told that the crowd presses round him and follows him, and that Jesus can scarcely restrain them. They listen to him eagerly, amazed at the "authority" of his teaching; they seek his healing power for the sick; they praise the miracles he performs. Such is the general picture evoked by the Gospels, which serves as a frame for the innumerable individual scenes from the story of Jesus. These people, however, do not constitute his disciples. To follow somebody from place to place does not mean discipleship.

In Judaism, too, there exists a close relationship between teachers and pupils.[1] A celebrated rabbi gathers pupils around him, who are introduced by him to the understanding of the Torah, who accompany him and are obliged to render him services. Just as the terms rabbi, teacher, master derive from the Jewish vocabulary, so do the New Testament terms "disciple" (i.e. pupil) and "following". It is no accident that we are occasionally told also of the disciples of the Pharisees (Mt. xxii. 16). The especial relationship between Jesus and his disciples, however, is in keeping with the special character of this rabbi (see above, page 57; pages 96 ff.). They do not become disciples by their own free choice, but by Jesus' "calling". We are nowhere told that he gives the disciples any special instruction in the law in the manner of the Jewish teachers, or that he makes them transmitters of his own interpretation of the law. Above all, their discipleship is not a transitional stage which ends with they themselves becoming teachers in their own right. Once and for all this sentence applies: "A disciple is not above his teacher, nor a servant above his master; it is enough for the disciple to be like his teacher, and the servant like his master" (Mt. x. 24 f.). The description "as his teacher—as his master" does not mean the promotion of the disciples to the rank of their teacher, but refers to the readiness to bear the same abuse which the teacher and master encountered, and to accept it as a mark of supreme distinction. It is in the sense of this permanent difference of rank, that in Matthew's Gospel the later Church came to accept the saying of the Lord as their rule: "But you are not to be called rabbi, for you have one teacher, and you are all brethren" (Mt. xxiii. 8), and has thereby drawn a distinct line between itself and the synagogue, with its hierarchy of office and privilege. This meaning of discipleship is expressed clearly and exhaustively in the Gospel of John, in its own particular way: "If you continue in my word, you are truly my disciples, and you will know the truth, and the truth will make you free" (Jn. viii. 31 f.).

A historical analogy which comes more readily to mind than that of the pupils of the rabbis is the analogy between the disciples of Jesus and those of John the Baptist, who are repeatedly mentioned in the Gospels (Mk. ii. 18; Mt. xi. 2; Lk. xi. 1; Jn. i. 35). Here, too, the use of the word "disciple" points to the fact that the Baptist movement, just as the movement of Jesus, originated within the framework of Judaism, and must not be considered as the creation of a religious community separate from it. The disciples of John, however, are no longer mere pupils in the school sense of the word, but are the followers of the movement originated by John. Just as Jesus himself came to his ministry through this movement, so some of John's disciples went over to him (Jn. i. 35 ff.; cf. also Acts xix. 1 ff.). But even the discipleship which John inspired does not offer a sufficiently close parallel to the distinctive traits of Jesus' movement to which we referred.

The Gospels state very clearly that the fact of someone becoming a disciple or being a disciple depends on Jesus' sovereign decision, and not on the free choice of individuals who are especially drawn to him. This is shown in all stories concerning the call of a disciple (Mk. i. 16 ff.; ii. 14; Lk. v. 1 ff.; Jn. i. 35 ff.). Jesus calls by the Sea of Galilee the two pairs of brothers, Simon and Andrew, and the sons of Zebedee, James and John, and they leave boat, nets, father and labourers and follow him.[2] The way in which the Gospels tell these stories makes it clear that they want to show by means of examples what a call to discipleship means.[3] This is why they do not tell the story as the historian would, who would be concerned with the disciples as individuals, and show their antecedents and their psychological preparation; nor are they interested in their heroic resolve. The main point is the master who calls. His word is heard: "Follow me!" (Mk. i. 17), and he draws the called person into the closest personal relationship with himself. This is also how the call comes to Levi (Mk. ii. 14). Again everything depends here too on Jesus' sovereign word. But this time it is a tax collector who is called, and thus Jesus' call represents a breaking of the barriers between the clean and the unclean, and becomes an act of grace.[4]

Little as these reports are meant to be read as chronicles—because they show by means of examples, what discipleship means—they nevertheless record something unique and unrepeatable. Jesus calls, appoints, selects from among the people, even from among his followers, certain individuals, and bids them follow him. The circle of his disciples is by no means limited to the twelve. This narrowing down of the term "disciple" does not occur until later in the course of the tradition. Originally it had a much wider application. Nevertheless, it does not include everybody who listens to Jesus' words, is moved and healed by them and follows him along with the crowd. Discipleship means decision, Jesus' decision as regards certain individuals, but then it means no less their own decision to follow him. It consists, in actual fact, in the determination to abandon everything and, in the first instance quite literally, to follow Jesus from place to place, and to accept the fate of the wanderer with all its privations.

What this "following" implies will have to be considered in good time. This a man has to accept, when he makes up his mind to follow Jesus and receives this reply: "Foxes have holes, and birds of the air have nests; but the Son of man has nowhere to lay his head" (Mt. viii. 20). In the same way the following double parable warns them not to be rash in their readiness to follow him: "For which of you, desiring to build a tower,[5] does not sit down and count the cost, whether he has enough to complete it? Otherwise when he has laid a foundation, and is not able to finish, all who see it begin to mock him, saying, 'This man began to build, and was not able to finish.' Or what king, going to encounter another king in war, will not sit down first and take counsel whether he is able with ten thousand to meet him who comes against him with twenty thousand? And if not, while the other is yet a great way off, he sends an embassy and asks terms of peace. So therefore, whoever of you does not renounce all that he has cannot be my disciple" (Lk. xiv. 28-33). "If any one comes to me and does not hate his own father and mother and wife and children and brothers and sisters, yes, and even his own life, he cannot be my disciple" (Lk. xiv. 26 f.). "Do not think that I have come to bring peace on earth; I have not come to bring peace, but a sword" (Mt. x. 34; cf. Lk. xii. 49). All these sayings are of extreme rigour; they demand the utmost.[6] Someone who wants to follow him, but wishes first to bury his father, receives the answer: "Leave the dead to bury their own dead." Another who wants first to take leave of his family is told: "No one who puts his hand to the plough and looks back is fit for the kingdom of God" (Lk. ix. 59-62).

Jesus does not make this demand on all. Some he leaves within their own circle, without taking them from their home, their work, their family.[7] He does not blame them for any lack of determination, or half-heartedness, nor exclude them from the kingdom of God. Nowhere in this respect is an exclusive line drawn between them and the disciples. It is precisely against such tendencies that these words seem to warn: "For he that is not against us is for us" (Mk. ix. 40).[8] On the other hand, the Gospels nowhere show the intention to include then and there tax collectors and sinners, and those who have experienced Jesus' healing powers, among his disciples; although they too, in their own spheres, are witnesses to Jesus, and he visits their homes (Mk. xiv. 3 ff.).

All this goes to prove that the disciples must be distinguished as a more intimate group from Jesus' followers in the wider sense. It is true that what he demands from them does not in fact differ from what he asks of everybody: to repent in light of the coming kingdom of God. To abandon everything and follow the summons (Lk. xiv. 16 ff.), to sell everything for the one precious pearl (Mt. xiii. 45 f.), this had been the call advanced to all. It recurs in the call to the disciples to follow him; in fact, it is often no longer possible for us to know with certainty whether some of Jesus' words were addressed to everybody or to his disciples only, just as the challenge to discipleship addressed to the rich young ruler in Matthew's Gospel is immediately followed by the word concerning the fetters of wealth in general: "Truly, I say to you it will be hard for a rich man to enter the kingdom of heaven. Again, I tell you, it is easier for a camel to go through the eye of a needle than for a rich man to enter the kingdom of God" (Mt. xix. 23 f.). The special demand made upon the disciples must, therefore, not be understood at all as a moral code for an élite, as a proclamation of an ascetic ideal which Jesus exacts only from the few, little as he elsewhere rejects earthly things as such: vocation and property, sex, marriage and family.[9] The kingdom of God is the sole foundation of Jesus' call to follow him. It imposes upon the disciples a special task, a special destiny, but also grants them a special promise. It is this task and this promise which are too much for the rich man who in Mark. x. 17-22 asks Jesus concerning the way to eternal life. Jesus' answer refers him back to God's commandments. Nothing indicates that this is not meant to be a clear and exhaustive answer. It is only when the rich man is not satisfied with it, and declares that he has from childhood kept all the commandments, that Jesus gives him the second reply: "If you would be perfect, go, sell what you possess, and give to the poor, and you will have treasure in heaven; and come, follow me." Surely this one thing that Jesus demands from him is not intended as an additional eleventh commandment. Nor should we suppose that there is any intention to shame the rich man and make him realise how poor his obedience to the first commandment, for example, has actually been. No, what makes the rich man fail is the call of the kingdom of God that now goes out to him in the call to follow Jesus.[10] He thus fails when confronted with the unheard-of offer of "eternal" life, and turns again to the emptiness of his worldly possessions.

The task of the disciples is clearly expressed in the words with which Jesus calls them away from their occupation of fishing: "I will make you become fishers of men" (Mk. i. 17; Lk. v. 10), a word which as in so many words of Jesus surprises us by its drastic nature. For to "catch men" is in ordinary language—in Hebrew as well as in Greek—a vernacular expression, used at times jokingly and sometimes disapprovingly, just as we may say, to "trap" a person, to "get hold of" him, to "hook" him. This rough, startling quality comes out in Jesus' words, though—it hardly needs to be said—it does not have the suggestion of outwitting the other person. The prophets already use as a threat the figure of fishers and hunters which Yahweh will send when the days of his judgment are come (Jer. xvi. 16 ff.; Ez. xlvii. 8 ff.).[11] Has this figure the same meaning when used by Jesus? As Jesus uses it, it certainly means to catch men for the coming kingdom of God. But with Jesus for the first time it rings with the note of salvation and promise. Only for him who refuses salvation will it become judgment. To proclaim the approach of the kingdom of God and to prove its healing powers, which are already active in the present, this is the service which demands from the disciples to be prepared for poverty and suffering (Mt. x. 6 ff.). It is therefore the first task of the disciples to bring peace and salvation to the towns, the villages and houses: "As you enter the house, salute it. And if the house is not worthy, let your peace come upon it; but if it is not worthy, let your peace return to you" (Mt. x. 12 f.).

The disciples are thus not only the recipients of the healing powers of the coming kingdom of God, those powers which are already present and mighty in Jesus' word and deed; rather they are most actively drawn into the service of his message and the proclamation of the kingdom's victory (Mk. iii. 14 f.; Lk. x. 17 ff.). We have certainly to take into account the fact that the description of the disciples, their commission and inspired deeds, have been coloured by the experiences of the early Church. But this by no means excludes the fact that the historical Jesus made his disciples share in his authority. It is easy to understand in this connection that the question of a special reward could arise amongst them, a very human question, it is true, but one which Jesus strictly forbids them, as is shown in his answer to the request made by the sons of Zebedee (Mk. x. 35 ff.).

The promise which Jesus gives his disciples is contained in these words: "And I tell you, everyone who acknowledges me before men, the Son of man also will acknowledge before the angels of God; but he who denies me before men will be denied before the angels of God" (Lk. xii. 8, 9; cf. Mk. viii. 38). Faithfulness and unfaithfulness towards their master here on earth will receive their confirmation and answer on the Day of Judgment. The community they have entered by becoming the disciples of Jesus is thus full of promise—and full of danger.

The importance and the task of discipleship is symbolically represented by the number of twelve disciples whom Jesus appoints: "And he appointed twelve, to be with him, and to be sent out to preach, and have authority to cast out demons" (Mk. iii. 14 f.). The twelve disciples are scarcely the creation of the post-Easter church, as has been suggested,[12] though they had certainly a representative significance in the earliest years. Their institution certainly goes back to the historical Jesus, because the fact that Judas Iscariot belonged to their circle was a serious stumbling-block to the later church. We also learn from the oldest source about the appearances of the Resurrected Lord, quoted by Paul in I Cor. xv. 3 ff., that he appeared to twelve disciples. Their circle must therefore have existed before Easter. The number twelve symbolises the twelve tribes of Israel (Mt. xix. 28; Lk. xxii. 30).[13] Jesus' disciples were thus conceived as the new people of God of the last days. This is, however, not to be understood in the sense of the "holy remnant" of the righteous, and is not true in the sense of any isolation from Israel, but is the visible symbol of Jesus' call, which goes out to the lost sheep of the house of Israel (Mt. x. 6; xv. 24).

We learn very little from the Gospels on the whole about the individual characters of the disciples. Apart from the above-mentioned brothers, we meet in several places lists giving their names (Mk. iii. 16 ff.; Mt. x. 2 ff.; Lk. vi. 14 ff.; Acts i. 13), which differ from one another as regards detail. It is striking that according to Acts i. 14 women too were found among them. Many of those mentioned by the synoptic Gospels remain obscure —until later legends took an interest in them. There are Jewish and Greek names. Matthew, who is probably identical with the Levi called in Mk. ii. 14 (cf. Mt. ix. 9), is a tax collector. Simon the Canaanite is a Zealot, as his surname shows (cf. Mk. iii. 18 and Lk. vi. 15)—both thus deadly enemies as regards their origin. Simon with his surname "Petros"[14] and Judas Iscariot, the betrayer of Jesus, are the most distinctly drawn profiles of all the disciples: Simon Peter, passionate in his dedication, yet wavering at the decisive hour, the spokesman for the other disciples, the first witness of the Resurrected, and after Jesus' death and resurrection the leader of the Church; and the sinister figure of the traitor—both, as we can well understand, of special significance in the recollection of the Church.

A survey of those named in the Gospels—in the Gospel of John there is the additional figure of Nathanael—reveals the fact that none of them belongs to the highest social circles. They are fishermen and tax collectors, perhaps also some craftsmen and peasants of Galilee. Their portrait remains in the first two Gospels plain and unadorned. Only Luke softens it, and removes, whenever possible, features that might offend.[15] Even the disciples, time and again, do not understand Jesus, lose courage when faith is required; they send away the children who are brought to Jesus (Mk. x. 13 ff.), or the blind beggar shouting by the roadside and demanding to see him (Mk. x. 48). Even the three who belong to the closest circle are unable to keep watch with their Lord during prayer in the garden of Gethsemane, but fall asleep. Peter disavows, Judas betrays the Lord. They flee when Jesus is taken prisoner. And yet they are "chosen" by Jesus, and Peter is able to say of them: "Lo, we have left everything and followed you" (Mk. x. 28).

The later Church has seen itself in the disciples, who follow Jesus on his earthly path. It thought of itself as the people of God of the last days, as the new Israel, but also identified its own post-Easter existence on earth with the situation of the disciples, called upon by their Lord to sacrifice, and to keep the faith. The name disciple thus comes to signify the believer as such (Acts vi. 1; ix. 11, 19, etc.). The temptation and distress of the disciples in the past, therefore become the model for the distress and the promise of the present believers. It was thus possible for Matthew to re-interpret the story about the calming of the storm, as a comparison with the reports of the other two Gospels shows, as the example and symbol of the following of Christ and of discipleship as such (Mt. viii. 23-26).[16] He deliberately precedes the story by the two short scenes concerning discipleship (Mt. viii. 19-22), and connects it with them by precisely this key word: "discipleship". He passes over details in the story which the text of Mark provides. On the other hand the cry of the disciples is in Matthew a real prayer—no longer, as with the other Gospels, just a call for help arising from fear and a feeling of helplessness—for now the prayer runs: "Save, Lord, we are perishing." Also in Matthew's story the disciples incur their master's reproach: "Why are you afraid, O men of little faith?" even before Jesus rebukes the wind and waves. This reproach forms now the centre, and the miracle itself follows. Thus temptation, faith and little faith, but also the authority of the Lord, who can create the great calm amid the storm of fear and temptation, have become the core of the story in order to shame and comfort the believers.

The farewell speeches of the Gospel of John—to mention just one example out of many—show too how the later Church saw itself portrayed in the picture of the disciples of the past. Here the situation, the distress and hope of the disciples *before* Jesus' death and resurrection, are seen as being one with the situation of the believers after Easter and before his return (Jn. xiii. 31 ff.; Jn. xiv-xvii).

Chapter VII

JESUS' JOURNEY TO JERUSALEM.
SUFFERING AND DEATH

EVEN the period of Jesus' Galilean ministry is not only one of success, but also of failure. We have no reason to speak in a romantic manner, like some of the older biographies of Jesus, of a Galilean spring so soon to be followed by the catastrophe in Jerusalem. Others think that a crisis occurred already during the first great period in Jesus' life: the suspicion of his opponents grew stronger, the people disappointed him by their unwillingness to repent, and the ruler, Herod Antipas, the tetrarch by the grace of Rome, took notice of him and decided to remove this "resurrected" John the Baptist. The texts, however, do not lend any reliable support to this representation of development in the life of Jesus. Nor do they justify the assumption that Jesus fled from Herod and temporarily left the country to go to the region of the Phoenician Tyre in the North, to the region of Caesarea Philippi, and to the country of the Decapolis on the other side of the Lake of Galilee, which was under direct Roman military rule, and that he finally set out on his journey to Judaea and Jerusalem in order to escape the pursuit of Herod.[1] The Gospels seem more likely to be historically correct when they report that success and failure, popularity and enmity, had been part and parcel of Jesus' life from the start, even when their frequently schematic description reveals the tendency to present Jesus' story from the very beginning as a story of suffering, and to make it lead up to the Passion at the end. (Already Mk. iii. 6 mentions a decision of his opponents to put him to death.)

The struggle of Jesus and the movement he set in motion were not directed against the political rulers, neither against Rome nor against Herod. It is characteristic that the Gospels, which elsewhere name a not inconsiderable number of villages and towns which he visited in Galilee—Nazareth, Bethsaida, Chorazin, Capernaum, in John also Cana—do not mention anywhere the

capital and residence of Herod, Tiberias, called after the Roman
Emperor Tiberius, nor the Hellenistic town of Sepphoris, neighbouring Nazareth. It is only through rumours that the tetrarch
hears about Jesus and wants to remove him, apparently because he
believes this supposed John *"redivivus"* to be the leader of a
rebellious movement. A short scene describes how a few Pharisees
come to Jesus and warn him: "Get away from here, for Herod wants
to kill you", and Jesus replies, "Go and tell that fox, 'Behold,
I cast out demons and perform cures today and tomorrow, and the
third day I finish my course. Nevertheless I must go on my way
today and tomorrow and the day following; for it cannot be that a
prophet should perish away from Jerusalem' " (Lk. xiii. 31-33).[2]
The real point of these words, which certainly contain as their
kernel an authentic saying, is obviously to reveal Jesus' true mission, which rejects a political misinterpretation of it; but also to
show his readiness to seek the decision on his mission in the only
place where it should be given, in Jerusalem.

This decision to go to Jerusalem is undoubtedly the turning-
point in Jesus' life. It must not, however, be too readily understood
along the lines of the later tradition, as though Jesus had sought
only his death in Jerusalem. It appears that way according to the
repeated prophecies of suffering and resurrection (Mk. viii. 31; ix.
31; x. 33 f.). They were clearly first formulated in retrospect in
view of the passion, in order to demonstrate Jesus' miraculous
knowledge of future events and the mysterious decrees of God
manifested in them. The third prophecy in particular has been
fashioned as a complete summary of the passion and Easter
story.[3]

The reason why Jesus sets out with his disciples on his journey
to Jerusalem cannot be doubted. It was to deliver the message of
the coming kingdom of God in Jerusalem also, Jerusalem which
Jesus himself calls the city of God, "the city of the Great King"
(Mt. v. 35). As for every Jew, Jerusalem is also for Jesus not only
the capital, but also the place which is in a special way connected
with Israel's destiny. That the road to Jerusalem had to lead to
new and serious conflicts with the spiritual and temporal rulers,
and that Jesus had to reckon with the possibility of his own violent
end, we have no reason to doubt, however justified our grounds for

disputing the historical validity of the individual prophecies concerning his suffering and resurrection. The sources do not tell us
clearly at what moment his readiness to accept death—a readiness
which Jesus, as we know, demanded from his disciples too—
turned into the certainty of his imminent end. We may, however,
assume that first and foremost his journey to Jerusalem was undertaken in order to confront the people there, in the holy city, with
the message of the kingdom of God, and to summon them at the
eleventh hour to make their decision. Luke says explicitly in several
places (xix. 11; xxiv. 21; Acts i. 6), that the disciples pinned to
this journey their hope that the kingdom of God was about to
appear. We do not know whether Jesus had previously been at
work in or near Jerusalem. His lament over Jerusalem, "How often
would I have gathered your children together, as a hen gathers her
brood . . ." (Mt. xxiii. 37 ff.), is most likely a quotation from some
part of the wisdom literature, but hardly proof of Jesus' earlier
activities in this town. Nor is the evangelist John here to be
considered a reliable historical witness. He makes the scene of
Jesus' activity alternate between Jerusalem and Galilee, and makes
him appear at three celebrations of the Passover festival. The places
of Jesus' activity have, with him, an obviously symbolical meaning.[4]
It is beyond doubt that only on the journey with his followers to
Jerusalem and the temple did Jesus seek the final decision.

The report of the Gospels beginning with Jesus' entry into
Jerusalem, above all the actual story of his suffering and death, is
distinguished from all the earlier reports by the fullness of detail
and the connection of events, which is here of such great importance. This at first creates the impression that the writers of the
Gospels had more copious and more reliable sources at their disposal for this last chapter of the life of Jesus, and that they were
therefore able to tell their story, to a greater extent than before,
in a more historical, biographical manner. But this impression is
only partly correct. Here, as elsewhere, the basis of the reports is
the individual pericope, and the presentation of events is to an
even greater degree than before inspired by the religious interest of
the Church.

The historical is therefore, here as elsewhere, interwoven with the
legendary, and the story is told in such a way that in it and behind

it the hand of God becomes visible, and Jesus appears as the one who carries out the decrees of God and suffers in their fulfilment. We therefore constantly meet the same theme: through Jesus' deeds and suffering "Scripture" had to be fulfilled. A great number of sayings from the prophets and the psalms runs through the story, not only as explicit quotations but also suggested in many individual features and allusions. Jesus' entry into Jerusalem is the fulfilment of Zechariah ix. 9: "Rejoice greatly, O daughter of Zion! Shout, aloud, O daughter of Jerusalem! Lo, your King comes to you; triumphant and victorious is he, humble and riding on an ass, on a colt the foal of an ass." The cleansing of the temple fulfils the word of Isaiah lvi. 7: "my house shall be called a house of prayer for all peoples." When Jesus describes the traitor, he says that the Son of man goes as it is written of him (Mk. xiv. 21), and clothes the announcement with the words of Psalm xli: "One of you will betray me, one who is eating with me" (Mk. xiv. 18). At the Last Supper the ancient word of the "blood of the covenant" (Ex. xxiv. 8) is echoed, and before Jesus is taken prisoner and the disciples flee, one hears an echo of Zechariah xiii. 7: "I strike the shepherd that the sheep may be scattered." In the scene at Gethsemane the words: "My soul is very sorrowful, even to death" are a direct allusion to Psalm xliii. 5. When we hear the death sentence of the High Court we should remember Psalm xxxi. 13: "as they scheme together against me, as they plot to take my life." On the occasion of Judas' betrayal, Matthew quotes expressly Zechariah xi. 12: "If it seems right to you, give me my wages . . . and they weighed out as my wages thirty shekels of silver."[5] When Jesus is scourged, the listener is reminded of Isaiah l. 6: "I gave my back to the smiters, and my cheeks to those who pulled out the beard; I hid not my face from shame and spitting." The story of Jesus' crucifixion and death above all is full of allusions, only a few of which, strangely enough, refer to the great prophetic chapter of the suffering servant of God (Is. liii). There are many more allusions to the "suffering" psalms. It is sufficient here to name only the most important ones. "They gave me poison for food; and for my thirst they gave me vinegar to drink" (Ps. lxix. 21). "They divide my garments among them and for my raiment they cast lots" (Ps. xxii. 18). "All who see me mock at me, they make mouths at me, they wag their heads"

(Ps. xxii. 7; cf. Lams. ii. 15). Already in Lk. xxii. 37 the Evangelist recalls the words: "And he was reckoned with the transgressors" (Is. liii. 12), which are quoted in some manuscripts of Mark xv. 28, at the crucifixion of Jesus between the thieves. The words, too, of the Crucified, which alone Mark and Matthew give, are the cry of prayer from Psalm xxii: "My God, my God, why hast thou forsaken me?" just as the word given by Luke as the last again comes from a Psalm: "Into thy hands I commit my spirit" (Ps. xxxi. 5).

This by no means complete enumeration of passages from the Old Testament quoted or alluded to in the story of the passion shows how this story is told and conceived, and how it is to be read and understood: not only as a chain of unfolding historical events, but as a combination of divine decrees which become meaningful in the light of God's prophecies, in spite of and in the very midst of worldly contradiction and injustice. It is dominated by the great and mysterious imperative of God, which turns the human actors in these events into divine instruments, without thereby releasing them from responsibility and guilt. At the same time it is to demonstrate that the terrible fate which Jesus meets does not happen to him accidentally, and does not disprove his claim to be the promised Messiah, but, on the contrary, confirms it; it therefore does not contradict but corroborates his status. "Was it not necessary that the Christ should suffer these things and enter into his glory?" So asks the Risen One of the disciples on the way to Emmaus, and expounds to them "in all the Scriptures the things concerning himself" (Lk. xxiv. 26 f.).

It is true that this insight into the attitude of the tradition towards history compels us to admit that we have little certain knowledge in the proper historical sense about the last chapter of the life of Jesus. For there can be no doubt that, to an undetermined extent, the proof derived from prophecy is not only an addition made by subsequent thought and interpretation, but has also played a creative role with regard to the story.[6] The considerable individual differences between the different accounts also go to prove how cautious and critical our historical judgment regarding the detail of the story has to be. All we can thus recognise are the outlines of the course of the historical events during Jesus' last stay in

Jerusalem until his end. Nevertheless, nothing would be more wrong than to deny that there is any historical truth in the story of the Gospels about Jesus' suffering and death, simply because the church's faith was specially concerned with this piece of tradition, and has filled it in with the aid of passages from the Old Testament.

Jesus' entry into Jerusalem in the company of his followers forms part of this last chapter of his life (Mk. xi. 1 ff.). It is the time of the Passover, when huge masses of pilgrims gather in the holy city to celebrate the liberation of the people from Egypt, and eschatological hopes run high, as we also know from later testimonies. The expectation of the coming kingdom of God also fills the heart of Jesus and his companions, who celebrate him, the prophet from Galilee, and acclaim him as the Messiah. It is controversial in how far Jesus himself intended this entry as a demonstration that he was the Messiah. Later tradition has, at any rate, understood the entry in this sense, and endowed it with miraculous features which bestow upon it this meaning. However, even if we here take into consideration the subsequent belief of the disciples, upon whom the deeper meaning of the events did not dawn until Jesus had been "glorified" (Jn. xii. 16), even then this entry of Jesus and his followers would be inconceivable without his powerful claim that the kingdom of God is dawning in his word, and that the final decision will turn upon himself. The struggle against the spiritual leaders of the nation was thereby opened by himself.

This is also borne out by the cleansing of the temple (Mk. xi. 15 ff.), which follows upon the entry into Jerusalem. It, too, is soon "overexposed" to the beam of Messianic expectation, as can be seen from the rendering in John (ii. 13 ff.).[7] And yet, according to the synoptic Gospels, it is more than an act of reform intended simply to restore the temple service to its original purity. The scene that Jesus saw in the outer temple court was not particularly offensive to a Jew. It is in keeping with the activities which up to the present day attend all pilgrimages. Merchants and money-changers do their business, offer for sale beasts for sacrifice, and exchange the foreign money of the pilgrims into ancient Hebrew or Phoenician currency, which was prescribed for commerce and the temple dues. Care was taken, as we know, that the sacred parts of the temple were not touched by this. But Jesus, brandishing his scourge, puts an end to these activities, and cleanses the sanctuary for the approaching kingdom of God. Here, too, we must not disregard this real context of what happened, nor the claim upon which this action is founded. With good reason, then, all the Gospels connect the story of the cleansing of the temple with Jesus' dispute with the leaders of the nation about the "authority" which entitles him to this action (Mk. xi. 27 ff.).[8]

The Gospels do not follow these two scenes immediately with the story of Jesus' arrest, his trials and suffering, but with a long chain of arguments, parables, and finally by the great apocalyptic speech in which Jesus announces the destruction of Jerusalem and the temple. The arrangement of the individual passages as regards time and place is in itself of no importance. They could have been placed in a different context, as can be seen from the deviations in Luke's arrangement.[9] In any case, the Gospels want to give us an impression of how the conflict between Jesus and his opponents now reaches its height, and how judgment is pronounced on the people with utmost severity, whilst the disciples are, at the same time, prepared for the approaching end. The story of the Passion proper does not commence till several chapters later in the first three Gospels—its supreme importance is thrown into relief by the fact that it follows upon the speech about the destruction of Jerusalem and the judgment of the world. These last observations, important as they are for the understanding of the formation of the tradition in the Gospels, are of no immediate use as regards the reconstruction of the story itself.

If we first of all continue to ask what was the course of events, we may assume with certainty that the Jewish authorities felt themselves compelled to intervene, by the provocation of the scenes at the entry into Jerusalem and at the temple. Jesus' strong influence on the people may have been the reason why the Jewish authorities did not strike at once (cf. Mt. xxi. 14 ff.; Lk. xix. 47 f.; Jn. xii. 19). Yet quick action, it seemed to them, was required, especially before the festival, "lest there be a tumult of the people" (Mk. xiv. 2). We find in this important reference in the Gospels of Mark and Matthew a recollection of the fact that Jesus' arrest and death occurred before the festival of Passover proper. This reference is in clear contrast to the chronology of events given elsewhere in the synoptic Gospels, according to which Jesus nevertheless celebrates the Passover meal with his disciples on the evening of Thursday, is arrested and sentenced by the High Court and Pilate during the night of the festival, and dies the death on the cross on the first great holiday, on the 15th of Nisan, according to the Jewish calendar. This chronology deviates from the one given by John, according to which Jesus dies on the 14th of Nisan (Jn. xviii. 28). The two chronologies cannot be made to agree.[10] It may rightly be pointed out, it is true, that the chronology of John is connected with a symbolic meaning—Jesus dies as the "lamb of God" (Jn. i. 29, 36) on the day on which the Passover lambs were slaughtered—nevertheless the correctness of this chronology is not thereby put wholly in question. We may be satisfied simply to accept any date shortly before the beginning of the festival. But there are also other passages in the synoptic Gospels which suggest that the last events of Jesus' suffering and death did not take place within the festival period. We shall presently deal with this point in connection with the questions of Jesus' Last Supper, his arrest and trial before the High Court. We may assume that the decision of the authorities to remove him before the festival (Mk. xiv. 2) was thus really carried out. The offer of Judas Iscariot, one of his own disciples, to deliver Jesus safely and unobtrusively into their hands, gave them the possibility to arrest him "with cunning".

Jesus, filled with the certainty of his approaching end, celebrates the last meal with his disciples. We can no longer be sure as to the exact procedure, for the texts are, in their present form, a reflection of the celebration of the Supper by the later Church, and a reflection of its liturgy. This, however, the texts do reveal for certain: Jesus celebrates the Supper with his disciples in the expectation of the approaching kingdom of God and of his parting from them. "Truly, I say to you, I shall not drink again of the fruit of the vine, until that day when I drink it anew in the kingdom of God" (Mk. xiv. 25).[11] These words are not found in the later liturgical tradition of the Lord's Supper, as can be seen from Paul, I Cor. xi. 23-25, and this fact itself may be taken to prove their authenticity. They place Jesus' death in the light of the coming kingdom of God, they distinguish Jesus and his destiny from that of the disciples—"I shall not drink again . . ."—but the saying welds the disciples who are left behind together, and gives them the promise of a new oneness with him in the kingdom of his Father. The antecedent words of the institution of the Sacrament, given in the tradition, express the meaning of this fellowship and its basis, even though the present form of the text reflects the liturgical tradition of the later Church: Jesus, in the form of bread and wine, has his disciples participate in his body, surrendered unto death, and in his blood (Mk. xiv. 24; I Cor. x. 16) shed for "many" (i.e. for all).[12] His death thereby comes to mean the renewal of the divine covenant entered upon at Sinai (Ex. xxiv. 8), or, as stated in the parallel text I Corinthians xi. 25, the foundation of the "new" covenant foretold by Jeremiah (xxxi. 31 ff.), the new dispensation. In these statements, found in increasing number in the Gospels, the creative faith of the worshipping community is certainly at work, which interprets Jesus' death retrospectively as the redemption of mankind. But the fact that this farewell supper had the meaning expressed by the eschatological words at its end is thereby not called in question.

It is very doubtful, however, that this supper was itself held as a Passover meal, although it certainly took place near the time of the Passover festival. What we do know for certain is only that the first three Evangelists wished to see and describe it as such. Yet already our reflections in connection with Mark xiv. 2 (see above, page 159) have caused some doubts in this respect. They are increased by the story of the institution itself. It lacks the elements which up to the present day belong to any Jewish Passover ritual: the interpretation of the Passover lamb, given by the master of the house during the meal with his family, in remembrance of the past liberation of the people from Egypt, and the interpretation of the unleavened bread, which is to recall the haste of the departure from Egypt, or the time of misery in the desert. Nothing of all this is mentioned. Instead—and this is completely without analogy in the Passover celebrations—Jesus gives himself, in the form of bread and wine, as one given over to death. It is not therefore surprising that Paul asserts no relationship whatsoever between the Lord's Supper and Passover. He too knows, it is true, the original Christian conception, that Christ is the Passover lamb which was sacrificed for us (I Cor. v. 7), but when this is mentioned, no reference is made to the Sacrament, just as, on the other hand, when he speaks of the Lord's Supper in connection with Old Testament texts, he does not recall the Passover story proper, although he mentions Israel's journey through the desert, her miraculous food from the divine manna, and her miraculous drink from the water-giving rock (I Cor. x. 1 ff.).[13] We may thus assume that the conception of Jesus' Last Supper as the Passover meal goes back to the theology of the first three Evangelists and that of the Christian groups behind them. This theology has not even penetrated into their own versions of the institution of the Sacrament, but only determines the surrounding frame. The governing considerations behind this interpretation cannot be doubted. They are those which we recognised as the background to John's chronology (see above page 160), and found expressed in I Corinthians v. 7, only that the synoptic Gospels apply them to Jesus' Last Supper, whereas Paul and John ascribe them directly to Jesus' death.

Jesus' Last Supper with his disciples is followed by the night of his solitary struggle in prayer in the garden of Gethsemane (Mk. xiv. 32-42). This story, too, should not be read simply as a historical record. The very fact that no human being witnessed Jesus' struggle is evidence of this. Yet this story, too, is a historical document in a higher sense: it presents Jesus, alone, at the fiercest point of his temptation, separated from his disciples, not as a "divine being", but in his complete humanity. The disciples cannot resist sleep, and fail in the hour of trial. Jesus, however, is the one who, in his agony, obediently accepts the will of his Father: "Abba, Father, all things are possible to thee; remove this cup from me: yet not what I will, but what thou wilt" (Mk. xiv. 36).[14]

Gethsemane is the place where Jesus is arrested by the band of his opponents under the leadership of Judas—a scene which, according to the description of the Gospels, finds Jesus prepared and the disciples unprepared. As elsewhere in the story of the Passion, the picture presented by the account is not one of Jesus and his followers on the one side, his enemies on the other. Rather it shows Jesus alone, and on the other side his enemies, led by one of the Twelve, and all around the disturbed band of his disciples, only one of whom tries, suddenly and helplessly, to intervene.[15] The scene is ghastly (Mk. xiv. 43-52): "Now the betrayer had given them a sign, saying, 'The one I shall kiss, is the man; seize him, and lead him away safely.' And when he came, he went up to him at once, and said 'Master.' And he kissed him. And they laid hands on him and seized him." Jesus permits it. His only words, according to the oldest record,[16] are these: "Have you come out as against a robber, with swords and clubs to capture me? Day after day I was with you in the temple teaching, and you did not seize me. But let the scriptures be fulfilled." The disciples flee; one, anonymous, naked, leaves his clothes behind. This is one of the few traces of an eye-witness.

The scene which follows, Jesus' trial before the Jewish High Court (Mk. xiv. 53 ff.), has been elaborated by the Gospels in the spirit of faith in Christ. The quite dramatically constructed report begins with the summoning of false witnesses who contradict one another: Jesus' own confession before the high priest that he is the Messiah, a confession made openly for the first time, forms its centre; it ends with Jesus being sentenced to death for blasphemy. The account thus becomes a testimony to Christ, in strong contrast to the rage and cruelty of his enemies.

Looked at from the historical point of view, the story arouses critical doubts. Here, too, the question arises as to the witnesses who would be assumed to have informed the disciples of the event later on. But above all, the details are in contradiction to our reasonably reliable knowledge of the Jewish procedure at Court, though this knowledge is derived from later accounts of scribes.[17] This procedure demands that capital crimes should be tried during daytime only, certainly not during festival times, and not be dealt with at a sitting of one day only. The immediate appearances of witnesses for the prosecution, moreover, who quote in a distorted form a saying of Jesus', certainly genuine, about the end of the old temple and the building of a new one,[18] would have been a serious breach of the law. Finally, there is not one single instance of a person's ever being accused of blasphemy and sentenced to death by the Jewish authorities because he claimed to be the Messiah. There is no mention of an abuse of the name of God. Moreover, in the case of blasphemy, the Jewish authorities would certainly have had the right to have Jesus executed, for instance to have him stoned (cf. Acts vi. 8 ff.; vii. 54 ff.). But Jesus is not stoned, but handed over by the High Court to the Procurator Pontius Pilate, and is crucified by him, a punishment which was the exclusive right of the Roman law court, and which was instituted for political crimes. Precisely here is the fixed point from which historical investigation must proceed. This fixed point is the criterion in the light of which the objections frequently taken to any doubting of the trial before the High Court do not carry much weight: such objections as that we would consider this an exceptional case, and that it is, moreover, most uncertain as to how far the later accounts of the Mishnah are valid for Jesus' time. If Pilate pronounced the death sentence, it does not at all exclude the possibility that the Jewish authorities delivered him as a political suspect into the hands of the Romans, in order to get rid of the hated prophet from Galilee. This is how, above all, Luke and John present the matter, certainly correctly as regards this point (Lk. xxiii. 2; Jn. xix. 12-15). Pilate found himself considerably embarrassed by this, as the records show. We have no reason to doubt this, even though the tendency of the Gospels is clearly to present the Procurator as a witness of Jesus' innocence, and thereby to exculpate Pilate, the representative of Rome, and at the same time to make him into the involuntary instrument of public opinion aroused by the Jewish leaders.[19] It is most probably authentic and not the invention of later poetic imagination that Pilate tried to extricate himself by offering to pardon Jesus, but that the incited people insisted upon the liberation of the Zealot Barabbas instead of Jesus—Barabbas who was rightly sentenced for the crime of which Jesus was wrongly accused.

Jesus is thus delivered up to the derision of the Roman soldiery, whipped and led to his crucifixion, forsaken even by his disciples. Peter, the only one who follows him up to the court of the high priest's palace, denies him there in front of maids and servants. One maid, it is said, recognises him as a follower of Jesus. With the other servants, too, the Galilean is given away by his language. But Peter, cursing and swearing, utters the word of denial: "I know not the man."[20] This scene was probably handed down to the later Church by Peter himself, and was for all time for the Church the terrible example of faithlessness shown to his master by the very disciple who, above all, had promised his Lord faithfulness unto death (Mt. xiv. 31), and who now failed, not before an authoritative court, but before the most unauthoritative forum of some servants and maids.

Jesus is brought from Pilate's official residence, the palace of Herod, in the north-west of the city,[21] to the hill of Golgotha, outside the city, the place of execution appointed by the High Court. On the way there, the report tells us, the procession, with Jesus breaking down under the weight of the cross, meets a man who is coming from the fields into the town. He is Simon of Cyrene, the father of Alexander and Rufus (Mk. xv. 21), who is forced by the soldiers to carry the cross for Jesus to Golgotha. What do these names, which only Mark mentions, mean? They must have been known to the church in which this ancient tradition circulated, a church of which Alexander and Rufus were perhaps themselves members. Thus, this part too bears the clear trace of an eye-witness account.

It was the custom to offer the condemned before his crucifixion a drink of strongly spiced wine, in order to dope his consciousness and thereby to mitigate his torture. But Jesus refuses the drink. The disposal of the garments by lot among the soldiers is also a Roman custom. For the Evangelists, both features were important in view of the prophecies of the Psalms of Suffering (Ps. lxix. 22; xxii. 19), which were to the early Church, as we have seen, the oldest book of the Passion. Above all, it was a Roman custom at executions to carry in front of the delinquent or to hang around his neck a sign with the inscription of his crime. In this case it is fixed on to the cross, according to John in Hebrew, Greek and Latin: "Jesus of Nazareth, the King of the Jews" (Jn. xix. 19 f.). The irony of this inscription is most strongly brought out by the writer of the fourth Gospel. For it pronounced judgment upon Israel, which has now rejected its Messiah. Hence the protest of the Jews, who demand from Pilate its correction: "Write not: King of the Jews; but that he said, I am King of the Jews" (Jn. xix. 21). But Pilate does not comply with their wish to change the inscription, and to put in its place the mere formulation of a presumptuous and illusionary claim. In defiance of the indignation of the Jews, and beyond the intention of the Roman governor himself, Pilate's inscription thus becomes the prophetic proclamation of Jesus' status for the whole world.

All the Gospels describe the course of the crucifixion itself with a minimum of words: "and they crucified him." Everyone was familiar with the ghastly process of this kind of execution, which was especially customary for slaves: the condemned was nailed with his arms spread out, to the crossbar; this was then fixed to the vertical post which was the height of a man; the feet were then fastened with nails or ropes to a specially attached piece of wood. But it is surely clear that there were more than external reasons for the sparseness of the description in the Gospels and the avoidance of detail.

The crucified, the Gospels report, is scoffed and abused: by the people who are passing by and looking on, by the priests and the scribes, and even by the two men on the right and on the left who are crucified with him. Again we are to be reminded of Psalm xxii. 7 ff., and made to consider that he who has been accused of abusing God is now abused himself, and God through him. Only Luke elaborates the scene further, and makes a difference between the unrepentant thief on the left, and the penitent thief on his right, who implores Jesus' help. The chorus of the scoffers demands from Jesus a miracle like the one Satan asked him to perform in the story of the temptation (Mt. iv. 1 ff.). Descend from the cross! Even in their scorn they must proclaim the truth from which they have erred. "He saved others, he cannot save himself." Indeed, the meaning here is clear: this he cannot do, here is the limit of his power. But this limit is obedience, the renunciation of his right and his power. Precisely this is the mystery of the Messiahship. The way the unbelievers are here compelled to proclaim, most paradoxically, the power and worth of Jesus, is expressed by J. S. Bach in his St. Matthew Passion, when he makes the wild chorus of the scoffers end with all eight parts singing in unison: "For he has said: I am the Son of God."

The description of his death varies not inconsiderably in the different Gospels. According to the first two Evangelists he dies with the cry from Psalm xxii. "Eli, eli, lama sabachthani?"—"My God, my God, why hast thou forsaken me?" It is a cry of prayer

—certainly not the cry of one who has despaired of God; and yet we must not take away from the harshness and depth of suffering expressed in the words, a suffering inflicted upon the dying not only by men but also by God. These words from the psalm cannot simply be replaced, for instance, by the following: "My flesh and my heart may fail: but God is the strength of my heart and my portion for ever" (Ps. lxxiii. 26), nor by the dying words as recorded by Luke (Ps. xxxi. 5). The tormentors of Jesus also hear his cry, but they misunderstand it as though he had called for Elias, the helper in the hour of need. They try—out of scorn or curiosity? —to refresh him with a drink of vinegar, in order to gain time for a miracle at the last moment. But Jesus dies with a loud cry.

The picture of his death is differently presented by Luke. As soon as the cross is set up, Jesus utters the prayer for his enemies: "Father, forgive them; for they know not what they do" (Lk. xxiii. 34).[22] Then, when the penitent malefactor recognises Jesus' innocence and majesty, he gives him the assurance: "Truly, I say to you, today you will be with me in paradise" (Lk. xxiii. 43). And finally come the words from Psalm xxxi: "Father, into thy hands I commit my spirit" (Lk. xxiii. 46). According to John, as he dies he utters three other statements, the words to his mother and the favourite disciple: "Woman, behold your son!" and "Behold your mother!" (Jn. xix. 26 f.); "I thirst" (Jn. xix. 28) and finally "It is finished" (Jn. xix. 30).

These are three great, and in themselves profoundly different, pictures of the crucified. They must not be taken as fragments of a historical record, and then pieced together to make a whole, however clearly all of them express, in their differences and despite their differences, the mystery of the person, mission and death of Jesus.

The miracles which accompany Jesus' death are also meant to proclaim this mystery: the darkness which spreads over the whole country in the hour of his death; the sudden tearing of the Temple curtain which veils the Holy of Holies, where the high priest offers the expiatory victim on the great Day of Atonement—an expression and a symbol of the fact that an old, senile order of things has now come to an end, and that a new, divine order has been founded (Heb. viii. 6-13). The confession uttered by the

Roman centurion when he sees Jesus die is also a miracle and a sign: "Truly this man was Son of God" (Mk. xv. 39). In the hour when Israel lets her Messiah die at the hands of the Romans, the first confession of faith in him comes from the lips of a pagan.[23]

As a rule the death of a crucified person occurs only after a long time of torture and exhaustion. Jesus dies after six hours, in the early afternoon. Executed persons are usually buried somewhere apart, without lament and funeral procession. By the courageous intercession of a distinguished, pious councillor, Joseph of Arimathaea, this final disgrace is avoided (Mk. xv. 42 ff.). He asks Pilate for Jesus' corpse, and buries him in his own rock tomb. Two women are witnesses. Their names and the mention of the burial place lead us on to the story of the resurrection. The report of Jesus' funeral is concise, unemotional and without any bias. But this is precisely how it could tell believers what J. A. Bengel has summed up in these words: *sepultura mortem ratam facit*—the tomb makes the death official.[24]

Chapter VIII

THE MESSIANIC QUESTION

S o far we have purposely not mentioned, or at least not definitely answered a question which is frequently considered the most important in the tradition, whether and in what sense Jesus regarded himself as the Messiah. It is generally called the question of Jesus' Messianic consciousness. In using this all too psychological formula, we should, however, remember that what mattered most for the Gospels and the tradition was the fact that Jesus *was* the Messiah; but as to the modern question of Jesus' "consciousness" they remain extremely indifferent and evasive. The topic itself and the records set very definite limits for us here, which we must always remember. Right from the start we also have to allow for the fact, which is also confirmed by the sources, that especially at this point tradition has been substantially shaped by faith. But can we seriously doubt that Jesus thought of himself as the Messiah and claimed to be such? This question, we shall proceed to show more clearly, cannot be answered as easily and certainly as is commonly believed.

Some may find it strange that we only now turn seriously to this question. Many are of the opinion that its place is at the beginning, and that without a definite answer to it, absolutely nothing in Jesus' message or history could be properly understood. Our answer is this: No, it should not be at the beginning, and the place which we have assigned to it reveals a material decision to which Jesus' teaching and works compel us, quite apart from any mere consideration as to a convenient arrangement of the chapters. For, as we have seen in our argument right from the beginning, it is the special character of his message and work, that Jesus is to be found *in* his word and *in* his actions, and that he does not make his own rank a special theme of his message prior to everything else.

In the light of the coming reign, and in the presence of God with his claims, each of his words and deeds has a decisive significance, both for the present and for the future. It is always concerned with the now and the today in face of eternity. His word is action and event, and his ministry a sign of the reign of God which is already dawning. In this sense everything he says and does is an expression of his mission. "Blessed are the eyes which see what you see and the ears which hear what you hear!" "Blessed is he who takes no offence at me!" God's spirit is at work in his deeds. Hence his reply to those who accuse him of being in league with the devil: "Truly, I say to you, all sins will be forgiven the sons of men, and whatever blasphemies they utter; but whoever blasphemes against the Holy Spirit never has forgiveness, but is guilty of an eternal sin" (Mk. iii. 28 f.).[1] He is the only sign which is given to this "adulterous and sinful generation", as once Jonah was a sign to the Ninevites, before the catastrophe came (Lk. xi. 20 ff.), but forgiveness and salvation take place through his word for the sick and the sinners, who came to him or were brought to him in faith. In Jesus himself the dawn of the kingdom of God becomes a reality.

In Jesus' attitude to the law, and in his efforts to put God's will into action, we have met again and again the claim and the secret of his mission. The "Truly, I say to you" in his preaching of the kingdom of God corresponds exactly with the "But I say to you" of his ethics. The calling of the disciples, the choosing of the Twelve, and the movement which he orginates, can only be thought of in connection with this claim. His entry into the Holy City, the conflict which he there initiates, the cleansing of the Temple all express it. No less do the appeals of the sick, the cries of the possessed which meet him wherever he goes, the hopes his followers place upon him, as do the fears and the opposition of the Jewish authorities who hand him over to Pilate, and finally his crucifixion as "King of the Jews"—all this is a reply to the claim which they meet in the person of Jesus.

In all this the question of this claim is only posed and not as yet answered. For what astonishes us most is that Jesus does not directly make this claim, but lets it be absorbed in his words and works without justifying either in virtue of some office well known to his hearers, and without confirming the authority which the people are willing to acknowledge in him. As little as he fulfils the demands of his opponents for proof of his claim, so little does he fulfil the expectations of his followers.

In the Gospels this very strange state of affairs has found expression in the paradoxical doctrine of the "Messianic secret" of Jesus. We meet it especially in the Gospel according to Mark. In Matthew and Luke we find it only in a milder version, while John has replaced it by the no less paradoxical doctrine of the "glory" of the Revealer *in* this incarnation and *in* this death. As we meet this theory in Mark, it clearly suggests the reflection and the interpretation of the post-Easter Church.[2] Here Jesus' whole history leads up to Easter. Until then the fact that he is the Messiah remains concealed and is not to be revealed. Again and again, however, it comes out in particular incidents and acts of Jesus. The evil spirits recognise him and know, fearfully, that the one who makes an end to their rule has come; the healed wish to make known his power; the disciples wish to confess and proclaim him the Messiah before his time. Jesus, however, repeatedly demands silence, and will not permit this confession and message until he has died and risen again. An example of this is his word to the disciples after they became for a moment witnesses of the coming glory of his resurrection in the story of the transfiguration: "And as they were coming down the mountain, he charged them to tell no one what they had seen, until the Son of man should have risen from the dead" (Mk. ix. 9). The stereotyped demands for silence[3] with which this whole Gospel is interspersed and which are often impossible to carry out, as well as the frequently repeated remarks about the disciples' lack of understanding (vi. 52; vii. 18; viii. 17 f., etc.), prove the uniform theological conception upon which the evangelist bases his work. Quite rightly, therefore, the oldest Gospel has been called paradoxically "a book of secret epiphanies".[4]

What then are the historical facts behind it? The idea of the Messianic secret in Mark so obviously presupposes the experience of Good Friday and Easter, and betrays itself as a theological and literary device of the evangelist, especially clearly where we recognise the hand of the author, that it is impossible to treat it forthwith as a teaching of the historical Jesus. If we were to follow any such assumption we should have to find quite different indications in the tradition, for example, that in his preaching Jesus had "spiritualised" the traditional conception of the Messiah. As often as this is maintained, so seldom do we find it confirmed in the sources. This leaves, it would seem, only the other explanation, that behind the doctrinal teaching concerning the Messianic secret there still dimly emerges the fact that Jesus' history was originally a non-Messianic history, which was portrayed in the light of the Messianic faith of the Church only after Easter.[5] However, the most serious doubts are to be raised against this assumption as well. With all due attention to the critical examination of tradition, we saw no reason to contest that Jesus actually awakened Messianic expectations by his coming and by his ministry, and that he encountered the faith which believed him to be the promised Saviour. The faith which is expressed by the two disciples at Emmaus: "But we hoped that he was the one to redeem Israel" (Lk. xxiv. 21) seems to express quite accurately the conviction of the followers of Jesus before his death. This, too, is the only explanation of the attitude of the Jewish authorities and of Pilate's verdict. And finally, if we bear in mind how closely prophecy and Messianic claim were linked in the words of the leaders of the numerous Messianic movements of that time, or at least in the faith of their followers, the picture which the Gospels present becomes thus thoroughly credible.

We should, therefore not speak about Jesus' non-Messianic history before his death, but rather of a movement of broken Messianic hopes, and of one who was hoped to be the Messiah, but who not only at the moment of failure, but in his entire message and ministry, disappointed the hopes which were placed in him. For this is the truly amazing thing, that there is in fact not one single certain proof of Jesus' claiming for himself one of the Messianic titles which tradition has ascribed to him. At any rate, nowhere does this seem to be of any importance either in his preaching of the coming of the kingdom of God, or in his endeavour to make God's will a reality to us now, although it is certain that his words and deeds are decisive both for the present and for the future.

In recognising this, we must not allow ourselves to be misled by the fact that the Gospels themselves contain many passages which are clearly Messianic. These should be regarded first of all as the Credo of the believers, and as the theology of the early Church. This applies to the quite divergent genealogies of Matthew as well as Luke, which try to describe Jesus as the son of David and as the child of the promise. And it applies equally to the infancy narratives of the same Gospels, which in the form of legends describe the secret of his origin; and it applies to the stories of his baptism and temptation, which again are not historical reports, but which, in the form of illustrative tales, explain Jesus' mission and person. We do not deny that the tradition here attaches itself to scenes whose historicity certainly need not be contested, starting with the baptism and continuing on to his crucifixion and resurrection. The possibility, however, of finding a historical kernel in these stories varies greatly in each case, and is generally slight. Any such attempt is purchased as a rule at the expense of cheating oneself out of the real meaning of the text. Anyone may see this more clearly in the description, say, of the story of the transfiguration of Jesus, which really only begins to speak to us when we cease to ask after the "historical facts" behind it. One of the neighbouring stories, that of Peter's confession, is no exception either. To be sure, it may point more directly to a historical scene, especially because of the striking fact that it gives the name of the place, Caesarea Philippi. But the manner in which it is told is completely shot through with the confession and the reflection of the later Church. It is no longer only a historical scene, but a historical record of a higher order, in which has been recorded Jesus' whole history, from the cross to the resurrection, as well as the history of a faith which first had to break down at the cross of Jesus, only to be rebuilt upon his cross and resurrection.

We cannot even except from this discussion those sayings of the Lord which we meet in the tradition as testimonies of Jesus to himself, by applying to him the Messianic titles—Messiah, Son of God, Son of David, Son of man. Here, too, it is evident that in all probability they received the form in which they appear in the tradition from the faith of the church which the resurrection had awakened. The right to make a far-reaching statement like this can only be assumed after a critical examination of the individual passages, to which the Third Appendix offers at least an introduction. If we keep in mind what we have mentioned once or twice before, that the tradition understood and transmitted Jesus' words not only as words spoken in the past, but as the words of the risen and present Lord, we can understand how it came about that his words appear here in this new form. Just because the resurrected and risen Christ was for the believers no other than the earthly Jesus of Nazareth, it was possible for exalted titles to find their way into words of Jesus spoken before Easter, titles which in reality anticipate the end of his life. They all speak of the authority which God gave to this Jesus, of the salvation which God has wrought through him for time and eternity, of the dignity of his person, the course he is to follow, and his work; but this is always done by keeping in view the close connection between his earthly life on the one hand and his end and the fulfilment of his mission on the other (Ch. IX). We do not contest here that we find in all these exalted titles the reactions and repercussions of what we meet constantly in Jesus' word before his death. Jesus' message and claim, that in his person and work the reign of God has already begun, and that now the decision is made for salvation or judgment, as well as the special and unique character of his relationship to his Father, which is expressed in many of his utterances—all this is included in the Messianic titles given to him by the Church. At the same time it is part of this special relationship that the earthly Jesus did not claim any of these titles for himself.

This opinion may seem strange, for we hear in Mark xiv. 61 f., in the story of Jesus' trial before the Sanhedrin, that, when asked by the high priest "Are you the Christ, the Son of the Blessed?" he replies for the first time quite openly: "I am." Similarly, in the scene of Peter's confession according to Matthew, he accepts Peter's confession of him as the Messiah (xvi. 17). Both passages, however, reflect clearly the confession to Christ by the later Church.[6] What applies to the title "Messiah" applies also to the title "Son". The expression "Son" used by itself is a Messianic title in the confessions of the early Church (see pages 226 f.). Unknown to Judaism in this form, we meet it in the synoptics only in two places. Both of these, as has been often observed, remind us of the style of John, but could hardly be used as proof in relation

to the historical Jesus. Neither is there a single instance in Jesus'
teaching in which he uses the Messianic title "Son of David" for
himself.

Among the statements concerning himself, only the title "Son
of man" has a special position. Its origin can be found, as we have
already seen (see pages 38 f.), in late Jewish apocalypticism. Its
meaning there is easily misunderstood, and does not mean a man
as opposed to a divine or heavenly being, but rather a mythical
transcendent figure; an exalted name, therefore, without equal,
certainly not a name for man in his low estate. The visionary of the
book of Daniel sees this figure as "One, who was like the son of
man". He descends in the clouds of heaven and is given an everlasting kingdom and dominion over all people (Dan. vii. 13 ff.).
The apocalyptic writer identifies him with the people of Israel,
but the later apocalypses show that this strange figure is a person
and identical with the Messiah (Enoch xlviii. 2 f.; lxii. f.; IV
Ezra xiii). The hope for the coming of the Son of man expresses
an expectation which goes beyond the narrow limits of Jewish
nationalism and embraces the whole world. With him the old
aeon ends and a new one begins. There can be no doubt that the
early Church in Palestine identified the figure of this Son of man,
who is to come to judge the world and to save those who are his,
with Jesus. This expectation was part of the oldest Christology of
the primitive Church. Its traces, however, were soon lost. For,
especially with the entry of the Gospel into the Hellenistic world,
the original meaning of the title "Son of man" was no longer understood, and the hopes which were placed upon him died away, or,
better, found a different expression. Only the first three Gospels
remain as a source of the expectation of the "Son of man". In the
Gospel according to John the title remains in the background,
behind the numerous other names for Christ's majesty, although
it can be found here too, still clearly dependent on the old tradition
of the original church, in several passages (Jn. i. 51; iii. 14; v. 27;
vi. 27). We no longer find it in Paul's writings, not to mention other
writings of the early church—except Acts vii. 56; Rev. i. 13.

All the more numerous, however, are the occurrences of the
name "Son of man" in the first three Gospels, and in the sources
used by them. It is, however, always in Jesus' own words; never is

he named in the narration as the Son of man, nor is he so called when being addressed or acclaimed. This seems to prove conclusively that the title Son of man must have been truly and incontestably Jesus' own designation of himself. But here, too, it would be advisable for historical investigation to proceed cautiously. The only thing we can be really sure of is that there are not a few instances of Jesus' use of the term "Son of man" which, quite in accordance with apocalyptic expectation, refer to the Son of man as him who comes on the clouds of heaven. Some of these passages may have been taken over with little alteration from Jewish apocalypticism into Christian tradition. Others, however, can be traced back without a doubt to Jesus himself. Among them there is especially the word addressed to the disciples: "And I tell you, everyone who acknowledges me before men, the Son of man also will acknowledge before the angels of God. But he who denies me before men will be denied before the angels of God" (Lk. xii. 8 f.; cf. Mk. viii. 38). It is worth noting that Jesus does not here call himself the Son of man, but speaks of him in the third person. At the same time, however, he links the judgment of the coming one very closely with his own person, and puts the decisions which are made concerning him in the closest connection with the future decisions of the judge of the world. This is where we come up against the original core of the tradition, Jesus' own words. The tradition has frequently removed the difference between Jesus himself and the Son of man, as the changing of numerous sayings in the Gospels already shows.

But we learn still more from the tradition. It offers other words about the Son of man which say nothing about the coming of the judge of the world, but which speak all the more about the many sufferings of the Son of man, about his rejection and death at the hands of the elders, the high priests and the scribes, and which say that after three days he will rise again (Mk. viii. 31, etc.). There is no parallel for these words in the apocalyptic literature. They are paradoxical in the extreme: the Son of man in the hands of men (Mk. ix. 31), the judge of the world to be judged himself. These prophecies of suffering bear the stamp not so much of the hope of the coming one, but rather of an experience which looks back to the earthly Jesus; the divine "must" in Jesus' passion and resurrection is their content. The story of Jesus' passion and resurrection has been absorbed by them in every detail. In terms of the history of the tradition this means: these words can hardly have been spoken by Jesus himself; they belong to a later stage of the tradition in which the completed story of Jesus gave a new form even to his words. Has then the idea of the Son of man lost thereby its original meaning? Certainly it has received a new content through Jesus. Yet, these words intend to impress upon us especially that he, not someone else, is the one whom we expected. The rejected and the crucified and no other is invested with the power of God to redeem and to judge.

Hence, we may understand that still other Son of man sayings in the tradition, without speaking of his coming or of his suffering and resurrection, can still talk of the earthly Jesus as the Son of man (Mk. ii. 10-28; Mt. viii. 20; xi. 19). How naturally has the title come to be vested with everything that could be said about Jesus, for "Son of man" and "Jesus" have become quite inseparably fused, and can, as the tradition shows, not infrequently be interchanged.

In any case it is obvious from the passages mentioned here that the tradition, particularly at this point, was in a state of transition, and that in it Jesus' message is not only passed on, but that, in this process of transmission, we are aware of an adaptation and interpretation of his person from the point of view of all that followed.

If we are right, it would mean that, although the historical Jesus spoke most definitely of the coming Son of man and judge of the world in the sense of the contemporary apocalyptic hope, and did so with the amazing certainty that the decisions made here with regard to his person and message would be confirmed at the last judgment, nevertheless he did not give himself the title Son of man. Also we can hardly assume that the earthly Jesus saw himself as destined to be the heavenly judge of the world.[7] This latter assumption is frequently supported in modern times by reference to the apocalyptic doctrine according to which the Son of man and judge of the world is concealed by God until the time of his revelation from heaven. Jesus is thought to have understood the time of his humiliation on earth in the light of this conception of concealment, and knew himself designated as the Son of man, to appear in glory in the future.[8] But which of Jesus' sayings gives us the right to fuse these two completely different conceptions and ideas of the concealment of this Son of man in heaven, as taught by apocalypticism, and the concealment of God's reign in the words and deeds of Jesus as proclaimed in his message? Not a single one of his words speaks of the *Messias designatus*.

We may thus assume with even greater certainty that it was in the first instance primitive tradition which, through faith in the risen Lord who will come to judge the world, added the name of majesty even to those sayings of the Lord in which it did not originally occur. These sayings, too, reflect the same process of adaptation and interpretation by the faithful which we were able to recognise in so many Messianic texts.

The result of these deliberations is in no way merely negative, but is pre-eminently positive as well. They recall us to the recognition which has governed our whole treatment of the message and history of Jesus, namely, that the Messianic character of his being is contained *in* his words and deeds and *in* the unmediatedness of his historic appearance. No customary or current conception, no title or office which Jewish tradition and expectation held in readiness, serves to authenticate his mission, or exhausts the secret of his being. It is impossible to solve this mystery with the logic, of whatever type, of any preceding doctrinal system. We thus learn to understand that the secret of his being could only reveal itself to his disciples in his resurrection.

Chapter IX

JESUS CHRIST

THE story of Jesus does not end with his death. It begins anew with his resurrection. The scattered and dispersed band of his disciples gathers together, and through their belief in him and their hope of his second coming, becomes a community. The spirit of their Lord, risen and lifted up, makes them sure that he is present and that the future is his. Their sealed lips are opened, and they show forth "the mighty works of God" (Acts ii. 11). Their witness awakens new faith, but at the same time arouses new opposition and persecution. The story of the Church begins, the story of its mission and expansion beyond the bounds of Palestine throughout the whole world. A story full of change and excitement it is, in which the world is called to face the gospel, while the Church is called by the world to deliver the message of Jesus Christ in ever new forms and languages. A story of tremendous accomplishment among nations and in the hearts of men, but at the same time a story of shortcoming and failure, of faithfulness and faithlessness, of insight and of error, of victories and defeats, in which often enough, if we measure them by the Church's commission and faith, the apparent victories of Christianity might be called its defeats, and its defeats victories. All this is a story of Jesus Christ and of his authority, but also a story of his never-ending passion.

This story lies beyond the limits of our present work. Only the outlines of its beginnings must be mentioned here. From the very beginning, the preacher Jesus of Nazareth enters into the message of faith and himself becomes the content of the preaching: he who called men to believe is now believed in. "And we have believed, and have come to know, that you are the Holy One of God" (Jn. vi. 69). A widespread modern view tries to explain this decisive turning-point, at which in point of fact the Christian faith is born, somewhat in this fashion: it sees Jesus' end on the cross as the tragic end of a prophet, who amid misunderstanding and persecution preached a great idea, and died for this idea, the victim of a terrible misunderstanding. Till quite recently, therefore, the fantastic idea could be entertained of re-opening the trial of Jesus and reviewing the historical error of Jewish and Roman justice. Such a viewpoint may then consider it the historic contribution of the disciples that they did not succumb to the fateful persecution and propaganda directed against their master, that they boldly withstood wickedness and lying, and after a short time of being paralysed by terror, bravely set to work to claim the abandoned inheritance of their Lord, and to make known his teaching in the world. In such an explanation of the origins of Christian history even the Easter faith of the disciples might seem to be included best, and made psychologically comprehensible, as a result and effect of the overwhelming impression which Jesus' personality had made on his disciples. "He was too great to die" (Lagarde).

Meanwhile, however plausible such a view may appear to many, the New Testament sources refute it, and not only the believer, but the historian, too, must here confess how little the sources at his disposal confirm such ideas, and how inadequate are the categories under which the historical origin of Christianity is here dealt with. But has the historian any better ones available, to understand the mystery of Jesus' resurrection and the origin of the Church? No one can deny that historical research and understanding are here confronted with immovable limits. But much is achieved simply in not overstepping these limits, as that all too clever explanation has tried to do.

I. THE RESURRECTION

The event of Christ's resurrection from the dead, his life and his eternal reign, are things removed from historical scholarship. History cannot ascertain and establish conclusively the facts about them as it can with other events of the past. The last historical fact available to them is the Easter faith of the first disciples. What the message and the experience on which it was founded mean is not hidden by the New Testament. This belief is not the particular experience of a few enthusiasts or a particular theological opinion of a few apostles, which in the course of time was fortunate enough to establish itself and make a big success. No; wherever there were early Christian witnesses and communities, and however varied their message and theology were, they are all united in believing and acknowledging the risen Lord. Paul has expressed this with the greatest possible emphasis—and he speaks here for the whole of primitive Christianity: "Whether then it was I or they (i.e. the other apostles), so we preach and so you believed" (I Cor. xv. 11). The same Paul says in this same chapter that faith absolutely stands or falls with this message of Christ's resurrection: "If Christ has not been raised, then our preaching is in vain and your faith is in vain. We are even found to be misrepresenting God, because we testified of God that he raised Christ, whom he did not raise up" (I Cor. xv. 14 f.). "If Christ has not been raised, your faith is futile and you are still in your sins" (I Cor. xv. 17). We are deceived and have deceived you; we are liars and enemies of God, who has nothing whatever to do with this our message. In that case we had better cast off this unreal Christianity as soon as possible and go back to those who have chosen the watchword, which seems so openly cheerful and is yet so full of hopeless resignation: "Let us eat and drink, for tomorrow we die" (I Cor. xv. 32).

In this passage, in which Paul pours forth a terrible cataract of awful consequences upon his hearers, he certainly does not speak as one anxiously arguing himself into a state of illusion, so as to escape these terrible possibilities that would turn everything to naught—on the contrary, he prefers to face them squarely rather than stand on unsure ground. What he is able to set against them is this, in all its simplicity: "But in fact Christ has been raised from the dead, the first fruits of those who have fallen asleep" (I Cor. xv. 20).

At the same time, just as certainly as—even in a completely historical sense—there would be no gospel, not one account, no letter in the New Testament, no faith, no Church, no worship, no prayer in Christendom to this day without the message of the resurrection of Christ, even so difficult and indeed impossible is it to gain a satisfactory idea of how the Easter events took place. There is an undeniable tension between the singleness of the Easter *message* and the ambiguity and historical problems of the Easter *narratives*. We cannot deal with this in all its detail here.

Every attentive and critical reader of the New Testament can gain a first impression of this problem of the Easter tradition, if he compares the appearances of the risen Christ which the apostle enumerates in the oldest and most reliable Easter text which was formulated long before Paul (I Cor. xv. 3 ff.), with the Easter stories of the Gospels.[1] The old form, which reads almost like an official record, mentions numerous appearances of the risen Christ which have left no trace in the Gospels. On the other hand, it knows nothing of the synoptic stories of the women at the empty tomb, for example, and the Emmaus disciples. We hear from Paul's version that Peter was the first witness of the risen Christ, and this is supported by Luke xxiv. 34, and by the leading position accorded to Peter in the early Church; but we do not now possess, at least not in the canonical Gospels, any story of this first appearance before Peter alone.[2] Most of the appearances enumerated by Paul point to Galilee, whither part at least of the disciples of Jesus returned after his crucifixion, before the church was formed in Jerusalem under the leadership of Peter and the rest of the Twelve.[3] But we have to reckon also with appearances in and around Jerusalem. As tradition shows, more importance was ascribed to these than to the Galilean appearances; this can easily be explained by the importance of the Church itself in the holy city. Mark reveals too, what Paul confirms, that Galilee was the land of the first encounter between the risen Christ and his disciples (Mk. xvi. 7); for the story he tells of the discovery of the empty tomb by the women is not a story of an appearance of Christ. Not till Matthew (xxviii. 9 f.) does it become one. John likewise, whose narrative is of course in detail quite different from that of the synoptic writers, has the risen Christ meet with Mary and Mary Magdalene and the assembled disciples. But both evangelists present Galilean Easter stories as well (Mt. xxviii. 16 ff.; Jn. xxi. 1 ff.). In contrast to the others, Luke has consistently placed all the appearances in Jerusalem and its immediate neighbourhood.[4]

The Easter narratives of the evangelists differ considerably in detail, and point back to a much less uniform tradition than their passion stories. This shows immediately that the tradition here was for a longer time in a fluid state. We have to reckon with gaps, but also with legendary additions. The Easter message is at any rate earlier than the Easter stories, and was echoed in them in very varied ways. They give empirical expression to the event of the resurrection in individual stories. This holds already for the story of the women at the empty tomb. As it is told this story, like the stories from the material peculiar to the other evangelists, is obviously a legend, the historical difficulties of which need not be assessed in detail here. We may also take it from the phrase at the end, that the women "said nothing to anyone" (Mk. xvi. 8), that it appeared only later in the tradition.[5] And indeed, how this story is told! The wonderful event of the resurrection is not even depicted, such is the reticence and awe. This is very different from later legends, which raise the miracle to the level of the fantastic, elaborate it without restraint, and make even guards and elders its witnesses.[6] All the more powerful does the message of Easter sound in this story as the angel speaks it: "Do not be amazed; you seek Jesus of Nazareth, who was crucified. He has risen, he is not here; see the place where they laid him" (Mk. xvi. 6). "Why do you seek the living among the dead?" (Lk. xxiv. 5).

The resurrection message and resurrection faith in the early church do not depend on uniform versions of the manner of the Easter event, or the physical nature of the risen Christ. This is already shown by the fact that what is certainly the oldest view held by the Church made no distinction between the resurrection of Christ and his elevation to the right hand of the Father,[7] while only later was there developed, in addition, the theory of the resurrected Christ walking the earth for a time and only subsequently ascending into Heaven.

From what has been said, it follows that we are to understand the Easter stories too as evidence of the faith, and not as records and chronicles, and that it is the *message* of Easter we must seek in the Easter *stories*. That is not to say by any means that the message of Jesus' resurrection is only a product of the believing community. Certainly the form in which it comes down to us is stamped with this faith. But it is just as certain that the appearances of the risen Christ and the word of his witnesses have in the first place given rise to this faith. What became clear and grew to be a certainty for the Church was this, that God himself had intervened with his almighty hand in the wicked and rebellious life of the world, and had wrested this Jesus of Nazareth from the power of sin and death which had risen against him, and set him up as Lord of the world. Thus, according to the interpretation of the early Church, Easter is above all else God's acknowledgment of this Jesus, whom the world refused to acknowledge, and to whom even his disciples were unfaithful. It is at the same time the intervention of God's new world in this old world branded with sin and death, the setting up and beginning of his kingdom. An event *in* this time and this world, and yet at the same time an event which puts an end and a limit to this time and this world. To be sure only faith experiences this (Acts x. 40 ff.), for it cannot be observed and demonstrated like any other event in time and space. And yet it concerns this world as an act of salvation and judgment, and must therefore be proclaimed to the ends of the earth. We note how Jesus' own message of the coming of the kingdom of God is heard here again in a new form, only that now he himself, together with his death and resurrection, has entered into this message and become the core of it.

The contrast between what men did and do and what God has done and accomplished in and through this Jesus, belongs therefore inalienably to all the New Testament testimony of the resurrection. In this the first Christians do not consider themselves in any way as confederates of God and comrades-in-arms with their Lord, as we might put it. They regard themselves as those who have been conquered, whose former lives and beliefs have come to naught. The men and women who encounter the risen Christ in the Easter stories, have come to an end of their wisdom. They are alarmed and disturbed by his death, mourners wandering about the grave of their Lord in their helpless love, and trying like the women at the grave with pitiable means to stay the process and odour of corruption, disciples huddled fearfully together like animals in a thunderstorm (Jn. xx. 19 ff.). So it is, too, with the two disciples on the way to Emmaus on the evening of Easter day; their last hopes, too, are destroyed. One would have to turn all the Easter stories upside down, if one wanted to present them in the words of Faust: "They are celebrating the resurrection of the Lord, for they themselves are resurrected." No, they are not themselves resurrected. What they experience is fear and doubt, and what only gradually awakens joy and jubilation in their hearts is just this: They, the disciples, on this Easter day, are the ones marked out by death, but the crucified and buried one is alive. Those who have survived him are the dead, and the dead one is the living.

Hence the miracle of the resurrection does not have a satisfactory explanation in the inner nature of the disciples, nor—and this is a quite unbiblical idea—does it have an analogy in the eternal dying and rebirth in nature. Past and present find their unity alone in the person of Jesus himself, this new Jesus of Nazareth, whom God by his resurrection and exaltation "has made both Lord and Christ" (Acts ii. 36). It is the resurrected Christ, therefore, who first reveals the mystery of his history and his person, and above all the meaning of his suffering and death. This is movingly told in the story of the disciples of Emmaus (Lk. xxiv. 13 ff.), who were joined on their way by the risen Christ, but did not know him. They tell the stranger at their side the terrible tale of their Master, which has disappointed all their hopes; indeed they can even tell the events of Easter morning, but only as a hopeless story, known to everyone except, apparently, this stranger, until he opens his mouth and reveals to them the deep redeeming meaning of the whole story: "O foolish men, and slow of heart to believe all that the prophets have spoken. Was it not necessary that the Christ should suffer these things and enter into his glory?" (xxiv. 25 f.). And so he fans the dying flame in their hearts anew, and they are aware of his presence at the evening meal. Truly, even the disciples at Emmaus cannot hold him as they might an earthly travel companion. The risen Christ is not like one of them. He vanishes from them again. But in the words that he speaks to them and in the supper he eats with them, they have the pledges of his resurrection and presence. Thus they return to the circle of their brethren as witnesses, and are met with the joyful confession from their midst: "The Lord has risen indeed, and has appeared to Simon" (xxiv. 34).

From amid the wealth of New Testament evidence about the substance and meaning of the resurrection, let us mention here further only the beginning of the First Epistle of Peter: "Blessed be the God and Father of our Lord Jesus Christ! By his great mercy we have been born anew to a living hope through the resurrection Jesus Christ from the dead" (i. 3). The community to whom this epistle is addressed is described as a group of strangers, their belief in the crucified and risen Christ making them "strangers scattered" (i. 1), whose inheritance is in heaven (cf. Phil. iii. 20). As such, however, they are "born again", endowed with the life of Christ. This fills them with a "lively hope", which, unlike earthly hopes, no longer changes into disappointment overnight. The First Epistle of Peter is able therefore to say of them, though it does not conceal from the believers the difficulties of their earthly road: "You who are guarded by the power of God" (i. 5).

2. THE CHURCH

The Church has its origin and its beginning in the resurrection of Jesus Christ. This is not to be taken as a calendar date, but as the governing factor in this origin and beginning. Luke is interested as no other New Testament writer in dates which pertain to general and sacred history, and fixes the day of the outpouring of the Holy Spirit at Pentecost. Yet his story of Pentecost shows that the resurrection and exaltation of Jesus and the sending of the Holy Spirit are inseparably bound together (Acts ii. 32 f.). The founding of the Church is therefore not the work of Jesus on earth, but of the risen Lord. This is stated unequivocally too, in the famous words of Jesus, much disputed from the point of view of the history of the tradition, which appear in the special material of Matthew.[8] There it is Jesus' answer to Peter's confession that he is the Christ: "Blessed are you, Simon, Bar-Jona! For flesh and blood has not revealed this to you, but my Father who is in heaven. And I tell you, you are Peter, and on this rock I will build my church, and the powers of death shall not prevail against it. I will give you the keys of the kingdom of heaven, and whatever you bind on earth shall be bound in heaven, and whatever you loose on earth shall be loosed in heaven" (Mt. xvi. 17-19). So much is clear in this saying, which more than any other has made history: Jesus speaks here of a future[9] which is still to come, and indeed both of an earthly and an ultimate future. The building of the Church on the rock of Peter will happen on earth, and the decisions which he makes to "bind" or to "loose" here upon earth will be recognised as valid at the last judgment of God in heaven.

The fact that in this saying we are dealing with very ancient tradition is betrayed at once by the Semitic character of the language down to the last detail. This is above all the case in the wordplay over the name, which is only possible in Aramaic,[10] and cannot be rendered in English (though, of course, it is possible in French: *"Tu es Pierre et sur cette pierre je bâtirai mon église."* The description also of Peter's official authority—"binding" and "loosing"—is the current Jewish expression for the doctrinal and disciplinary powers of the rabbis; as also the words in Matthew xxiii. 13 speak of the "power of the keys" misused by the scribes. Nevertheless, there arise most serious doubts as to whether the historical Jesus himself really did speak these words. This is not only because they have no parallel in the other Gospels, and because this is the only place in the whole synoptic tradition where the word *"ekklesia"* appears in the sense of the church as a whole. (Only in Mt. xviii. 17 do we come across the word *"ekklesia"* again, in connection with Church regulations, but used here in the sense of an assembly of the Church.) But the authenticity of the passage in Matthew xvi is questioned chiefly because it is not easily compatible with Jesus' proclamation of the imminent coming of the kingdom of God. The word that we render in English by "church" has its origin in the Old Testament Jewish language, and signifies God's people of the end of time, the elect people, the holy ones of God. This meaning unquestionably underlies the conception contained in the word *"ekklesia"* in Matthew xvi. 18, but it has here already been solidified as an institution, which, being invested with full authority in doctrinal and legal matters, and bound up with the monarchical office of a particular apostle,[11] has its clearly defined place between the resurrection and the last judgment. It is therefore difficult to ascribe to the earthly Jesus this saying about the "Church"; rather is it the tradition which has put these words in his mouth, and not a very widely-spread special tradition at that, which is scarcely in keeping with other information about Peter and the early Church.[12]

Certainly the words of Matthew xvi. 18 f. form, in any case, a testimony to the founding of the Church on the resurrection of Jesus, and to the consciousness of the early Christians that they were the community of the end of time, against whom the powers of the underworld can achieve nothing. In this community the power of the Spirit promised for the end is active in prophecy, prayer and miracles; baptism, too, is again carried out as the eschatological sacrament for the forgiveness of sins and admission into the people of God, but now "in the name of Jesus". In this community, too, the supper is partaken together, in joy and jubilation, in expectation of the coming of the Lord.

But this very community who await the coming Lord and, in the spirit, are already certain of his presence, bind themselves consciously, at the same time, to the way and the message of the earthly Jesus, and take his orders and promise as a guide for their own earthly way; not in spite of their hopes which are fixed on the future, but precisely because of them. Their expectation of the coming of the Lord gains its power and its reason for existence in their knowledge of past and present. From now on the great theme of the early Christian mission is the proclamation and delivery of the message of the redemption, which happened through the cross and the resurrection, and the kingship of Jesus Christ over the world.

3. THE CONFESSION OF FAITH

By the events of Easter and the certainty of the resurrection of Jesus Christ from the dead, he who proclaimed the coming of the kingdom of God, as we have already said, became the one proclaimed, the one who called to faith became the content of the faith. Jesus' words and the gospel about Jesus Christ have become a unity. To many this process appears as Christianity's great fall. From that time on, so they say, the simple preaching of Jesus was overgrown by mythology and dogma, so that even in Paul it is no longer recognisable. "Back to Jesus!" became, therefore, the great formula. Yet we should not give in to this watchword too readily, and take it for granted that we end up with Jesus by following this supposedly so certain path. The example of the theology built upon the quest of the historical Jesus should warn us. It might be wiser to enquire after the motive and meaning of the early Christian confessions, in which that faith found expression.

To judge by their nature and by the way they understood themselves, these confessions,[13] which the early Christians set forth in many different forms, in short formulae for confession of faith

or sermon, in hymns and prayers, are an answer to the word of
God which had already gone forth. They all give this Jesus of
Nazareth a name of honour: Christ (Messiah), Son of David, Son
of God, Son of man, Lord, and call him in this way the bringer of
eternal salvation. Are they thereby giving him an honour which the
earthly Jesus, as we have seen, did not desire for himself? The
Gospel of John answers this question when it tells, in a seemingly
paradoxical manner, of Jesus saying: "Yet I do not seek my own
glory" (viii. 50), and alongside this: "He who does not honour
the Son does not honour the Father who sent him" (v. 23). In this
sense Jesus' resurrection and exaltation is praised as the act of God,
who has raised the humbled one, obedient to the death of the cross,
to his right of kingship, and given him the "name above every name",
the name of the divine "Lord": "Therefore God has highly exalted
him and bestowed on him the name which is above every name, that
at the name of Jesus every knee should bow, in heaven and on earth
and under the earth, and every tongue confess that Jesus Christ is
Lord, to the glory of God the Father" (Phil. ii. 9-11). The same kind
of thing is true of other confessions. God has given him the name
of son: "Thou art my son, today I have begotten thee"; hence
he is so called in the confession (Heb. i. 5; v. 5; etc.). Therefore
Peter, on his confession "You are the Christ, the Son of the living
God", receives the answer: "Flesh and blood have not revealed this
to you, but my Father who is in heaven" (Mt. xvi. 16 f.). From this
standpoint we understand why the traditional accounts of Jesus
have woven record and confession into one. By this they show that
they took Jesus himself, in all his words and even apart from them,
as *the* Word of God to the world (Jn. i. 1; I Jn. i. 1); Jesus himself,
prior to and in all his works *the* work of God in the world; Jesus
himself prior to and in all the stories the decisive and final history
of God in the world.

So the confession of the early Church is heard in many varied
forms at baptism and the Lord's Supper, in preaching and teaching,
but also in the struggle against false teaching, in the struggle with
demonic powers, and again in the witness of the martyrs.[14]

The language in which it is heard changes. It is the language of a
particular time and situation, one language, where the gospel is
preached before Jews, another where it had to come to grips with

mystery religions, with gnostic ideas of redemption, with the cultured religiosity of the Stoics and with the emperor-cult. The Christian faith, one might say, takes possession of heathen ideas and "baptises" them, but heathen things very often change the face of Christianity. Thus, from the first, theology is summoned to the field, and the struggle within Christianity itself begins, a struggle for truth, which yet many a time cannot defend itself from what is false. This is all a highly complicated and involved process, which we cannot trace in detail here.

If we confine ourselves here to the beginning, and the motives which are at work in it, we realise that the testimony of early Christian faith had to find expression in many different ways, as the first three evangelists show, and the fourth even more; Paul again, and the writings of the post-apostolic time in a different way. We have already seen how the name "Son of man" was no longer understood in Hellenistic Christianity and soon disappeared. The word "Christos", too, i.e. the Anointed One (Messiah), becomes widely used as a proper name. The title "Son of God" in Greek circles takes on a new meaning, and especially in later theology becomes a conception with which various speculations about the divine being and divine nature of the Saviour become closely connected. The honorific title "Kyrios" (Lord) also undergoes a profound change in the transition from Jewish to Hellenistic Christianity.[15]

The vital point is that no title or name, from all that have come down to us from Judaism or been taken over from the religious language of Hellenism, retains its meaning unchanged. Wherever such names become titles of honour for this Jesus of Nazareth, the crucified and resurrected, they take on the mystery of his person and history, and acquire a new sense. "Messiah-Christ" is now no longer he who appears in might and fulfils Israel's hopes, but the "Lowly One" (Mt. xxi. 5; xi. 29) who must suffer, in order to enter into his glory (Lk. xxiv. 26). "The Son of David" becomes the symbol of his earthly, human form (Mt. i. 1 ff.; see below on Mk. xii. 35 ff. Appendix IIIc, pages 227 f.). The "Son of man", coming on the clouds of heaven to judge the world, becomes the earthly one who is delivered into the hands of men (see pages 176 f., 228 ff.). The "Son of God" is he who "has been as we are, yet without sinning" (Heb. iv. 14 f.), "born of woman, born under the law" (Gal. iv. 4), who, "although he was a Son, learned obedience through what he suffered" (Heb. v. 8; Mt. iv. 1 ff.). The hymn which Paul has left us in Philippians ii. 6 ff. says the same thing: the path of Christ and the nature of Christ mean renunciation of divine form, giving up self, taking the form of a servant, obedience even to the death of the cross. *This* is he who is exalted by God and bears the name above every name, "Lord". Again the Gospel of John has given special expression to this paradox, when it avows in the prologue: "And the word became flesh and dwelt among us full of grace and truth; we have beheld his glory, glory as of the only Son from the Father" (Jn. i. 14), when the crucifixion of Jesus itself is here called his lifting up (iii. 14; xii. 32 f.), and when the risen Lord is recognised by his disciples by the print of the nails (xx. 24 ff.).

Always the confession of the disciples is the answer to the act of God and to the word which went forth in Jesus Christ. It is Jesus himself who asks them: "But who do you say that I am?" (Mk. viii. 29; cf. Jn. vi. 67). The answer they give is "No" to the ways the world offers them, and thus "Yes" to Jesus Christ: "Lord, to whom shall we go? You have the words of eternal life; and we have believed and have come to know, that you are the Holy One of God" (Jn. vi. 68 f.).

In the same Gospel Jesus gives his disciples the promise that the knowledge of the believers will go further. The Spirit which he will send, shall guide them into all truth (Jn. xvi. 13). But this way into the future will at the same time be none other than the way back to the word of Jesus, for the Spirit shall "bring to your remembrance all that I have said to you" (xiv. 26).

LIST OF ABBREVIATIONS

Z.N.W.	Zeitschrift für die neutestamentliche Wissenschaft und die Kunde der älteren Kirche
Z.Th.K.	Zeitschrift für Theologie und Kirche
Th.R. N.F.	Theologische Rundschau, Neue Folge
Th.L.Z.	Theologische Literaturzeitung
Z.K.G.	Zeitschrift für Kirchengeschichte
Ev. Theol.	Evangelische Theologie
N.T.St.	New Testament Studies
J.B.L.	Journal of Biblical Literature
R.G.G.	Die Religion in Geschichte und Gegenwart
Th.W.z.N.T.	Theologisches Wörterbuch zum Neuen Testament

COMMENTARIES AND FREQUENTLY QUOTED WORKS

Erich Klostermann, *Markus* (4th ed. 1950), *Matthäus* (3rd ed. 1938), *Lukas* (2nd ed. 1929) in *Handbuch zum Neuen Testament*, founded by Hans Lietzmann, edited by Günther Bornkamm.

Ernst Lohmeyer, *Markus* (11th ed. 1951), *Matthäus* (1956) in *Kritisch-exegetischer Kommentar über das Neue Testament*, founded by H. A. W. Meyer.

Julius Schniewind, *Markus* (5th ed. 1949), *Matthäus* (4th ed. 1950) in *Das Neue Testament Deutsch*.

Adolf Schlatter, *Der Evangelist Matthäus* (1929; 3rd ed. 1948).

Julius Wellhausen, *Einleitung in die drei ersten Evangelien* (2nd ed. 1911), *Markus* (2nd ed. 1909), *Matthäus* (2nd ed. 1914), *Lukas* (1904).

Hermann L. Strack and Paul Billerbeck, *Kommentar zum Neuen Testament aus Talmud und Midrasch*, I-IV (1922-1928, Reprint 1951), cf. Billerbeck.

Emil Schürer, *A History of the Jewish People in the Time of Jesus Christ*, 2nd and revised ed., tr. by J. Macpherson, S. Taylor and P. Christie, 5 vol., 1885-90, Index 1891.

Wilhelm Bousset, *Die Religion des Judentums im späthellenistischen Zeitalter*, edited by Hugo Gressman (3rd ed. 1926).

Paul Volz, *Die Eschatologie der jüdischen Gemeinde* (2nd ed. 1934).

William Wrede, *Das Messiasgeheimnis in den Evangelien* (2nd ed. 1913).

Gustaf Dalman, *The Words of Jesus*, tr. by D. M. Kay, 1909.

Rudolf Bultmann, *Jesus and the Word*, tr. by Louise Pettibone Smith and Erminie Huntress, 1934, paperback reprint, 1958.

—— *Geschichte der synoptischen Tradition*, 3rd ed. 1958, tr. by John Marsh, 1960.

—— *Theology of the New Testament*, tr. by Kendrick Grobel, 2 vols, 1951-55 cf. Theology.

Martin Dibelius, *From Tradition to Gospel*, tr. from the 2nd revised ed. by Bertram Lee Wolff, 1935.

—— *Jesus*, tr. by Charles B. Hendrick and Frederick C. Grant, 1949.

—— *Botschaft und Geschichte, Gesammelte Aufsätze*, I (1953), II (1956).

Maurice Goguel, *The Life of Jesus*, tr. by Olive Wyon, 1933, paperback reprint, 1960.

Joachim Jeremias, *The Eucharistic Words of Jesus*, tr. from the 2nd German ed. by Arnold Ehrhardt, 1955.

—— *The Parables of Jesus*, tr. by S. H. Hooke, 1955.

Werner Georg Kümmel, *Promise and Fulfilment* (*Studies in Biblical Theology*, No. 23), tr. from the 3rd German ed. by Dorothea M. Barton, 1957.

Eduard Schweizer, *Lordship and Discipleship* (*Studies in Biblical Theology*, No. 28), 1960.

NOTES

Chapter I

Regarding the problems of the first chapter cf. in recent literature: C. H. Dodd, *History and the Gospels* (1938); E. Kasemann, "Das Problem des historischen Jesus", *Z. Th. K.*, 51. Jahrg. 1954, 125 ff.; Nils Alstrup Dahl, "Der historische Jesus als geschichtswissenschaftliches und theologisches Problem", *Kerygma und Dogma*, 1. Jahrg. 1955, 104 ff.; E. Fuchs, "Die Frage nach dem historischen Jesus", *Z. Th. K.*, 53. Jahrg. 1956, 210 ff.; Joachim Jeremias, "The Present Position in the Controversy Concerning the Problem of the Historical Jesus", *Expository Times*, LXIX (1957-8), 333-9; James M. Robinson, "The Quest of the Historical Jesus Today", *Theology Today*, XV (1958), 183-98, and *A New Quest of the Historical Jesus* (*Studies in Biblical Theology*, No. 25), 1959.

1. As to the non-Christian sources cf. pp. 27 f.

2. Cf. A. Seeberg, *Der Katechismus der Urchristenheit* (1903); C. H. Dodd, *The Apostolic Preaching and its Development* (6th ed. 1950); E. Stauffer, *New Testament Theology* (tr. by John Marsh, 1956), 233 ff.; R. Bultmann, *Theology of the New Testament*, II (1955), 119 ff.; E. Schweizer, *Lordship and Discipleship*, Chh. V-VII.

3. M. Kähler, *Der sogenannte historische Jesus und der geschichtliche, biblische Christus* (2nd ed. 1896), 80, note 1 (republished 1953: 59 f., note 1).

4. Compare for example the Mishna-tractate Aboth ("the Fathers") in *The Mishnah*, tr. by H. Danby (1933), 446 ff.

5. Regarding the question of Paradosis and Kyrios, cf. O. Cullmann, *The Early Church*, ed. by A. J. B. Higgins (1956), 59 ff.

6. We all remember the phrase popular in sermons and in teaching, "Jesus had just . . ." with which the preacher is in the habit of introducing the recapitulation of the section preceding his text, and with which he means to give a particularly vivid introduction to the text of the day. We can be sure that the real message contained in such passages is entirely neglected.

7. Cf. K. L. Schmidt, *Der Rahmen der Geschichte Jesu* (1919); M. Dibelius, *From Tradition to Gospel* (1935); R. Bultmann, *Die Geschichte der synoptischen Tradition* (3rd ed. 1958, tr. by John Marsh, 1960); *Form Criticism*, containing R. Bultmann, *The Study of the Synoptic Gospels*, tr. by F. C. Grant, 1934; J. Schneiwind, "Zur Synoptiker-Exegese", *Th. R.* N. F. 2 (1930), 129 ff., especially 161 ff.; F. C. Grant, *The Earliest Gospel* (1943).

Chapter II

1. Detailed study of the non-Christian sources in M. Goguel's book, *The Life of Jesus* (1933), 70 ff.

2. Josephus' scanty knowledge of Christianity is probably due to the fact that

the church in Jerusalem had already emigrated east of Jordan before the outbreak of the Jewish war and was not involved in it. There is no need for me to enter upon the later Christian interpolations in the historical works of Josephus. They are to be found especially in the Slavonic translation of his *Jewish War*, cf. M. Goguel, *The Life of Jesus*, 75 ff., 82 ff.

3. Cf. H. L. Strack, *Jesus, die Häretiker und die Juden* (1910); A. Meyer, *Handbuch zu den Neutestamentlichen Apokryphen* (1904), 47 ff.; J. Klausner (Jewish), *Jesus of Nazareth* (tr. by H. Danby, 1925), 18 ff.; S. Krauss (Jewish), *Das Leben Jesu nach jüdischen Quellen* (1902).

4. Also the numerous non-canonical Gospels of later times and the scattered apocryphal words of our Lord are in themselves of no value as sources and do not need to be considered here.

5. Only a few first attempts to fit the story into the framework of world history are to be found in Luke (ii. 1 ff.; iii. 1 ff.).

6. Still basic is the extensive work by E. Schürer, *A History of the Jewish People in the Time of Jesus Christ* (1885-90); E. Meyer, *Ursprung und Anfänge des Christentums*, Bd. II (1921); A. Schlatter, *Geschichte Israels von Alexander dem Grossen bis Hadrian* (3rd ed. 1925); M. Noth, *The History of Israel*, tr. by Stanley Godman (1958, rev. ed., 1960), 355 ff. Especially important for the question of the origin of Judaism and the social and religious structure of Samaria and Galilee are the historical and territorial studies of Albr. Alt, *Kleine Schriften*, II (1953), 316 ff., 363 ff. The most important sources for the history of the Jewish people at the time of the Maccabaeans are the first and second books of the Maccabees and, continuing from there, the two historical works of Josephus, *De Bello Judaico* and *Antiquitates Judaicae*.

7. The expression "abomination that makes desolate" used for the first time in Dan. ix. 27; xii. 11, for the desecration of the temple by Antiochus (cf. I Macc. i. 54, 59; vi. 7), has also in later Judaism been interpreted to mean the threatened erection of a statue of Caligula in the temple in A.D. 40. In Mk. xiii. 14 (cf. II Thess. ii. 3 f.) it occurs to describe the Antichrist.

8. Cf. C. Watzinger, *Denkmäler Palästinas*, II (1935) 31 ff. Herod also had the ancient memorials of Israelite history decorated and restored.

9. The question whether the Sanhedrin had the power to inflict the death penalty is contested. In my opinion, H. Lietzmann, *Der Prozess Jesu (Sitzungsber. d. Berl. Ak.,* 1931 XIV, 313 ff. and *Z.N.W.,* 30 (1931) 211 ff. and 31 (1932), 78 ff.), was justified in opposing F. Büchsel (*Z.N.W.,* 30 (1931), 202 ff.) by answering in the affirmative. Cf. also M. Goguel, *Z.N.W.,* 31 (1932), 289 ff.; H. J. Ebeling, *Z.N.W.,* 35 (1936), 290 ff.

10. This tax is a special tax "per head" raised for the imperial fiscus (see pp. 120 f.). This "Census" was levied for the first time in the year A.D. 6 by the Syrian legate Sulpicius Quirinus. Concerning the movement of the Zealots, cf. O. Cullmann, *The State in the New Testament* (tr. by Stuart D. Currie), 8 ff.

11. Ps. lxxxix. 10 ff.; civ. 6 ff.; Is. li. 9 f. We meet the theme of "the fight with the dragon" not only in statements about the creation, but it serves also to describe historical events like the destruction of the Egyptians and Israel's

deliverance at the Red Sea. It is used mainly, however, for the description of eschatological events. Cf. H. Gunkel in *R.G.G.*, 2nd ed., Vol. IV, 381 ff.

12. For the following, cf. W. Bousset, *Die Religion des Judentums im späthellenistischen Zeitalter* (edited by H. Gressmann, 3rd ed. 1926); P. Volz, *Die Eschatologie der jüdischen Gemeinde im neutestamentlichen Zeitalter* (2nd ed. 1934); G. F. Moore, *Judaism in the First Centuries of the Christian Era. The Age of the Tannaim*, I-III (1927-30).

13. The tension between Jewish faith and Platonic thinking is quite apparent in an attempt at a synthesis of both in the theology of Philo of Alexandria (first century A.D.).

14. M. Dibelius, *Jesus* (1949), 43.

15. The most important preserved texts are translated into English in R. H. Charles, *The Apocrypha and Pseudepigrapha of the Old Testament in English*, 1913, II, 163 ff.

16. Regarding the Pharisees and the Sadducees, cf. J. Wellhausen, *Pharisäer und Sadduzäer* (1874); I. Abrahams, *Studies in Pharisaism and the Gospels* (1917); G. Hölscher, *Geschichte der israelitischen und jüdischen Religion* (1922), 218 ff.; J. Jeremias, *Jerusalem zur Zeit Jesu*, II (*Die sozialen Verhältnisse*), B 1 (1929); G. F. Moore, *Judaism in the First Centuries of the Christian Era*, I, 56 ff.

17. Cf. E. Schürer, *A History of the Jewish People in the Time of Jesus Christ*, Div. II, Vol. II, 52 ff.; G. F. Moore, *Judaism in the First Centuries of the Christian Era*, I, 281 ff.; R. Bultmann, *Primitive Christianity in its Contemporary Setting* (tr. by R. H. Fuller, 1956), 59 ff.

18. Their name can be assumed to be a derivation of the proper name Zadok, perhaps of that of the high priest of Solomon and ancestor of a family of priests (II Sam. viii. 17; I Kings ii. 35; Ezekiel xl. 46); cf. G. Hölscher in Pauly-Wissowa's *Realenzykl.*, XII, 2169 ff.; O. Staehlin, Pauly-Wissowa's *Realenzykl.*, II Reihe, I, 1691.

19. Cf. J. Jeremias, *Jerusalem zur Zeit Jesu*, II (*Die sozialen Verhältnisse*), B 1, 88 ff.; G. Bornkamm, πρεσβύτερος *Th. W.z.N.T.*, VI, 651 ff., esp. 659.

20. To be precise: *their* Pentateuch; it differs considerably from the Jewish version.

21. The literature is already immense. Cf. Krister Stendahl (ed.), *The Scrolls and the New Testament* (1957); W. Baumgartner, *Th.R.* 17 (1948-49), 329 ff.; *Th.R.* 19 (1951), 97 ff.; H. Bardtke, *Die Handschriften am Toten Meer* (1952); G. Molin, *Die Söhne des Lichtes, Zeit und Stellung der Handschriften vom Toten Meer* (1954); Millar Burrows, *The Dead Sea Scrolls* (1955) and *More Light on the Dead Sea Scrolls* (1958); Theodor Gaster, *The Jewish Sect of Qumran and the Essenes* (1956); Chaim Rabin, *Qumran Studies* (1957); Frank M. Cross, *The Ancient Library of Qumran and Modern Biblical Studies* (1958).

22. The members of the movement call themselves among other names "sons of Zadok". This, however, does not mean that there is any connection with the priestly party of the Sadducees. Cf. H. J. Schoeps, *Urgemeinde, Judenchristentum, Gnosis* (1956), 71 ff.

23. E.g. between forbidding swearing in the Sermon on the Mount (Mt. v. 34) and the rejection of the use of the oath among the Essenes; in both groups a sharp criticism of the service of the temple and of sacrifice. The old assertion that Jesus himself was an Essene, found originally in studies of the life of Jesus during the period of the Enlightenment, has found once again its protagonists. Cf. A. Dupont-Sommer, *The Dead Sea Scrolls. A Preliminary Study* (1952); E. Wilson, *The Scrolls from the Dead Sea* (1955), 84 ff. On the other hand, see K. G. Kuhn, *Sonntagsblatt*, published by H. Lilje, on April 29, 1956.

24. Cf. J. Jeremias, "Der Gedanke des 'Heiligen Restes' im Spätjudentum und in der Verkündigung Jesu", *Z.N.W.*, 42 (1949), 184 ff.

25. Cf. O. Cullmann, "Die neuentdeckten Qumrantexte und das Judentum der Pseudoklementinen" (*Neutest. Studien für R. Bultmann*, 1954), 35 ff.; and "The Significance of the Qumran Texts for Research into the Beginnings of Christianity", *J.B.L.*, 74 (1955), 213 ff.; H. J. Schoeps, *Urgemeinde, Judenchristentum, Gnosis*, 68 ff.

26. M. Dibelius, *Die urchristliche Überlieferung von Johannes dem Täufer* (1911); E. Lohmeyer, *Das Urchristentum*, I (1932); C. H. Kraeling, *John the Baptist* (1951).

27. In this matter A. Schlatter is probably right, *Der Evangelist Matthäus* (1929), 80 f.; it is possible that the combination of baptism by the Spirit and by fire points to Christian baptism. If we can trace only the announcement of fire baptism back to the tradition of "Q", and hence the idea of Spirit baptism in Matthew and Luke has been taken over from Mark, then the word fire itself contains "the conception of judgment and of salvation". Cf. R. Bultmann, *Geschichte der synoptischen Tradition*, 261 ff.

28. He is called "the Baptist" even in Josephus (*Antiquitates Judaicae*, XVIII, 116).

29. The necessary combination of cleansing and conversion is also especially stressed in the newly discovered rules of the sect (DSD, 3: 4-5; 5: 10.13 f., Brownlee).

30. Billerbeck I, 102 ff.; J. Jeremias, "Der Ursprung der Johannestaufe"; *Z.N.W.*, 28 (1929), 312 ff.; and "Proselytentaufe und Neues Testament", *Theol. Zeitschr.*, 5 (1949), 418 ff.

31. Regarding the baptismal sects, cf. J. Thomas, *Le Mouvement baptiste en Palestine et Syrie* (1935).

32. N. A. Dahl, "The Origin of Baptism", *Norsk teologisk tidsskrift*, 56 (1955) 36 ff., believes that the Essenes as well as John, quite independently, show traces, although in a modified form, of the religious regulations for the cleansing of the priests before the service in the temple.

33. Cf. Lk. v. 33; xi. 1; Acts xix. 3. Concerning the reflection of the rivalry between the followers of Jesus and those of John the Baptist in the tradition of the synoptics, cf. R. Bultmann, *Gesch. d. syn. Trad.*, 22; 177 ff.; 261 ff.; in the Gospel according to John: Bultmann, *Das Evangelium des Joh.* (1941) 4, note 7; 29 ff.; 57 ff.; etc.

34. The fact that John only appears in a late period of the Mandaean literature and that their baptismal rites are dependent on those of the Syrian Church

H. Lietzmann, "Ein Beitrag zur Mandäerfrage", *Sitzungsber. d. Berl. Akad. d. Wissensch.*, *philos.-histor. Kl.*, 27, 1930), is no disproof of the view that the Mandaeans originated from the Jewish baptismal movements of the Jordan Valley. Cf. H. Schlier, "Zur Mandäerfrage", *Th.R. N.F.*, 5 (1953), 1 ff.; 69 ff.; Saeve-Soederbergh, *Studies in the Coptic Manichaean Psalmbook* (1949).

35. Cf. also Jn. i. 6-8; iii. 28 ff.

36. "Q", as is shown in Matthew and Luke, has already assembled a whole collection of sayings under the heading "Jesus and the Baptist".

37. Cf. E. Käsemann, "Das Problem des historischen Jesus", *Z.Th.K.*, 51 1954), 149.

38. Note how the Evangelist changes the tenses of the Isaiah text from the future into the tense of the fulfilled event, in contrast to the Septuagint.

Chapter III

1. Cf. M. Dibelius, "Jungfrauensohn und Krippenkind", *Botschaft und Geschichte (Ges. Aufsätze)*, I (1953), 1 ff.

2. The assertion that Jesus was Aryan was stated for the first time by H. St. Chamberlain in *Foundations of the Nineteenth Century*, tr. by John Lees, I (1910), 00 ff. This theory was occasionally accepted not only in the Germany of the Third Reich but also elsewhere. Cf. regarding this question, as well as what follows, M. Goguel, *The Life of Jesus*, 254 ff., 572 ff. It is unnecessary here to disprove this point. More difficult is the question of Jesus' descent from David and his birth in Bethlehem, reported by Mt. and Lk.). The synoptics do not doubt it, nor do some of the early Christian formulas of faith (Rom. i. 3; II Tim. ii. 8; and elsewhere). (It appears, however, doubtful, in Jn.; cf. vii. 41 f.) But in spite of its age, the tradition can be suspected to have grown from a dogmatic conception of the Messiah. The two genealogies which differ from each other (Mt. i. 1 ff.; Lk. iii. 23 ff.) are products of Christian scribal research. As originally conceived, they are difficult to combine with the virgin birth, no matter how old the attempts at such a reconciliation may be. (Cf. already Mt. i. 16, and commentaries thereon.) The places in Galilee in which Jesus works prove that he belongs to the Israelite part of the population. Regarding this, cf. A. Alt in *Kl. Schriften*, II (1953), 436 ff.

3. The oldest text of Mk. vi. 3 may have run: "Is this not the son of the carpenter and of Mary, etc." This is less strongly attested than the other: "Is this not the carpenter, the son of Mary?" This latter, however, can be expected to have been corrected to conform with the doctrine of the virgin birth. Cf. E. Klostermann, *Markus*, 55.

4. Doctrinal considerations in the interest of maintaining the continued virginity of Mary have made these brothers into half-brothers or cousins of Jesus. This opinion is based on the fact that Hebrew and Aramaic have no special term for a more distant degree of relationship, and occasionally the word "brother" can be used for it (e.g. Gen. xiii. 8). *Adelphoi* may therefore be an inaccurate translation. However, there is nothing to justify this supposition. "*Adelphoi*" never means "cousins" in the New Testament (Greek "*anepsioi*,"

Col. iv. 10). And further, in Lk. ii. 7, Jesus is called the "firstborn" son of Mary. Cf. Th. Zahn, "Brüder und Vettern Jesu", *Forschungen*, VI (1900), 225 ff.; A. Meyer in Hennecke, *Neutestamentl. Apokryphen* (2nd ed. 1924), 103 ff.

5. Especially in Jn. cf. i. 40 ff., 47 f.; ii. 24 f.; iv. 17 ff.

6. In Mark the story is obscured by uncertainty ("Lord, is it I?"). Only in Matthew (xxvi. 20 ff.) and John (xiii. 21 ff.) is the traitor openly named.

7. Cf. J. Schniewind, *Markus*, 55.

Chapter IV

1. "Faith in the Gospel" (in the sense of the gospel of salvation about Jesus Christ) is a term used later in the Church's mission (cf. E. Klostermann, excursus on Mk. i. 1; R. Bultmann, *Theology*, I, 87 ff.).

2. βασιλεία τοῦ θεοῦ and βασιλεία τῶν οὐρανῶν are therefore the same. The conception basileia has been translated by "reign", or "kingdom" without distinction in meaning. The translation "reign" is certainly more to the point, for it expresses the fact that the βασιλεία has not been constituted by its citizens (inhabitants of the realm), but by the will and the rule of its king (in this way alone does it correspond with Oriental ideas), and should not be pictured according to the analogy of a particular, defined territory. Only for this reason can we speak (in the temporal sense) of the "nearness" and the "coming" of the βασιλεία, and thus the word be used as practically synonymous with God. But this does not exclude the physical idea. For God's reign is synonymous with God's new world. Hence the use of expressions such as "entering into the kingdom", the "keys of the kingdom of heaven", the "lying-at-table", "eating and drinking in the kingdom of heaven", etc. (the latter correctly but one-sidedly stressed in E. Lohmeyer, *Kultus und Evangelium*, 1942, 72 ff.). Cf. further Schniewind, *Markus*, excursus to i. 14 f.; K. L. Schmidt, in the article βασιλεία *Th.W.z.N.T.*, I, 582 ff.

3. Examples in Billerbeck, I, 172 ff.; cf. K. G. Kuhn, *Th.W.z.N.T.*, I, 570 ff.

4. This interpretation, backed by J. Weiss, J. Wellhausen, H. Windisch, and O. Cullmann, is however not certain. See further: G. Schrenk, *Th.W.z.N.T.*, I, 608 ff.; W. G. Kümmel, *Promise and Fulfilment*, 121 ff.

5. R. Bultmann, *Theology*, I, 5 f.

6. For the understanding of this expression which is often misunderstood because of the King James translation ("within you"), cf. W. G. Kümmel, *Promise and Fulfilment*, 32 ff.

7. This is how M. Dibelius quite correctly interprets this passage in *Jesus* 72 f. In the text according to Matthew Jonah's three days in the belly of the whale are interpreted as an allegory of the time between Christ's death and resurrection (xii. 40 f.).

8. Cf. A. Jülicher, *Die Gleichnisreden Jesu*, I, II (2nd ed. 1910); R. Bultmann, *Geschichte der synoptischen Tradition* (3rd ed. 1958), 179 ff.; C. H. Dodd, *The Parables of the Kingdom* (4th ed. 1938); J. Jeremias, *The Parables of Jesus* (1955).

9. Cf. H. Greeven, "Wer unter euch . . . ?" *Wort und Dienst (Jahrbuch d. Theol. Schule Bethel* (1952), 86 ff.

10. Jülicher has cleared up this misunderstanding once and for all.

11. J. Jeremias, *The Parables of Jesus*, 14 ff., translates γίνεσθαι ἐν παραβολαῖς with "being obscure", but this translation is hardly possible. Both halves of the verse speak of ways of giving instruction (cf. Jn. i. 17). Also, the meaning of παραβολαί has already been fixed by Mk. iv. 10 and can only mean the parables as a teaching form, which here are understood to be riddles, according to current, generally understood and legitimate interpretation of the Hebrew word "*maschal*". Neither should this saying be freed, as Jeremias tries to do, of a purpose clause's intention of hardening the heart.

12. C. H. Dodd, J. Jeremias.

13. This has been convincingly worked out in N. A. Dahl, "The Parables of Growth". (*Studia Theologica*, 1951, 132 ff.).

14. J. Schniewind, *Markus*, 75.

15. For the following cf. N. A. Dahl, "The Parables of Growth" (*Studia Theologica* 1951, 132 ff.)

16. J. Jeremias in interpreting the parables differentiates quite rightly between the "*Sitz im Leben Jesu*" and the "*Sitz im Leben*" in the later tradition. It is no longer the people of old which is being addressed, but the Church today.

17. The meaning of the kingdom of God in Jesus' message was fatally misunderstood by the theology of the nineteenth century, which, in dependence upon Kant's teaching of the supreme good, and in accordance with the belief in progress of their time, defined the kingdom of God as the highest moral ideal. It is man's duty to bring about its realisation. A. Ritschl argues similarly, *Instruction in the Christian Religion*, tr. by A. S. Swing in *The Theology of Albrecht Ritschl* (1901) paragraph 5 (pp. 174 f.) with special reference to the parables in Mk. iv. They "mean by the fruit always the product of man brought forth by his own individual efforts (!) which in their turn are called forth by the divine seed, i.e. the inspiration of the divine words of revelation". Logically, with such an interpretation, Christian doctrine became a cultural programme, and Christianity itself, as Richard Rothe had previously stated, a purely historical entity—a historical entity which, by means of a rational world culture informed by faith, was to dissolve itself into the life of the nations. The secularisation of the idea of the kingdom of God had thus been introduced and sanctioned even by theology. Since Christianity was now merely an element in the building up of a Christian-Western tradition, as, in fact, it is regarded to this day in the widest areas of "Christian" society, the time could be foreseen when, so to speak, the historical cables could be cut and Christian reminiscence could be thrown overboard. The dividing line, so tenaciously defended, between the bourgeois-Christian faith in progress and a secularised political doctrine of salvation, which determinedly abandons the ballast of religious tradition and replaces the idea of a kingdom of God by the idea of a classless society, then becomes purely fictitious. The flank is turned when the kingdom of God is made merely "a product of man, which is being brought forth by his own individual efforts". The first penetrating criticism

of the conception of the kingdom of God in Ritschl's theology was made by Joh. Weiss, *Die Predigt Jesu vom Reiche Gottes* (1892, 2nd ed. 1900).

18. Here too the interpretation of the parable (Mt. xiii. 36 ff.) is a later addition. This is shown (a) in the allegorisation of all individual features, (b) in the stock of ideas and words typical for Matthew, (c) the sacrifice of the real point of the parable—i.e. the admonition to be patient. Cf. the careful analysis in J. Jeremias, *The Parables of Jesus*, 64 ff.

19. Numerous Greek and Jewish instances in F. Hauck and G. Bertram, μακάριος, *Th.W.z.N.T.*, IV, 365 ff.; cf. e.g. the collection of beatitudes in Sir. 25, 7-10.

20. The traditional text in Mt. (v. 3 ff.) offers nine beatitudes, the last two of which are variations of each other; Lk. (vi. 20 ff.) offers four beatitudes and four woes.

21. Mt. v. 3 "poor in (their) spirit" reflects the true meaning of the Hebrew *anaw*. It prevents the misunderstanding that Jesus' beatitude is aimed at poverty itself.

22. Cf. M. Dibelius, *Der Brief des Jakobus* (1921), 37 ff.; E. Percy, *Die Botschaft Jesu* (1953), 45 ff.

23. In recent years E. Percy, *Die Botschaft Jesu*, has stated that "poor" always means a real case of need in the Biblical psalms and the later Jewish literature, and can never be identified directly with "pious" or "righteous". I certainly grant this. Yet suffering is considered to be a typical instance of that fate which gives to the righteous, on the ground of their obedience and humility, a claim to the promise given to the poor of future help and exaltation. Thus is explained the reference by the author of Psalm lxxxvi (1 f.) to his misery and at the same time to his confidence in God. From then on "poor" and "pious" can be used in a parallel sense (cf. Ps. cxxxii. 15 f.; Ps. Sol. x. 6), and poverty becomes a religious conception. This happened not only in the pursuance of the theodicy idea, but also through the very acute perception that in the time of increasing Hellenisation and sociological-economic changes the stigma of godlessness is attached to wealth, and that poverty is the fate of those who keep the law. There is a widespread belief that in Jesus' time there were in the Jewish nation certain circles of the *Anawim* (the poor), "the quiet in the land", who lived apart from Pharisaism and Zealotism, humbly keeping the law and waiting for the fulfilment of their eschatological hopes. Dibelius calls them Messianic pietists. It is said that Jesus comes from those circles. Cf. W. Sattler, "Die Anawim im Zeitalter Jesu Christi", *Festgabe für A. Jülicher* (1927), 1 ff.; M. Dibelius, *Jakobusbrief*, 39 ff.; E. Lohmeyer, *Galiläa und Jerusalem* (1936), 64 ff., 85; H. Lietzmann, *The Beginnings of the Christian Church*, tr. by Bertram Lee Woolf (reprint 1953), 38. This assumption, however, is unconfirmed. Cf. E. Percy, *Die Botschaft Jesu*, 68 ff.

24. In Matthew the beatitudes are no longer only a word of comfort to those who find themselves in need (Lk.), but a part of the catechism, explaining how the disciples are required to live ("A catalogue of Christian virtue", M. Dibelius, *Jesus*, 106).

25. The passive voice is used to speak indirectly of the name of God.

26. Cf. J. Jeremias, "Der Gedanke des 'Heiligen Restes' im Spätjudentum und in der Verkündigung Jesu", *Z.N.W.*, 42 (1949), 184 ff.

27. Only much later was the idea of a world mission accepted by the original Church, against opposition. Cf. G. Bornkamm, "Christus und die Welt in der urchristlichen Botschaft" in *Das Ende des Gesetzes (Paulusstudien)*, 1952, 157 ff. Cf. especially the most recent and important study by J. Jeremias, *Jesus' Promise to the Nations* (*Studies in Biblical Theology*, No. 24, tr. by S. H. Hooke, 1958).

28. See above, pp. 18 f.

29. προάγουσιν has exclusive, not temporal significance. Cf. J. Jeremias, *The Parables of Jesus*, 100, note 53, further elaborated in the 4th German ed. (*Die Gleichnisse Jesu*, 1956, 108, note 6).

30. Cf. Billerbeck, Vol. IV, 1154 ff.

31. Only the later Church has thus applied the picture of the (heavenly) bridegroom to Jesus, cf. J. Jeremias, *Th.W.z.N.T.*, IV, 1094 ff. Mt. xxii. 1 ff., as against Lk. xiv. 16 ff., shows how the great supper becomes an allegory of the wedding feast of the Messiah, which God prepares for his son. See above, pp. 18 f.

32. In Matthew the parable of the lost sheep is found in a different context (xviii. 12 ff.).

33. Cf. J. Behm, μετανοέω, μετάνοια *Th.W.z.N.T.*, IV, 972 ff.; especially E. K. Dietrich, *Die Umkehr (Bekehrung und Busse) im Alten Testament und im Judentum* (1936); E. Sjöberg, *Gott und die Sünder im palästineschen Judentum* (1938), 125 ff.; H. Braun, " 'Umkehr' in spätjüdisch-häretischer und frühchristlicher Sicht", *Z.Th.K.*, 50 (1953), 243 ff.

34. Joma VIII, 9; cf. also Aboth R. N. 40.

35. Cf. J. Jeremias, *The Parables of Jesus*, 145 ff.

36. Roughly £3½ million as against £7.

37. H. G. Wood, "Interpreting the Times", *Th.L.Z.*, 1955, 628 f. relates both to military events in the struggle of the Romans against rebels (mentioned earlier by R. Eisler). This, however, is not certain. In any case, the bloodbath of the Galileans can be connected with the procurator's proceedings against the Zealots. Josephus reports nothing of this occurrence. Professor Wood's essay is reprinted complete in *N.T.St.*, 2 (1956), 262 ff.

38. To be understood in this sense in Lk. xviii. 6.

39. Even Luke, as also many after him, found himself unable to deal with the parable, and interpreted the Lord in v. 8 to be the lord in the parable instead of Jesus, and only lets Jesus speak in his own words from v. 9 on. In the passage which follows, he adds in the briefest form, ad vocem habitations, the right use of Mammon, faithfulness in little things and in big things, in the true and the untrue, with the goods of others and with your own. This is a series of individual sayings used in allegorical fashion, which originally have nothing to do with the parable. For the analysis of this parable cf. J. Jeremias, *The Parables of Jesus*, 33 ff., 126 ff.

40. Jesus counted without any question on the imminent ending of the

world (W. G. Kümmel, *Promise and Fulfilment*, 19 ff., 54 ff.). It was left to the later Church to adjust itself to the delay in the parousia. They did this, however, without losing faith in their expectation. It is evident that they did not forget Jesus' warning to be wise and to be prepared, as the parable of the ten virgins shows, a parable which in my opinion does not go back to Jesus himself, but is strongly allegorical (Mt. xxv. 1 ff.). In my essay, "Die Verzögerung der Parusie", in the volume *In memoriam Ernst Lohmeyer* (1951), 119 ff., I have tried to show that it is hardly possible to find an earlier core of the text (as does J. Jeremias, *The Parables of Jesus*, 41 ff.). It is an essential part of the text that the wise virgins have deliberately prepared themselves for a long absence of the bridegroom, while the foolish ones counted on his coming in the near future, and had therefore not provided themselves with enough oil. Hence the point of the story is different from the one in the parable of the watchful servants (Mt. xxiv. 45 ff.), who are called wise just because they counted on the bridegroom's arrival in the near future. Luke has interfered most with the tradition of the Gospels, and has eradicated the conception of "nearness" in not a few passages. Cf. H. Conzelmann, *Die Mitte der Zeit* (1954, Eng. tr. 1960), 80 ff. With reference to the subject in general, cf. E. Grässer, *Das Problem der Parusie-Verzögerung in den synoptischen Evangelien und in der Apostelgeschichte* (1957).

41. It is quite clear here that Jesus' words have been transferred to the later Church: Lord, Lord is no longer only a polite form of address (like rabbi), but confession and address to the judge of the world. Those who stand before the Lord in this scene of the judgment of the world are Christian charismatics.

42. Concerning the history of the tradition, cf. R. Bultmann, *Gesch. d. synoptischen Trad.*, 124 f.

43. W. Bousset, *Jesu Predigt im Gegensatz zum Judentum* (1892), 63.

44. Cf. P. Feine, *Theologie des Neuen Testaments* (8th ed. 1950), 73.

45. P. Wernle, *Jesus* (1916), 237 f.

46. J. Weiss, *Die Predigt Jesu vom Reiche Gottes* (2nd ed. 1900), 100 f. For further literature see W. G. Kümmel, *Promise and Fulfilment*, 141 ff.

47. C. H. Dodd, *The Parables of the Kingdom*. Further information in W. G. Kümmel, *Promise and Fulfilment*, 16, note 3.

48. H. D. Wendland, *Die Eschatologie des Reiches Gottes bei Jesus* (1931), 45 f.

49. W. G. Kümmel, *Promise and Fulfilment*, 88 ff.

50. Concerning Mk. xiii, cf. W. G. Kümmel, *Promise and Fulfilment*, 95 ff. (earlier literature to be found there); cf. also G. Harder, "Das eschatologische Geschichtsbild der sogenannten Kleinen Apokalypse Markus 13", *Theologia Viatorum*, IV (1952), 71 ff.

51. Cf. M. Dibelius, *Jesus*, 71 ff.

Chapter V

1. As stated in M. Goguel, *The Life of Jesus*, 344, who here maintains a correspondence between Jesus' views and those of the Sadducees.

2. This holds good despite one isolated saying of a rabbi (R. Simeon, circa

A.D. 180), who defines with similar words the Sabbath as a blessing and a gift to man. Cf. Billerbeck, II, 5.

3. Cf. merely the cleansing rites (Lev. xi-xv) and the rites of the great feast of the atonement (Lev. xvi). For details cf. W. Eichrodt, *Theologie des Alten Testaments*, I (1933), 60 ff.; F. Hauck, *Th.W.z.N.T.*, III, 419 ff.; and regarding Judaism: R. Meyer, *Th.W.z.N.T.*, III, 421 ff.

4. *Z.Th.K.*, 51 (1954), 146.

5. In comparing the New Testament passages on divorce, it can be seen that the early Church abandoned Jesus' rigorous point of view in extreme cases. Matthew shows this for the Jewish Christian congregation, and Paul for the Hellenistic. The latter permits divorce in the case of a mixed marriage, where one partner is Christian and the other heathen, but only if demanded by the heathen partner (I Cor. vii. 10 ff.). He leaves, however, no doubt as to the Lord's uncompromising view on the matter (v. 10). He shows thereby that God's own will must not be modified, little though Paul insists on its observance in an extreme, particular case. Cf. G. Bornkamm, "Die Stellung des neuen Testaments zur Ehescheidung", *Ev. Theol.*, 1948, 283 ff. Mark and Paul, incidentally, have transferred Jesus' words from Jewish to Greek-Roman legal conditions. Here not only the husband but also the wife is entitled to a divorce.

6. Cf. E. Käsemann, *Z.Th.K.*, 51 (1954), 148 ff.

7. Matthew alone offers 30 examples (Mt. v. 18, 26; vi. 2, 5, 16, etc.).

8. Ch. V, section 2, is the substance of my essay, "Die Gegenwartsbedeutung der Bergpredigt" (*Universitas*, 9, 1954, 1283 ff.). Regarding the history of the exposition of the Sermon on the Mount, cf. Appendix II (see below, pp. 221 ff.).

9. Cf. E. Thier, *Einführung zu K. Marx, Nationalökonomie und Philosophie* (1950); K. Löwith, *Meaning in History* (1949, reprint 1957), 44; *Marxismus-Studien* (*Schriftenreihe der Studiengemeinschaft der Evangel. Akademien*), 1954; see there especially H. D. Wendland, "Christliche und kommunistische Hoffnung", 214 ff.

10. The conception of "alienation" in Marx must come directly from Schelling, and hence indirectly from gnosticism.

11. Read the conversation between Ivanoff and Rubaschow in the second trial in A. Koestler, *Sonnenfinsternis*.

12. See pp. 223 f.

13. Even the "fulfilment" does not refer to Christ's representative obedience, but to Jesus' teaching, which brings out the full meaning of the law and the prophets. Only in this way does v. 19 make sense in this connection. Pauline ideas (as Rom. viii. 3 ff.) may not be transferred without further examination into the Gospel of Matthew.

14. Here, as so often elsewhere, the exegete can only render a passage, after reflection, in his own words. Mere quotation of the text does not suffice. Of course the text itself does not mention this reflection, but it calls for it by the interweaving of beatitudes and demands. The thesis of the "hidden eschatology" in the Sermon on the Mount is directed particularly against the opinions of J. Weiss and A. Schweitzer, who saw the ethic of the Sermon on the Mount as an "interim

ethic" (Schweitzer), i.e. as the exceptional emergency laws for the "last period",
i.e. the time immediately preceding the imminent end of the world.

15. Cf. M. Dibelius, *The Sermon on the Mount* (1940), 101 f.

16. Cf. M. Dibelius, *The Sermon on the Mount*, 104 ff., esp. 137 ff.; also
Dibelius, "Das soziale Motiv im Neuen Testament", *Botschaft und Geschichte*, I,
178 ff.

17. The text is quoted according to Matthew. Each of the first three evangelists
has handed down his interpretation of the passage, with the result that they differ
not inconsiderably from each other. Cf. G. Bornkamm, "Das Dopplegebot der
Liebe", in *Neutestamentliche Studien für R. Bultmann* (1954), 85 ff.

18. Cf. E. Stauffer, Article ἀγαπάω, *Th.W.z.N.T.*, I, 38 ff.

19. S. Kierkegaard, *Leben und Walten der Liebe* (translated by Schrempf), 85.

20. S. Kierkegaard, *Leben und Walten der Liebe*, 19f.

21. At this point Matthew lets Jesus by way of explanation tell the parable of
the wicked servant (see pp. 85 f.). How much his composition is at the same
time interpretation becomes evident in that he places this particular parable after,
and the parable of the lost sheep (which occurs in Luke in a different order,
Ch. xv. 1 ff.), before, the passage in which he treats the question of the right
discipline for the congregation!

22. U. v. Wilamowitz-Möllendorf, *Platon*, I (1919), 384.

23. Cf. A. Nygren, *Agape and Eros*, tr. by Philip S. Watson (1953).

24. The strange story of the cursing of the fig-tree, Mk. xi. 12 ff., 20 ff., is
thought to be originally a parable which has only become a miraculous punishment
in the tradition. Cf. E. Klostermann, *Markus*, 116 f.

25. In Mt. v. 25 f., primitive laws of the Orient are presupposed: the adversaries go together to the Kadi. It is different from our custom, where two quarrelling parties never exchange another word until the day they meet in the court of
justice. Jesus' words are originally an illustration reminding people to think in
time of the end, the day of judgment (cf. Lk. xii. 58 f.).

26. We prefer to remember the verses by M. Claudius in his splendid
Christmas-Cantilene: God is for ever God in all his ways / and does not deal with
man according to his station or his title. / Herod and his armies are passed over /
but the shepherds in the fields by their flocks / are the chosen ones—Instead of
Herod we may safely say Augustus and Tiberius.

27. Formulated according to Hans von Campenhausen, "Die Kirche und der
Staat nach den Aussagen des Neuen Testaments" in *Die Autorität der Bibel heute*
(1951), 341.

28. Cf. E. Stauffer, *Christ and the Caesars*, tr. by K. and R. Gregor Smith
(1955), 127 ff., and on the other hand, M. Dibelius, "Rom und die Christen im
ersten Jahrhundert" in *Botschaft und Geschichte*, II, 177, note 2; H. v. Campenhausen, "Die Kirche und der Staat nach den Aussagen des Neuen Testaments" in
Die Autorität der Bibel heute (1951), 341 f.

29. Stauffer, *Christ and the Caesars*, 134.

30. Cf. A. Schweitzer, *The Mysticism of Paul the Apostle*, tr. by William Montgomery (2nd printing 1956), 314; M. Dibelius, "Rom und die Christen in ersten Jahrhundert" in *Botschaft und Geschichte*, II, 178.

31. I owe this explanation of Mk. xii. 17 to a letter from Professor W. Eltester of Tübingen. He points out to me that it has recently made its appearance in English literature. Cf. D. Cairns, *The Image of God in Man*, London (1953), 30. Mention is made there also of Dorothy Sayers, *The Man Born to be King*, 225, and of Tertullian, *De idololatria*, 15 (I 47, 25). The parallelism of τὰ τοῦ καίσαρος and τὰ τοῦ θεοῦ would support this explanation. Incidentally, as I have noticed later, the same interpretation can be found in M. Claudius, *Zweiter Brief an Andres*. I thank Professor G. Wehrung for the further reference to Jul. Lütgart, *Natur und Geist Gottes* (1910), p. 21, and especially to the *Sachsenspiegel*, Book III, Art. 42, § 5; Eike von Repgow concludes from this interpretation that slavery results from wrongful power.

32. "The eschatological proclamation of the coming kingdom of God remains here, as in most passages, in the background." M. Dibelius, "Rom und die Christen im ersten Jahrhundert", *Botschaft und Geschichte*, II, 178.

33. No more can it claim for itself the word of the Johannine Jesus before Pilate: "My kingship is not of this world" (Jn. xviii. 36). Certainly his kingship has a different source and is of a different nature from earthly power. But although it is not *of* this world, it is set up *in* this world, in the testimony to the truth, and may very profoundly affect those who exceed their political power in a most irksome and unpleasant way, whether they like it or not, and whatever their attitude to this challenge of truth may be. Pilate too is called outside the safe world of politics, which is satisfied with its own laws, and challenged. And because he does not meet this challenge, he falls a prey to the hither and thither, the ups and downs of political considerations, and becomes hopelessly enslaved by its implications, fears and calculations. He falls a prey to dangerous political dealings regardless of the truth. He now alternates between fear and arrogance; between fear of the raging of the Jews and the fear of the emperor, to whom they could denounce him, and, on the other hand, the arrogance which makes him think *he* could offer Jesus his life. Even at the point, however, where the sovereignty of the state rejects the challenge of truth, as it clearly did in Pilate's case in the story of the Passion, that sovereignty does not become questionable either for Jesus or for the Church.

34. Translation in F. C. Grant, *Hellenistic Religions. The Age of Syncretism* (1953), 152 ff.

35. *Dissertationes*, I, 9, 6 f.

36. Acts xiii. 33; Heb. i. 5; v. 5; vii. 28 (Cf. Mk. i. 11).

37. E.g. in Prokofieff's ballet, The Prodigal Son. Typically enough, life in the foreign country with its feasting and its revels is rendered in the most vivid colours. In contrast, the scene of the return home with the entrance and dance of the "virtues" is dull and lifeless.

38. Compare Mk. i. 15 and Mt. iv. 17; Mk. ix. 42 and Mt. xviii. 6; Lk. viii. 13 and Mk. iv. 17.

39. Jesus' word: "I will come and heal him" (Mt. viii. 7) can also be understood to be an astonished question: "I—come and help him?" The meaning of the captain's answer changes according to the meaning of what Jesus says. It can either be deprecatory, "I, the heathen, am not worthy to receive you into my house." Or, confirming Jesus' surprise, "You are right, but there is no need for it."

40. These are the nature miracles: (1) The calming of the storm (Mk. iv. 35 ff.); (2) The walking on the waves (Mk. vi. 45 ff.); (3) The feeding of the 5,000 (or the 4,000) in the desert (Mk. vi. 31 ff.); (4) The raising from the dead (Mk. v. 21 ff.; Lk. vii. 11 ff.; Jn. xi. 1 ff.). Leaving out the parallels in non-biblical, profane literature, of which there are not a few, one should notice here especially the Old Testament analogies and themes. Regarding (1) cf. Ps. lxv. 7, "Who dost still the roaring of the seas, the roaring of their waves, and the tumult of the peoples." Regarding (2): Job ix. 8: "Which trampled the waves of the sea" (cf. xxxviii. 16); regarding (3) the story of the supply of manna to the people of Israel in the desert (Ex. xvi. 4, 13-15; Ps. lxxviii. 24; xxii. 27); regarding (4) I Kings xvii. 17 ff.; II Kings iv. 8, 17 ff. It is no mere chance that precisely these miracles are often understood in the tradition as transparent events which tell more than a miraculous episode which happened only once. This is true especially in John. The story of the feeding is the setting for the sayings about the bread of life, which Jesus not only *gives*, but *is* (vi. 1 ff.; 26 ff.). It also becomes clear in the way in which Matthew (viii. 23 ff.) understands the story of the calming of the storm to be a symbol for discipleship (see above pp. 151 f.), and the way he enriches the story of the walking on the waves by the scene of the sinking Peter (Mt. xiv. 28 ff.), again a symbol of faith on trial. From the very beginning, the story of Peter's miraculous catch of fish (Lk. v. 1 ff.), and the miracle at the marriage of Cana (Jn. ii. 1 ff.), have this transparent sense.

41. Jesus certainly does not speak of his own faith here (cf. J. Schniewind, *Markus*, regarding this passage). Characteristically, the New Testament speaks of it only very seldom. Rather his word emphasises the father's inability to believe.

42. This word should not without further ado be taken to mean "the divine food" in the sense of Jn. iv. 34.

43. Note that all the passages quoted here arise out of the context of the first commandment (Deut. vi. 4 ff.).

44. Horace, Carm., I, 2.

45. Instances in F. Heiler, *Das Gebet* (5th ed. 1923), 211 (omitted in abbreviated English edition).

46. There is no need to contest this as does J. Jeremias, *The Parables of Jesus,* 115 ff.

47. Cf. H. Greeven, "Wer unter euch . . . ?", *Wort und Dienst (Jahrbuch d. Theol. Schule Bethel,* 1952).

48. Much the same applies to the words of institution of the Lord's Supper.

49. Regarding the following, cf. K. G. Kuhn, *Achtzehngebet und Vaterunser und der Reim* (1950). In the older literature G. Dalman, *Worte Jesu* (2nd ed. 1930), 283 ff. (lacking in the English translation of the 1st ed.).

50. The much discussed and not precisely defined word ἐπιούσιος in the

fourth petition is best understood as an expression for a frugal portion, and therefore in the meaning of the King James translation: our daily bread.

51. Cf. E. Lohmeyer, *Das Vater-Unser* (1946), 40.

52. J. A. Bengel, *Gnomon*, to Mt. vi. 13.

53. Concerning the following, cf. G. Bornkamm, "Der Lohngedanke im Neuen Testament", *Ev. Theol.*, 1946, 143 ff.

54. Cf. J. Jeremias, *The Parables of Jesus*, 135 f.

Chapter VI

1. Concerning the following, cf. G. Kittel, ἀκολουθεῖν, *Th.W.z.N.T.*, I, 210 ff.; H. H. Rengstorf, μαθητής, *Th.W.z.N.T.*, IV, 417 ff.

2. In Lk. v. 1 ff. the calling of Peter is associated with the legend of Peter's miraculous catch, a legend to which the saying about catching men may have given rise. The catch of fish is to be understood as a symbol of future events. Cf. Bultmann, *Geschichte d. syn. Trad.*, 232.

3. Cf. A. Schlatter, *Der Evangelist Matthäus* (1929), 118 f., 302; R. Bultmann, *Gesch. d. syn. Trad.*, 26 f.

4. Cf. E. Schweizer, *Lordship and Discipleship*, 13.

5. πύργος may be a tower or farm buildings. The latter perhaps applies in Lk. xiv. 28, Walter Bauer's *Greek-English Lexicon of the New Testament*, tr. by W. F. Arndt and F. W. Gingrich, p. 738.

6. The mysterious word Mt. xix. 12 seems to speak of those who renounce marriage for the sake of the kingdom of God. Cf. H. v. Campenhausen, *Die Askese im Urchristentum* (1949), 27 ff.

7. Cf. M. Dibelius, *Jesus*, 58 ff.

8. There is a divergence between Mk. ix. 40 and the "Q" version of the saying (Mt. xii. 30). We find both versions of the saying in Lk. (Lk. ix. 50; xi. 23). If the negative version ("He who is not with me is against me, and he who does not gather with me scatters") demands the unconditional decision for Jesus, then the positive version rebukes the censorious spirit in the disciples who have made of this discipleship their own personal privilege.

9. Cf. the study of H. v. Campenhausen, *Die Askese im Urchristentum* (1949).

10. Cf. H. v. Campenhausen, *Die Askese im Urchristentum*, 5 ff.

11. Cf. J. Schniewind to Mk. i. 17.

12. Bultmann, *Gesch. d. syn. Trad.*, 171; *Theology*, I, 37.

13. Mt. xix. 28; Lk. xxii. 30 grants to the disciples the office of rulers (to judge = to rule) over the twelve tribes of Israel for the period "when the Son of Man is seated on the throne of His glory" (Mt. xix. 28). Both versions of the passage, different in themselves, can be understood, as in Bultmann, *Gesch. d. syn. Trad.*, 170 f., to be the words of the risen Christ and to reflect the expectation of the primitive Church. This, however, does not eliminate the fact that the twelve were appointed by Jesus. The fact that Mt. xix. 28 does not go back to Jesus is clearly

shown in Matthew by the use of the unusual term παλιγγενεσία, which cannot be translated back into the Aramaic, as well as by the expression "in my kingdom" in Luke. Kümmel, however, differs from this in his *Promise and Fulfilment*, 41.

14. Cf. O. Cullmann, *Peter: Disciple, Apostle, Martyr* (tr. by Floyd V. Filson, 1953); and Cullmann, *Th.W.z.N.T.*, VI, 99 ff.

15. E.g. he omits Jesus' reprimand after Peter's confession, as well as the note about the flight of the disciples at Jesus' arrest. They are also shown to greater advantage in the Gethsemane scene than in the other Gospels, cf. also Lk. xxii. 28, 31 f.

16. Cf. G. Bornkamm, "Die Sturmstillung im Matthaus-Evangelium", *Überlieferung und Auslegung im Matthäus-Evangelium*, 1960, 48 ff.

Chapter VII

1. The latter is supported by H. Lietzmann in *The Beginnings of the Christian Church*, 57.

2. The reconstruction of the passage, which has been changed into a prophecy of suffering and Easter, is contested. I follow J. Wellhausen, *Lukas*, 75 f.; H. Lietzmann, *The Beginnings of the Christian Church*, 57, and M. Goguel, *The Life of Jesus*, 349 f. Cf. also R. Bultmann, *Gesch. d. syn. Trad.*, 35.

3. And this summary only begins when Jesus is delivered to the high priests and the scribes, and not at the point of his entry (into Jerusalem), the planning of his death, the anointing in Bethany, the last supper and Gethsemane; cf. R. Bultmann, *Gesch. d. syn. Trad.*, 297 ff. J. Jeremias, *The Eucharistic Words of Jesus* (1955), 66 ff. Furthermore, the Johannine passion narrative (xviii. 1 ff.) begins only at this point to run parallel to the synoptics. The tendency of the tradition to cause Jesus to speak as early and frequently as possible of his death and resurrection is evident. Cf. already Mk. ii. 19 f., Mt. xii. 40, etc. According to Lk. iv. 24, the theme of his rejection occurs already in Jesus' first sermon in Nazareth. Cf. also Jn. ii. 4: "My hour (i.e. the hour of his death) has not yet come"; and further, ii. 18 ff.; iii. 14 ff., etc.

4. Cf. M. Dibelius, *Jesus*, 62.

5. Zech. xi. 13 is behind the story of Judas' end (Mt. xxvii. 3 ff.); in Acts i. 18, it is told in a quite different manner.

6. Cf. M. Dibelius, *From Tradition to Gospel*, 178 ff.; also Dibelius, *Botschaft und Geschichte*, I (1953), 221 ff.; Bultmann, *Gesch. d. syn. Trad.*, 303 ff. (refers to older literature); K. H. Schelkle, *Die Passion Jesu* (1949), 81 ff.

7. John has placed it in line with his own plan at the beginning of the story of Jesus (ii. 13 ff.).

8. John has woven the demand for a sign even into the story of the cleansing of the temple itself (ii. 18 ff.).

9. Thus, the parable of the Great Supper (Mt. xxii. 1 ff.) is found in Luke as early as Lk. xiv. 16 ff.; the discussion about the greatest commandment (Mk. xii. 28 ff.) already in Lk. x. 25 ff., the speech against the Pharisees (Mk. xii. 37 ff.)

already in Lk. xi. 37 ff., and the story of the anointing (Mk. xiv. 3 ff.) already in Lk. vii. 36 ff.

10. We shall not enlarge here upon the many attempts made to harmonise.

11. The text in Luke (xxii. 15-18), which differs not inconsiderably in its wording, and which makes the eschatological saying, which is given twice, precede the actual words of institution, is probably secondary. He historicises, by expressly inserting Jesus' words and actions in the framework of the Passover, through the use of a prophecy of suffering. Elsewhere, too, in Luke's version we are faced with problems regarding the history of its text and tradition, which we do not need to examine here.

12. "The many" (also without article) has in Hebrew and Aramaic an inclusive significance (= all). Cf. J. Jeremias, *The Eucharistic Words of Jesus*, 123 ff.

13. Also the eucharistic words in Jn. vi. 53 ff., which are inserted in Jesus' discourse on the bread of life, mention the feeding by manna, not the Passover, which John, however, understands differently from Paul, to stand in definite contrast to the Lord's Supper.

14. Luke has embellished this scene in the style of the martyr literature. Cf. M. Dibelius, "Gethsemane", *The Crozer Quarterly*, XII (1935), 254 ff.

15. According to Matthew it is Peter who intervenes. According to Luke it is Jesus who heals the wounded; John even gives the name of the servant.

16. In Matthew (xxvi. 47 ff.) the scene has been further enlarged (cf. also Jn. xviii. 1 ff.).

17. Cf. G. Hölscher, *Sanhedrin und Makkot (ausgewählte Mischnatraktate 6)*, 1910, 33 ff.; Billerbeck, I, 1020 ff.; H. Lietzmann, "Der Prozess Jesu" (*Sitzungsberichte der Berliner Akademie*, 1931, XIV); the historicity of the scene before the Sanhedrin is defended by Joseph Blinzler, *Der Prozess Jesu* (1951), esp. 143 ff., 149 ff. Also regarding this question see above note II, 9.

18. Cf. Mk. xv. 29; Jn. ii. 19; Acts vi. 14.

19. The tendency to political apologetic is strongest with Luke; here the accusation of the Jews is openly branded as a lie (xxiii. 2 refers back to xx. 20 ff.), the Jews are the real rebels (xxiii. 18 f.). Pilate, however, definitely declares that Jesus' claim to be the Messiah is not a political crime (xxiii. 3 f.), and declares Jesus' innocence three times (xxiii. 22). Neither does he sentence Jesus, but "delivers" him to the will of the Jews. *They* bring Jesus to the cross. This explains the alteration of the mocking of Jesus by Roman soldiers into a corresponding scene at the court of Herod. Cf. H. Conzelmann, *Die Mitte der Zeit* (1954, Eng. tr. 1960), 117 ff. In John we have the most splendid description of the Pilate scene (xviii. 28.–xix. 16). Concerning this, cf. R. Bultmann, *Das Evangelium des Johannes* (1941), 501 ff.; H. Schlier, *Die Zeit der Kirche* (1956), 56 ff.

20. Mk. xiv. 71 should not be translated according to Luther: "But he began to curse *himself* and to swear." The Greek verb is equivalent to the Hebrew heherim, i.e. to pronounce a ban on another person. This is confirmed by the expression "I do not know this man", a formula of excommunication known in the synagogue (Billerbeck, I, 469). Cf. here also Mt. vii. 23; xxv. 12. The terrible

crescendo of Peter's threefold denial consists, not in any cursing of himself, but in a cursing of Jesus.

21. It is most probable that the Roman procurator in Jerusalem had his seat by what we call today the Jaffa gate, according to Josephus, *Bellum Judaicum*, II, 14, 8 (301). The popular belief which is also supported by others today, that Jesus was condemned to death in the castle Antonia, north of the temple, can be traced back to *c.* 1200. This belief also places the beginning of the Via dolorosa here (by the castle).

22. This word is missing in some of the old manuscripts.

23. Matthew adds one special cosmic-apocalyptic miracle: the opening of the graves and the appearance of the dead in the holy city. To understand these verses, which already quite early were interpreted as Christ's descent into Hades, cf. H. Riesenfeld, *The Resurrection in Ezekiel XXXVII and in the Dura-Europos Paintings* (1948), 35 ff.

24. Bengel, *Gnomon* to Rom, 6, 3.

Chapter VIII

1. In Matthew and Luke this saying appears in different form: they speak of the forgivable blasphemy of the Son of man and the unforgivable blasphemy of the Holy Spirit (Mt. xii. 31 f.; Lk. xii. 10). This changed form may have been based on a version which gave the singular "son of man" instead of "sons of man". This was then misunderstood as a Messianic title of Jesus, and the conception of a pardonable blasphemy of the "Son of man" added. (This is supported by J. Wellhausen, *Matthäus*, 63; *Einleitung*, 66 f.; and Bultmann, *Gesch. d. syn. Trad.*, 138.) The meaning of the saying has thus been considerably changed. Mark speaks of the blasphemy of the Spirit of God, whose power is at work *now* in Jesus' deeds. Matthew and Luke have added a Christological thought, characteristic for the later period: "Son of man" is here Jesus in his still hidden, humble form of the Messiah. Only after his resurrection and ascension is that spirit revealed against whom any blasphemy is unforgivable. The "Spirit", therefore, in both versions of the saying, refers to different periods of the revelation. Cf. to Mk. iii. 28 f., also C. K. Barrett, *The Holy Spirit and the Gospel Tradition* (1947), 103 ff., who applies the blasphemy of the "Spirit" in Matthew and Luke to the sin of deserting their faith committed by baptised members of the church, in contrast to the blasphemy against the Son of man committed by the heathens *before* their baptism.

2. W. Wrede has shown this in an exemplary fashion in *Das Messiasgeheimnis in den Evangelien* (1901, 2nd ed. 1913). Cf. also M. Dibelius, *From Tradition to Gospel*, 229 f.; Bultmann, *Gesch. d. syn. Trad.*, 370 ff.

3. E.g. Mk. v. 43; vii. 36; viii. 26; cf. Wrede, *Das Messiasgeheimnis in den Evangelien*, 33 ff.; Dibelius, *From Tradition to Gospel*, 80 f.

4. Dibelius, *From Tradition to Gospel*, 230.

5. The same in Wrede, Bultmann.

6. Regarding Mk. xiv. 53 ff.; cf. pp. 163 f.; regarding Mt. xvi. 17 ff.; cf. pp. 187 f.

7. M. Dibelius, *Jesus*, 95 f., similarly E. Percy, E. Schweizer, etc.

8. Thus with Dibelius, *Jesus*, 97, 102.

Chapter IX

1. Cf. Mk. xvi; Mt. xxviii; Lk. xxiv; Jn. xx. f. Regarding the following cf. H. v. Campenhausen, "Der Ablauf der Osterereignisse und das leere Grab", *Sitzungsberichte der Heidelberger Akademie d. Wiss., philosophisch-historische Klasse* (1952), 4.

2. E. Stauffer, "Zur Vor- und Frühgeschichte des Primatus Petri", *Z.K.G.*, 62 (1943-44), 11 ff.; O. Cullmann, *Peter* (1953), 59 f., advocate the quite possible hypothesis, that the original conclusion of Mark's Gospel was lost, and with it the story of the appearance to Peter related in it. Lk. v. 1 ff.; Jn. xxi. 15 ff. may reflect Peter's first meeting with the risen Lord. Cf. v. Campenhausen, "Der Ablauf der Osterereignisse und das leere Grab", *Sitzungsberichte der Heidelberger Akademie d. Wiss., philosophisch-historische Klasse* (1952), 14 f.; Bultmann, *Gesch. d. syn. Trad.*, 275 ff. assumes also the story of Peter's confession to be originally an Easter story which was projected back into the life of Jesus.

3. There are some indications that the disciples returned to Jerusalem at Pentecost, cf. G. Kretzschmar, "Himmelfahrt und Pfingsten", *Z.K.G.*, 66 (1954-55), 209 ff., esp. 252 f.

4. Mk. xiv. 28 is missing in Luke; Mk. xvi. 7 is changed in Lk. xxiv. 6. Behind this we see a fixed conception of history in which Jerusalem occupies a special place. Cf. H. Conzelmann, *Die Mitte der Zeit* (1954, Eng. tr. 1960), 113 ff.

5. In my opinion H. v. Campenhausen, "Der Ablauf der Osterereignisse und das leere Grab", *Sitzungsberichte der Heidelberger Akademie d. Wiss., philosophisch-historische Klasse* (1952), 24 f., 34 f., is wrong in contesting this interpretation. I also consider his attempt to establish a historical kernel of the story, to which he also attributes "up to a certain degree" a legendary character (p. 37), not very successful.

6. Thus in the Gospel of Peter, viii f. But Matthew too introduces the keepers of the sepulchre as witnesses (xxviii. 11 ff.). Cf. v. Campenhausen, "Der Ablauf der Osterereignisse und das leere Grab", *Sitzungsberichte der Heidelberger Akademie d. Wiss., philosophisch-historische Klasse* (1952), 26 ff.

7. Cf. Jn. iii. 14; xii. 32, 34; Acts ii. 33; v. 30 f.; Phil. ii. 9; Heb. i. 3-13; viii. 1, etc. Cf. Bultmann, *Theology*, I, 45, 82.

8. From the innumerable commentaries on Mt. xvi. 17-19, may I only mention among the more recent ones A. Oepke, "Der Herrnspruch über die Kirche Mt. xvi. 17-19 in der neuesten Forschung", *Studia Theologica*, Lund (1948-50), 110 ff.; O. Cullmann, *Peter* (1953), 158 ff. (We find here also a detailed history of the exegesis of the passage.) Both Oepke and Cullmann support along with others the historical authenticity of the saying. On the other hand, H. v. Campenhausen in *Kirchliches Amt und geistliche Vollmacht* (1953), 140 f., says "In spite of recent attempts to maintain this, it should not be doubted that Jesus' statement as to the founding of the church upon Peter is unthinkable." Cf. also R. Bultmann, "Die Frage der Echtheit von Mt. xvi. 17-19", *Theol. Blätter*, 20 (1941), 265 ff.;

W. G. Kümmel, *Kirchenbegriff und Geschichtsbewusstsein in der Urgemeinde und bei Jesus* (*Symbolae Biblicae Upsaliensis I*, 1943), 32 ff.; H. Strathmann, "Die Stellung des Petrus in der Urkirche", *Zeitschrift für System. Theologie*, 20 (1943), 223 ff.

9. All the verbs have a future implication. One can hardly interpret δώσω with Jeremias, *Th.W.z.N.T.*, III, 749, in a "volitional" way. W. G. Kümmel, *Kirchenbegriff und Geschichtsbewusstsein in der Urgemeinde und bei Jesus* (*Symbolae Biblicae Upsaliensis I*, 1943), 52, note 74, correctly rejects such an interpretation.

10. The Aramaic gives in both instances Kephā. The play of words can still be brought out in the Greek (πέτρα "rock" and Πέτρος). We cannot be so sure that the naming definitely goes back to the earthly Jesus, though this is often maintained. As the meaning of the name surely has in view the conception of the church expressed in Mt. xvi. 18, I am inclined to believe that Peter was given his name by the risen Lord. The tradition varies as to the occasion of the naming: Mk. iii. 16, at the calling of the twelve; Jn. i. 42, at the first meeting; Mt. xvi. 18, at Peter's confession (Jesus uses this second name nowhere else in addressing Peter).

11. This fact, for example, does not receive enough attention from Oepke and Cullmann, as they only operate with the idea of the people of God.

12. Cf. here especially the research of Strathmann. In the interpretation of the saying on Peter and the Ekklesia, Roman Catholic and Protestant theology are nearer each other than they have been for some time (the "rock" means neither Christ—as stated already by Augustine, whose opinion Luther followed—nor Peter's faith or his preaching office, as the reformers thought, but Peter himself, as leader of the church). The two theologies differ, of course, in the opinion of the authenticity of the saying, but they are especially opposed to each other as to whether it is right to transfer the authority given to Peter to the bishop of Rome (this interpretation appears for the first time about 200, but is not regularly claimed by the popes for themselves until the early middle ages). Cf. Cullmann, *Peter*, 158 ff., 213 ff.

13. Cf. W. Bousset, *Kyrios Christos* (2nd ed. 1921); W. Staerk, *Soter*, I (1933); R. Bultmann, *Theology*, I, 42 ff., 121 ff.; E. Stauffer, *New Testament Theology*, 233 ff.; O. Cullmann, *The Earliest Christian Confessions* (tr. by J. K. S. Reid, 1949); V. Taylor, *The Names of Jesus* (1954); E. Schweizer, *Lordship and Discipleship*, 43 ff.

14. Cf. O. Cullmann, *The Earliest Christian Confessions*, 18ff.

15. Some theologians (Bousset, Bultmann) think that the title Kyrios first originated in Hellenistic Christianity. This opinion, however, raises serious doubts. Cf. most recently E. Schweizer, *Lordship and Discipleship*, 56 ff.

Appendix I

INTRODUCTION TO THE HISTORY AND SOURCES OF THE SYNOPTIC GOSPELS

Our presentation is based on the first three Gospels, which in research bear the name "the Synoptics", because their records run parallel to each other and agree to such a degree that it is possible, for easier comparison, to put their texts together in a "synopsis" (synopsis = seeing together). For reasons mentioned earlier (page 14), we have not brought in John as an independent source, but only occasionally to make a point clear. It is true that the fourth Gospel contains historical reports, the value of which must be examined individually, but Jesus' word and history are here so strongly interwoven with the vision of the risen and glorified Lord that it would be wiser not to base our exposition on this Gospel in the same way as on the others. Also as far as its age is concerned, John's Gospel is the latest, written about A.D. 100, while Mark must have been written about A.D. 70 and the other two soon after, in the period, say, between A.D. 75 to 95.

The beginnings of the tradition about Jesus are largely obscure for us. To study its history, we have to turn first of all to the synoptics. Here we are given the chance of gaining access, at least with some certainty, not only to the literary sources behind them, but also to penetrate further into the period of oral and pre-literary tradition. Careful research regarding the question of the sources of the first three Gospels has led to a first and important result which today is recognised by most scholars, the so-called "two-document hypothesis". This states (1) that Mark is the oldest Gospel, and that it has been woven by the two others—although in their characteristically different ways—into the composition of their Gospels, and (2) that Matthew and Luke used, apart from Mark (to be called M in the following), yet a second common source which because of its contents is customarily called—especially in German research—the discourse source, the logia source, the sayings source (Q). This hypothesis in fact best explains the facts: (1) almost the whole of Mark's Gospel can be found again in the two others, (2) basically the order of events in them, in spite of much regrouping of individual items, is the same as in M, and (3) the wording of the Gospels agrees to such an extent that we are justified in maintaining the priority of the Second Gospel as well as the literary dependence of the two others upon it. In contrast to M, we do not possess Q in its literary form, but rather have to deduce it from the tradition common to Matthew and Luke. Only on the assumption of this second source can the agreements be satisfactorily explained, as neither Gospel appears to know or use the other.

Quite apart from M and Q, Matthew and Luke provide special and important material of their own (e.g. numerous parables from Mt. xiii; xx. 1 ff.; xxv. 31 ff.; Lk. x. 29 ff.; xv. 11 ff., xvi. 1 ff., 19 ff.; also the infancy narratives Mt. i-ii; Lk i-ii, and the Easter stories, except for the story of the finding of the empty tomb which comes from M). On account of this special material found in Matthew and Luke which cannot be ascribed either to M or Q, English scholars, especially, have assumed the existence of further sources, and have extended the "two document hypothesis" to a "four document hypothesis" (cf. B. H. Streeter, The Four Gospels, 1924). This, however, remains an assumption which is contradicted by the widely varying character of this special material from the point of view of the history of the tradition.

In the two sources, M and Q, we are faced with a host of new questions which no longer can be answered with certainty. This applies already to Mark. The fact that (1) even the text of Mark, as we know it, contains a small amount of special material (e.g. Mk. iv. 26 ff.), (2) in certain cases only one of the two others follows Mark (e.g. Mk. vi. 17 ff. = Mt. xiv. 3 ff., also the entire passage Mk. vi. 45–viii. 26 is missing in Lk.; on the other hand, we find only in Lk. a parallel to Mk. ix. 38 ff.; xii. 41 ff.); and finally (3) certain pericopae like Mk. xii. 28 ff.; Mt. xxii. 34 ff.; Lk. x. 25 ff. differ considerably from each other in all three Gospels, suggests with a considerable degree of probability that Matthew and Luke used another version of Mark's Gospel, which differs here and there from the one known to us. The attempt, however, to reconstruct the original Mark is a hopeless endeavour. Yet the observations mentioned show that M, both before and after its appropriation by Matthew and Luke, suffered additions and changes in certain particulars. The additions and changes were, however, so insignificant that on this ground the "two document hypothesis" could not be shaken.

The problems which face us in Q are more difficult to answer. It is certain that this source, in contrast to M, contains predominantly sayings material. It contains, however, some stories also (e.g. Mt. iv. 1 ff. = Lk. iv. 1 ff.; Mt. viii. 5 ff. = Lk. vii. 1 ff.). Q, however, cannot be regarded as a Gospel complete in itself. To be such it would require at least a continuous Passion and Easter story. Of this, however, we find no trace at all. (Cf. N. A. Dahl, "Die Passionsgeschichte bei Matthäus", *N.T.St.*, 2, 1955, 17 ff.) Moreover, it is impossible to imagine Q without a certain order, determined above all in respect of its themes—an order which made possible the use of this collection in the Church, particularly for teaching purposes. Its form, however, was still so fluid that Matthew and Luke could exercise a far greater degree of freedom in the arrangement of this source within their Gospels than in the case of M (short summary of passages attributed to Q in E. Klostermann, *R.G.G.*, 2nd ed., II, 426). From the differences, in some respects considerable, in the rendering by Matthew and Luke of the tradition which can be traced back to Q, we may conclude that the two evangelists had before them two different versions of the collection of sayings (cf. e.g. Mt. v. 3 ff. and Lk. vi. 20 ff. [see also note 20 to Chapter IV]; cf. also the varying texts of the Lord's Prayer, Mt. vi. 9 ff., Lk. xi. 2 ff.). All this shows that Q is still relatively close to the oral tradition, and remained exposed to its continuing influence. This influence is to be taken into account again and again elsewhere in the Gospels. The age of Q can no longer be determined with certainty. As certainly as the beginnings of the collection of sayings go back to the early time, so equally clearly does it contain passages which were not formulated until later.

The literary characteristics of Matthew and Luke show not least in the different ways in which they combine M, Q and their own special material. Matthew prefers to treat the sayings material by putting it together in long discourses (Sermon on the Mount, Chh. v-vii; the mission of the disciples, Ch. x; the parables, Ch. xiii; rules for the Christian community, Ch. xviii; the denunciation of the Pharisees, Ch. xxiii; Christ's coming again and the eschatological parables, Ch. xxiv-xxv). These discourses are usually concluded with stereotyped expressions (vii. 28; xi. 1; xiii. 53, and elsewhere). He fits these "speeches" into the framework given by Mark. Luke works differently. He too retains the framework of Mark (cf., however, the two great exceptions, Lk. vi. 16 ff. following

Mk. iii. 19 and the so-called "travel account", Lk. ix. 51 ff. following Mk. ix. 41), but otherwise has a stronger preference for biographical detail, among which he intersperses the sayings material.

The question of the literary sources of the Gospels is, however, only a stage on the road to the illumination of the beginnings of the tradition about Jesus. So-called form-criticism has been the first to follow this road methodically (M. Dibelius, R. Bultmann and others). It has shown that from the character of the Gospel tradition we can recognise reasonably clearly the laws and forms of the pre-literary oral tradition. One observation is of special significance. It is that at the beginning of the tradition we find, not a historical sequence of events, but the individual pericope—the individual parable, the individual saying or story, which only in the Gospels, often in very different ways, is given its setting and, with a very modest editing, arranged coherently. These little individual parts of the tradition have to be considered by themselves. They differ from each other clearly, according to their various categories, and each receives its definite form according to its content and purpose in the life of the Church. We find numerous parallels to these forms and laws of tradition, particularly in the rabbis' method of teaching, in the apocalyptic tradition, but also in popular oral tradition in general. No specialised knowledge is needed for the understanding of this general statement. Any attentive reader can find confirmation in the Gospels for the fact that parables, proverbial sayings, discourse and disputation, miracle stories, short anecdotes, etc., have their own definite style. This self-sufficient character of each individual passage, and the typical style of the reports (see above pages 25 f.), show how little interest the tradition has in presenting them in a proper historical chronological sense. The historian, too, is obliged again and again to defer his enquiries as to the historical facts in what is done and said. All the more important is the question of the connection between each part of the tradition and certain interests in the life of the Church and the expression of that life (preaching, teaching, polemic, apologetic, confession, cult, etc.). There can be no doubt that the Gospel tradition was thus closely related to the Church's life, had grown out of it and was designed for it. Therefore the question concerning the tradition's "setting in life" (*Sitz im Leben*) must be asked. In many cases a convincing answer can be given. This problem takes us to the very source of the Jesus tradition.

The Evangelists were the first to mould this tradition into a continuous story of Jesus, Mark being the first of them to do so, as far as we can see. But with him and his successors also the governing interest is a theological not a historical one. The tradition about Jesus is servant to the faith and, indeed, has been from the beginning. The latest research is turning, therefore, more and more vigorously to the task of working out the basic theological conceptions of the Gospels, different as they are from one another (cf., for instance, concerning Mark: J. M. Robinson, *The Problem of History in Mark, Studies in Biblical Theology*, 21, 1957; W. Marxsen, *Der Evangelist Markus, Forschg. z. Rel. u. Lit. d.A.u.N.T.*, N.F., 49), 1956; concerning Lk.: H. Conzelmann, *Die Mitte der Zeit*, 1954, Eng. tr. 1960; concerning Mt.: G. Bornkamm, "Kirche und Enderwartung im Matthäus-Evangelium" in *Überlieferung und Auslegung im Matthäus-Evangelium*, 1960, 48 ff. The book by K. Stendahl, *The School of St. Matthew*, 1954, shows that there is a separate school behind Matthew). We cannot enter into detail as far as these individual questions are concerned. But so much is clear, that the Gospels in many different ways give us an insight not only into the tradition about Jesus, but also into the way in which that tradition has been assimilated to and interpreted by the very different contexts of the primitive Jewish-Christian and gentile Christian Church.

It cannot be denied that the individual Gospels established themselves with various degrees of success in the Church, although we are not to assume any immediate intention to "canonise" them (the Biblical canon developed in stages from the end of the second century onward). For Mark this is proved by Matthew and Luke, but Luke can already speak in his prologue (i. 1-4) of "many" predecessors of whom—apart from Mark—we no longer know anything. Matthew very soon became the leading Gospel of the Church. John is of a quite different type. It is a characteristic example of the further development, at least of one completely different type of Gospel literature.

Apart from our "canonical" Gospels, the process of formation of Gospels continued. Proof of this are the numerous "apocryphal" Gospels, of which some are known to us only by name, some only from fragments (texts in English translation in M. R. James, *The Apocryphal New Testament*, 1924). The historical value of this (generally later) literature, however, is small. It offers a tradition predominantly overgrown with legend and is quite tendentious. The same applies to the tradition about Jesus which was otherwise preserved (in the Fathers, in papyri, etc.), apart from our canonical Gospels. They are of value for the history of the church and of the sects, and contain information on the history of the tradition, but are of no actual use for the history for which we search and which we would like to find *in* the oldest tradition.

From the abundant literature, I give here the numerous more recent textbooks of introduction to the New Testament (Jülicher-Fascher, 7th ed. 1931; Feine-Behm, 9th ed. 1950; Knopf-Lietzmann-Weinel, 5th ed. 1950; W. Michaelis, 2nd ed. 1954, etc.). Further, F. C. Grant, *The Earliest Gospel*, 1943; V. Taylor, *The Formation of the Gospel Tradition*, 1953. For the general reader: M. Dibelius, *A Fresh Approach to the New Testament and Early Christian Literature*, 1937; R. Bultmann, *The Study of the Synoptic Gospels* in *Form Criticism*, tr. by F. C. Grant, 1934.

Appendix II

THE HISTORY OF THE EXPOSITION OF THE SERMON ON THE MOUNT

(First published in "Die Gegenwartsbedeutung der Bergpredigt", *Universitas*, 9 (1954), 1283 ff.)

Let us recall some of the most important and influential expositions which the Sermon on the Mount has received in a long history, and especially in modern times. In following this history we find ourselves faced with the question whether the times when the Sermon on the Mount has had special historical significance were not always those in which men allowed themselves to be challenged by Jesus' demand and commandment in a radical and direct fashion, and sought, with the most thorough-going personal decision, to put the Sermon on the Mount into practice, quite literally in their own day—in their refusal to take an oath, by their renunciation of personal property, their "no" to military service. Were not these the truly historical moments, in which the attack upon this world was actually launched and in which the crumbling foundations of its supposedly sacred political, social, moral and religious traditions were shaken; where the volcano of the Sermon on the Mount erupted, or at least where its menacing glow of fire became visible, whose light revealed the precarious ledge upon which Christianity had settled down to a comfortable existence, and upon which unconcernedly it let the flocks of its faithful graze?

In these moments the attack was always directed towards a Church which, with its sophisms and theologisms, sanctioned the existing world and its "orders", and which had put the dynamic power of the Sermon on the Mount, so to speak, under lock and key. We are reminded in this connection especially of Tolstoi's exposition of the Sermon on the Mount. In examining it more closely we soon realise that in it all Jesus' commandments are reduced to a purely negative statement: thou shalt not resist evil. In the light of this sentence the state, law, property and culture appeared to Tolstoi to be simply attempts and expedients on the part of society to resist evil and thus to confirm its rule. Therefore there can be in Tolstoi really no question of taking Jesus' commandment of love in the positive sense. It is no accident that the Sermon on the Mount becomes for him "the metaphysics of a moral economy", in which it is really no longer a case of the relationship between God and man and between man and his brother, but rather of a kind of technique of passivity which is to lead man to a rational existence.

Tolstoi, as we know, did not consider revolution to be the inevitable result of his protest against the existing world order—a protest which was based on Jesus' Sermon on the Mount. Rather he chose the way of the recluse. Marxism, in his view, was only the attempt to replace one existing despotism by another. Nevertheless, he helped to prepare the ground for communism and bolshevism. The slogan of the retreat from the world quickly became the slogan for the attack upon the world. Though this movement of the proletarian-communist revolution refused radically, in contrast say to the fanatics of the time of the reformation, to base its doctrine upon religious principles, backed by the Sermon on the Mount, it has nevertheless used Jesus' Sermon on the Mount to hold up a mirror before capitalist-Christian society. "Does not every minute of your ordinary life give the lie to your theories? Do you consider it wrong to go to court when you have been wronged? But the apostle says that this is wrong. Do you offer the right cheek when someone smites you on the left, or do you not follow it up with legal action for bodily injury? But the Gospels forbid it. . . . Does not the major part of your trials and civil laws deal with property? But it has been said to you that your treasures are not of this world" (K. Marx, *Ges. Ausg.*, I, page 246).

As we know there is no lack of examples in the literature of socialism and in particular of religious socialism (cf. most recently L. Ragaz, *Die Bergpredigt Jesu*, 1945), in which Jesus was proclaimed to be the revolutionary against ownership, society and the power of the state, as well as the advocate of the suppressed and underprivileged, and, if not its leader, at least was recognised as an ally in the struggle for a new social order. This is how Kautzky and others described him, and in this sense the Jacobins of the French Revolution claimed him for themselves as *le bon sansculotte*. It is easy enough for us to recognise in all these utterances the frequently horrible and grotesque misrepresentation of Jesus' person and message. But can we thus dismiss the disquieting question which Christianity is being asked? Time and time again Christianity, especially with the assistance of its theology, has known so well and still knows how to intercept, so to speak, the thrust of Jesus' challenge, to divert it and to settle down peacefully in spite of it.

The Christian and theological struggle against fanaticism and anarchy, especially against those who place their revolutionary aims and dreams under the flag of Christ, is however not only an expression of a fatal complacency, but a duty to which we are pledged by clearly legitimate and continuing historical and theological reflection. It was an extremely painful experience for F. Naumann when he realised on his visit to Palestine at the turn of the century the complete discrepancy between Jesus' historical environment and the political, social and cultural situation of our technical age, and therewith the impossibility to expect from Jesus direct and detailed instructions as to the problems we are asked to solve (cf. Th. Heuss, *Friedrich Naumann*, 2nd ed. 1949, 133 ff.).

About the same time Joh. Weiss and Albert Schweitzer made the great discovery, so decisive for later theology, that Jesus' person and message not only belonged to a different historical environment, but to an apocalyptic conception of history which has become quite alien to us. Against this background and in this setting they tried to understand the Sermon on the Mount as the law for an exceptional situation in a world which lies in the blaze of the cosmic catastrophies accompanying the end of the world and the speedy dawn of the kingdom of God. This was the meaning of Schweitzer's famous expression concerning the "interim ethic" of Jesus, which has lost its original meaning through the fact that the end of the world, expected by Jesus and his disciples, never came.

Theology could not be satisfied with this exposition either, which looks so illuminating at first sight. For there can be no doubt that this interpretation of the Sermon on the Mount attributes to it an apocalyptic temperature, so to speak, which it does not possess. And it is not true that it has about it the burning odour of the cosmic catastrophy, however much it heralds the coming kingdom of God and calls us to the righteousness without which no one shall enter the kingdom. Or in other and less figurative words: this interpretation would appear to make the apocalyptic end of the world the ground of Jesus' demands, whereas the love of our neighbour and of our enemy, purity, faithfulness and truth are demanded simply because they are the will of God. The inner relationship between Jesus' requirement and his message of the coming of the kingdom of God are not brought out clearly in the apocalyptic interpretation of the Sermon on the Mount.

Other explanations have been put forward too: e.g. the opinion that Jesus' demands are completely misunderstood, if they are looked upon as binding directions for a certain course of action. The Sermon on the Mount really aims at a change of mind. True, we must reply, but this antithesis between frame of mind and deed is unquestionably a wrong way out of the difficulties into which the Sermon on the Mount leads us. For if one thing becomes clear it is this, that Jesus takes the intention for the deed and consistently demands obedience in actual deed. "Whosoever hears these my words and does them . . ."!

Finally a completely different solution of the problem of the Sermon on the Mount, which has maintained itself since Lutheran orthodoxy up to our present time, is the opinion that the Sermon on the Mount is not in any way aimed directly at obedience in deed, but designed to hold up a mirror to our sins, so as to lead us in this way to him who alone as our representative has fulfilled for us the righteousness demanded by God. This is the way that the Sermon on the Mount, seen from the point of view of the gospel and especially of Paul, should be understood: as a presentation of the one man, Jesus Christ, who has completely fulfilled the law, and as a promise of the new man which we shall become through faith in the righteousness bestowed upon us by Christ (Thurneysen). All too clearly, however, reflection on the position in which the Sermon on the Mount places us has been confused here with the exposition of the words themselves. Where this distinction is not observed, we are most certainly in danger, to put it drastically, of putting the Sermon on the Mount away in storage by means of dogmatics.

Looking back on all the aforementioned expositions of the Sermon on the Mount in their diversity, we soon discover a dangerous tendency running through them all, which at least in its effect can be noticed again and again. They all aim at limiting its application, they all contain a characteristic "only". Jesus' demands are only applied to the situations of this world (the political revolutionaries), they apply only on the historical assumptions of an age not yet mechanised and under an apocalyptic view of history; they demand only a change of mind; they are to be understood only as a mirror of sin, only as a description of the new man who is

Jesus Christ alone. This manifold "only" is obviously highly suspect. Again and again it became a shock absorber, which made the real meeting with Jesus' word bearable and therefore illusory, and which, in advance, dissolved this meeting into historical and theological reflections.

Appendix III

THE MESSIANIC TITLES IN JESUS' REFERENCES TO HIMSELF

(a) The Son. The title "the Son", used by itself, is found in numerous of Jesus' references to himself in John's Gospel; in the synoptics, however, only in two places: Mt. xi. 27; Mk. xiii. 32. Mt. xi. 27 reads: "All things have been delivered to me by my father; and no man knows the Son, except the Father; and no one knows the Father, except the Son, and anyone to whom the Son chooses to reveal him." (With regards to differing textual variants, cf. Klostermann, *Matthäus*, page 103.) This word of revelation speaks, as has frequently been noticed, entirely in the manner of John, in complete contrast to the other sayings of the Lord in the synoptics. This is borne out not only by the pair of terms Father-Son, but also by the reciprocal conception "to know". E. Norden, *Agnostos Theos* (1913), 277 ff., M. Dibelius, *From Tradition to Gospel*, 279 ff.; Bultmann, *Gesch. d. syn. Trad.*, 171 f. and *Th.W. z. N.T.*, I, 713 f.; E. Klostermann on this passage; W. G. Kümmel, *Promise and Fulfilment*, 40 f.; and others all agree that this passage can hardly be called a saying of the historical Jesus. The same unusual use of the name "Son" appears elsewhere only in Mk. xiii. 32: "But of that day or that hour no one knows, not even the angels in heaven, nor the Son, but only the Father." For dogmatic reasons this word was early subject to correction (Luke left it out altogether), as objection was taken to the Son not knowing. Nevertheless, even this saying, at least in the form in which it has been handed down to us, especially in the use of the name Son, shows the traces of the Christology of the primitive Church (cf. Kümmel, *Promise and Fulfilment*, 42; G. Harder, *Theol. Viatorum* 1952, 95 f.). Infrequently though the Messianic title Son (of God) is found in the references to himself of the historical Jesus, the more its use can be explained from the Credo of the Church in which it has its own secure place—based on Ps. ii. 7.

(b) The Servant of God. Similarly, there is no definite proof that Jesus designated himself as Messiah in the sense of the prophecy of Deutero-Isaiah concerning the suffering servant of God

(Is. liii). Quite rightly this great and mysterious chapter is one of the essential passion texts of Christianity, with its message of the servant of God with no form or comeliness, despised and rejected by men, who has borne our griefs and carried our sorrows, smitten by God and wounded for our transgressions. He shall make his soul an offering for sin, and the righteous servant shall justify many. But, however much the text may say to interpret the secret of Jesus' death as a substitutionary atonement, this interpretation strangely enough does not appear at the beginning of the Christian tradition. We find it for the first time in Acts viii. 32 ff.; Rom. iv. 25; I Peter ii. 22-25; Heb. ix. 28 and in later documents. Even in the passion narrative we meet, as we have already seen, only a few scattered echoes of Is. liii (see above, page 156), but many more of the Suffering Psalms. From the words of Jesus which have been handed down, we can only name one which makes use of Is. liii. "For the Son of man also came not to be served, but to serve, and to give his life as a ransom for many" (Mk. x. 45). We must, however, along with many recent exegetes regard this saying, especially since Luke transmits it in simpler form (Lk. xxii. 27), as a homiletical saying of the primitive Church in Palestine, which interpreted Jesus' life and death in the sense of Is. liii.

As to the age and origin of the saying from the Palestinian tradition cf. J. Jeremias, "Das Lösegeld für Viele", *Judaica*, 3 (1947-48), 249 ff.; E. Lohse, *Märtyrer und Gottesknecht* (1955), 117 ff. (Yet the age of the passage does not prove its genuineness.) Cf. also E. Schweizer, *Lordship and Discipleship*, 49 ff., and his and E. Lohse's criticism (*op. cit.*, pages 104 ff.) of the opinion put forward in recent years, especially by J. Jeremias (παῖς θεοῦ, *Th.W.z.N.T.V*, 680 ff.), that the doctrine of the Messiah suffering in our stead was known already to pre-Christian Judaism, and was a starting-point for Jesus' understanding of himself as the Messiah.

(c) Son of David. We find the title "son of David" in Jesus' own words only in Mk. xii. 35 ff. Jesus challenges here the right of Jewish doctrine to the claim that the Messiah is a son of David, with the words of Ps. cx, "The Lord said unto my Lord, Sit at my right hand until I make your enemies your footstool". And the scene closes with the question, "David himself calls him Lord; so how is he his son?" (Mk. xii. 35-37). The meaning of this passage seems to be to contest the title son of David for the Messiah altogether, pointing out that David himself, in referring to him in the psalm, uses the higher title, "the Lord". It is questionable, however, whether this view is appropriate to the views of the Gospels and the primitive Church, which considered it beyond doubt that the Messiah was the son of David. More likely is the interpretation which finds the point of the saying in the *relationship* between the Messiah's being the son of David and also the Lord. What does it mean that the Lord of David is at the same time his son? The title "son of David", however, is here no longer used in the typically Jewish sense as a title for the Messiah, but in its later Christian meaning, according to which his descent from David shows the Messiah in his humanity and lowliness, in contrast to his exaltation and dominion (Rom. i. 3; II Tim. ii. 8; Ignatius Eph. xviii. 2; xx. 2; Tr. ix. 1; Sm. i. 1). This re-coining and fresh application of the old Jewish title certainly goes back to the theological reflection of the later Church. From this reflection originates also this piece of the tradition.

(*d*) The Son of Man. The sayings of the Lord handed down to us in the synoptic Gospels in which Jesus speaks of the Son of man are not uniform in themselves:

(1) A first group speaks of the coming Son of man strictly in the sense of apocalyptic expectation (Mk. viii. 38; xiii. 26; xiv. 62; Mt. xxiv. 27, 37, 39, 44). Here the Son of man is the future judge and saviour, coming from heaven to earth. Suddenly, like a flash of lightning, and equally obvious to all, he will return. We must be ready for his coming. In all these passages the Son of man is referred to in the third person. Nothing is said here of an identity between Jesus and the Son of man, although the believing community was certain of it. As to the source of these texts, they come almost without exception from either Mark or from Q. Some of these words may have been formed by the Church. We can assume with certainty, however, that Jesus himself spoke in this manner of the coming of the Son of man. This applies especially to the words in which he speaks about the answer of the judge of the world to the confession or denial of the disciples here on earth (Lk. xii. 8; Mk. viii. 38). Striking is here the distinction between the "I" of the earthly Jesus and the Son of man who is to come.

(2) A second group of sayings speaks quite differently of the coming suffering, death and resurrection appointed by God for the Son of man (especially Mk. viii. 31; ix. 31; x. 33 f.). In contrast to the first group, nothing is said here of his parousia (i.e. of his coming), and of the judgment he will execute. They speak all the more of the trial by men here on earth, to which the Son of man

will be delivered according to God's will, before he rises again. Even if we do not doubt that Jesus reckoned on his violent death, these prophecies of his suffering and resurrection can hardly be considered to be Jesus' own words. They presume a detailed knowledge of the Passion and Easter story. The difference between the two groups of sayings is obvious. As much as the one lacks references to the suffering and resurrection of the Son of man, so little does the other refer to his coming. They also differ as to their sources: the second group belongs exclusively to Mark's tradition, not to Q.

(3) Between the two groups mentioned above stands a third, numerically smaller, group, which speaks neither of the coming nor of the suffering of the Son of man. To this group belong the words which speak of the authority of the Son of man to forgive sins (Mk. ii. 10), of him as the Lord of the Sabbath (Mk. ii. 28), of the Son of man who is reproached as gluttonous and a drunkard, a friend of tax collectors and sinners (Mt. xi. 19), but homeless and with nowhere to lay his head (Mt. viii. 20). It has been suggested that these sayings were only subsequently developed into allusions to Jesus' Messiahship by the tradition. Originally, it is said, the title "Son of man" was not found here, but rather "child of man" (i.e. man), which only through wrong translation came to be linked with Jesus (cf. J. Wellhausen, Einleitung, 128 ff.). This, however, is extremely improbable in the case of Mk. ii. 10, 28. Rather here we have to do with sayings of the Church which invest the earthly Jesus with the authority of the ascended Lord, on which authority they base the right to forgive sins and to enjoy Sabbath freedom. This authority in turn is exercised by his Church (cf. Mt. ix. 8). The authority exercised also by the Church is therefore no universal human right. Neither is the assumption that Mt. viii. 20 has been wrongly translated, convincing (thus in Bultmann, Gesch. d. syn. Tradition 27). According to this assumption this passage is believed to have been originally a wisdom saying, speaking in general about the unsettled existence of man in contrast to the animals, who each have their own shelter (cf. e.g. Job xiv. 1), and which was afterwards applied to Jesus as the Son of man. We lack, however, adequate parallels for this assumption; moreover, the assumed process of development of the saying up to the point where it is used in our text (Mt. viii. 20; Lk. ix. 58) seems to me all too complicated. A simpler and more probable explanation is, in my opinion, that here, as in Mt. xi. 19, a

Messianic title has been introduced into a saying of the Lord, to which originally it did not belong. This was made possible by the Church's complete identification of "Jesus" with "Son of man", a fact for which we find ample proof in the tradition. This also explains why one evangelist not infrequently simply uses "I" while the other uses the title Son of man (e.g. Mt. x. 32 f., as against Lk. xii. 8 f.; Mk. viii. 38), and how, on the other hand, this title could take the place of a mere "I" in one of Jesus' words (e.g. Mt. xvi. 13, as against Mk. viii. 27).

The most generally found assumption, that Jesus himself supported his Messianic claim with the title Son of man (thus, among many others, also V. Taylor, *The Names of Jesus*, 1954, 25 ff.), presents us most decidedly with problems which are difficult to solve. Was it really his intention to make use of an ambiguous secret name which could be understood either as a Messianic title or just as well in the sense of "the man", without any Messianic implication whatsoever (as already argued by P. Fiebig, *Der Menschensohn*, 1901, 100)? Or did he wish, by using this self-designation, to stimulate his hearers to "draw their own conclusions" (E. Percy, *Die Botschaft Jesu*, 259)? I find both these assumptions impossible to imagine and impossible to support with any text whatsoever. Quite unconvincing also is the opinion that he described himself as the one destined to be the future Son of man. Nowhere are there any statements as to how we are to understand the relation between Jesus' earthly existence and his own role as the heavenly judge of the word. There is no mention made either—not even in the prophecies of his suffering—of, say, his being taken up into heaven after a preliminary period as Messiah-designate only (these criticisms are raised quite rightly by Bultmann, *Theol*. I, 28 ff.).

For the reasons specified I consider it probable that the historical Jesus never used the title "Son of man" for himself. The answer to our question as to why we meet this title so frequently in Jesus' references to himself can only be that this title above all others is for the oldest Palestinian Church, to which we owe the transmission of the words of the Lord, an expression of the essence of their faith, and was to be invested with the authority of Jesus himself. The strong formative influence of the faith and expectation of the original Church upon the tradition of the sayings of the Lord seems to me all the more conceivable, since the question of the Son of man, in the late Jewish as in the early Christian sense, was concerned with a name and a subject of eschatological certainty and expectation. We may assume, therefore, that the prophets of the early Church have played a considerable part in the formation of the words concerning the Son of man, who preached to the congregation the word of the crucified, the resurrected and the coming Lord, in the same way as the visionary in the revelation of John sees one "like a son of man" (i. 12 ff.), and received from him the word which he is to deliver to the congregations.

INDEX OF SUBJECTS

INDEX OF NAMES

INDEX OF BIBLICAL REFERENCES

APOCRYPHA AND APOCRYPHAL WRITINGS